PRACTICING
NEW HISTORICISM

PRACTICING
NEW HISTORICISM

CATHERINE GALLAGHER & STEPHEN GREENBLATT

The University of Chicago Press
Chicago and London

The University of Chicago Press, Chicago 60637
The University of Chicago Press, Ltd., London
© 2000 by The University of Chicago
All rights reserved. Published 2000
Paperback edition 2001
Printed in the United States of America
09 08 07 06 05 04 03 02 01   2 3 4 5

ISBN: 0-226-27934-0 (cloth)
ISBN: 0-226-27935-9 (paperback)
Chapter 1, "The Touch of the Real," © 1997 by the Regents of the
University of California. Reprinted from *Representations* (no. 59, summer
1997): 14–29, by permission.

Library of Congress Cataloging-in-Publication Data

Gallagher, Catherine.
    Practicing new historicism / Catherine Gallagher and Stephen
Greenblatt.
        p.   cm.
    Includes index.
    ISBN: 0-226-27934-0 (alk. paper)
    1. Criticism. 2. Historicism. I. Greenblatt, Stephen 1943–. II. Title.
PN8I. G237   2000
801´.95— dc21

                                                          99-42410

To the editorial board of *Representations,*

past, present, and future

Contents

Acknowledgments

We have been fortunate in our wonderful colleagues and students at Berkeley and Harvard, and we have greatly profited as well from the probing questions asked by those who have heard versions of several of these chapters delivered as lectures. Stephen Greenblatt wishes to acknowledge a particular debt of gratitude to the Istituto Italiano per gli Studi Filosofici, the Wissenschaftskolleg zu Berlin, and the Rockefeller Foundation Study and Conference Center, Bellagio. We have received especially valuable suggestions and advice from Paul Alpers, Sarah Beckwith, Harry Berger Jr., Stephen Best, William Bouwsma, David Brewer, Caroline Walker Bynum, Rosanna Camerlingo, Margaret Carroll, T. J. Clark, Catherine Creswell, Mimi Danson, Mario Domenichelli, Daniela Fink, Guido Fink, Philip Fisher, Dolores Freese, Lisa Freinkel, Lowell Gallagher, Carlo Ginzburg, Kevis Goodman, Francis Grady, Anthony Grafton, Margreta de Grazia, Valentin Groebner, Hans Ulrich Gumbrecht, Carla Hesse, Martin Jay, Jeffrey Knapp, Joseph Koerner, Paul Kottman, Lisa Lampert, Thomas Laqueur, Colleen Lye, Clarence Miller, Chris Nealon, Walter Ong, S. J., Annabel Patterson, Jürgen Pieters, Robert Pinsky, Chris Prendergast, Michael Rogin, Elaine Scarry, David Schalkwyck, Regina Schwartz, James Shapiro, Debora Shuger, Pippa Skotnes, Gary Smith, Richard Strier, Ramie Targoff, and Bernard Williams.

Introduction

This book is probably more in need of an introduction than most: two authors, two chapters on anecdotes, two on eucharistic doctrine in the late Middle Ages and the Renaissance, and two on nineteenth-century materialism. Or, to put it somewhat differently, two chapters on anecdotes, and four on bread, potatoes, and the dead. The underlying coherence of all this may not be self-evident.

We began by wanting to explain how new historicism had changed the field of literary history. The project was, on our part, a belated act of recognition. When years ago we first noticed in the annual job listing of the Modern Language Association that an English department was advertising for a specialist in new historicism, our response was incredulity. How could something that didn't really exist, that was only a few words gesturing toward a new interpretative practice, have become a "field"? When did it happen and how could we not have noticed? If this was indeed a field, who could claim expertise in it and in what would such expertise consist? Surely, we of all people should know something of the history and the principles of new historicism, but what we knew above all was that it (or perhaps we) resisted systematization. We had never formulated a set of theoretical propositions or articulated a program; we had not drawn up for ourselves, let alone for anyone else, a sequence of questions that always needed to be posed when encountering a work of literature in order to construct a new historicist reading; we would not be able to say to someone in haughty disapproval, "You are not an authentic new historicist." The notion of authenticity seemed and continues to seem misplaced, for new historicism is not a coherent, close-knit school in which one might be enrolled or from which one might be expelled. The term has been applied to an extraordinary assortment of critical practices, many of which bear little resemblance to our own. This book will not attempt to capture that rich variety; here we will speak only for ourselves, to whom "new historicism" at first signified an impatience with American New Criticism, an unsettling of established norms and procedures, a mingling of dissent and restless curiosity.

To be sure, we talked constantly about our methodological principles. We eagerly read works of "theory" emanating principally from Paris, Konstanz, Berlin, Frankfurt, Budapest, Tartu, and Moscow, and met regularly with a group of friends to argue about them. At this distance we remember best the heated discussions of Althusser and Lacan, but, for all of our passionate interest, terms like "Institutional State Apparatus" or the "*objet a*" have not found their way comfortably into our own teaching or writing. One of the recurrent criticisms of new historicism is that it is insufficiently theorized. The criticism is certainly just, and yet it seems curiously out of touch with the simultaneous fascination with theory and resistance to it that has shaped from the start our whole attempt to rethink the practice of literary and cultural studies. We speculated about first principles and respected the firmer theoretical commitments of other members of our discussion group, but both of us were and remain deeply skeptical of the notion that we should formulate an abstract system and then apply it to literary works. We doubt that it is possible to construct such a system independent of our own time and place and of the particular objects by which we are interested, and we doubt too that any powerful work we might do would begin with such an attempt.

The group of friends who had been meeting to discuss theory began to read each other's work, probing with genial ruthlessness the underlying assumptions of each paper we ventured to submit. It turned out to be important that the participants in these bracingly frank discussions were not only theoretically diverse but also came from a range of disciplines, since it quickly became apparent that positions that served as stable footing in one disciplinary inquiry were shifting sands in another. There was no requirement, of course, that we all find common ground; the historical evolution of the disciplines made and continues to make such uniformity inherently unlikely. But we had to explain ourselves to colleagues who did not necessarily share our enabling assumptions and who did not feel constrained by propriety to take on faith what we could not effectively justify.

The group came to understand also that there was, in interdisciplinary studies, a tendency to invoke, in support of one's own positions, arguments from other disciplines that sophisticated thinkers in those other disciplines had in fact been calling into question. We had, as it were, been complacently dressing ourselves in each other's cast-off clothes, until, looking around the room, we erupted in laughter. The spectacle was not entirely grotesque: some of the intellectual hand-me-downs looked surprisingly good on our friends, and we experienced the odd sensation one might feel at seeing one's own discarded possessions sold at auction for a handsome profit. In a few cases, such as the formal analysis of the inner structure of literary works, we wanted to take back what we had been rather too hasty to give away. The effect on the two of us was to underscore the difficulty of constructing an overarching theory, prior to or independent of individual cases, that would integrate historical and literary interpretation, generate powerful new readings, and survive the withering critiques leveled at it from outside. We became rather good at slipping out of theoretical nooses.

After several years of regular meetings, acknowledging the transforming importance that the informal discussions had had for each of us and the vital energy that they had contributed to our work, the group began to think about ways of extending its existence, for we knew from prior experience that the charismatic moment that bound us together, though in this case unusually intense and prolonged, could not endure. We would need a structure that would provide a set of ongoing challenges and hence a raison d'être. We settled on the idea of a journal,[1] for we could constitute ourselves as the editorial board and hence continue as well as broaden our discussions, but we needed to come up with an idea and a title. After considerable debate, we settled on representation as the central problem in which all of us—literary critic and art historian; historian and political scientist; Lacanian, Foucauldian, Freudian, neopragmatist; deconstructor and unreconstructed formalist—were engaged. It was tempting then to call the proposed journal "Representation," but the uneasiness some of us felt with theoretical abstraction, our skepticism about the will to construct a unified theory, led us to adopt the plural. Whatever progress we were likely to make in grappling with the contested status of representation would occur, we were convinced, only in close, detailed engagement with a multiplicity of historically embedded cultural performances: specific instances, images, and texts that offered some resistance to interpretation.

About a year after launching *Representations,* the group decided that it would be good to have an editorial statement, as many journals do, staking out our theoretical position, but we found once again that we could not agree on a satisfactory unitary formulation. If a literary critic came up with something that sounded plausible, the historians would sharply dissent, while the historians' terms would in turn be challenged; nor were the disagreements strictly disciplinary. There were fracture lines everywhere, and yet we were convinced that we were wrestling with a shared set of issues and that it was important to continue the inquiry; to continue the inquiry but not to conduct a system: a few of us at least were beginning to extol the methodological eclecticism of our intellectual climate as salutary in itself. Attempts to systematize deconstruction provided a cautionary example, for they seemed to us a betrayal of its Pyrrhonian energy (as if someone in the early seventeenth century had tried to rewrite Montaigne in order to make him sound like Thomas Aquinas). Each of us, it turned out, still held unshared convictions that we could not sacrifice for the sake of an editorial statement. Several of us particularly wanted to hold on to our aesthetic pleasures; our desire for critical innovation; our interest in contingency, spontaneity, improvisation; our urge to pick up a tangential fact and watch its circulation; our sense of history's unpredictable galvanic appearances and disappearances. The editorial statement went unwritten.

The issues could all be traced in some sense back to the explosive mix of nationalism, anthropology, poetry, theology, and hermeneutics that found originary expression in Giambattista Vico and was recombined by the German historicists of the late eighteenth and early nineteenth centuries. Brooding on the wild variety of environments in which human societies have evolved, Johann Gottfried von Herder posits what he calls a principle of diversification that ensures the widest possible variety of adaptations to the natural world: "The practical understanding of man was intended to blossom and bear fruit in all its varieties: and hence such a diversified Earth was ordained for so diversified a species."[2] The observation, at first glance modest enough, entails a radical departure from centuries of speculation about the optimal climatic conditions for the emergence of the optimal society (speculation that had a pronounced tendency to locate those conditions within a narrow compass, usually in the vicinity of the city where the writer happened to be sitting).[3] It entails as well the abandonment of the project of charting the *translatio imperii,* the great westward trajectory of civilization from Athens to Rome to, say, London.

There is no longer a unitary story, a supreme model of human perfection, that can be securely located in a particular site. Any individual culture, no matter how complex and elaborate, can express and experience only a narrow range of the options available to the human species as a whole, a species that is inherently— that is, abstracted from any particular historical manifestation of its being—without qualities. "Born almost without instinct," humans are astonishingly malleable; our identity is formed "only through lifelong training toward humanity, and this is the reason our species is both perfectible and corruptible."[4] Though there are instances in which particular social adaptations are dismaying, Herder eschews the Enlightenment project of finding a universal norm for the realization of human potential. To be sure, for Herder enlightenment exists, just as beauty exists—his vision is fueled by faith that history is essentially progressive and that "the increased diffusion of true knowledge among people has happily diminished their inhuman, mad destroyers"[5]—but it cannot be fixed in any single place or time: "The chain of culture and enlightenment [*Kette der Kultur und Aufklärung*] stretches to the ends of the earth."[6]

Herder finds in the phenomenon of extreme human diversity not an incoherent Babel or the breeding ground of murderous conflict but rather a principle of hope:

> Man, from his very nature, will clash but little in his pursuits with man; his dispositions, sensations, and propensities, being so infinitely diversified, and as it were individualized. What is a matter of indifference to one man, to another is an object of desire: and then each has a world of enjoyment in himself, each a creation of his own.[7]

Hence the goal should never be to reduce the variety of human adaptations to a single triumphant form or to rank the cultures of the earth as if they were all competing for the same prize. To the question posed by the Berlin Academy—"Which was the happiest people in history?"—Herder replies that all comparison is disastrous:

> Happiness does not depend on a laurel wreath, on a view of the blessed herd, on a cargo ship, or on a captured battle flag, but on the soul that needed this, aspired to this, attained this, and wanted to attain nothing more. Each nation has its own *center* of happiness *within itself.* . . .[8]

The task of understanding then depends not on the extraction of an abstract set of principles, and still less on the application of a theoretical model, but rather on an encounter with the singular, the specific, and the individual.

Much of this resonates in powerful ways with the impulses and perceptions that lay behind the journal *Representations*: the fascination with the particular, the wide-ranging curiosity, the refusal of universal aesthetic norms, and the resistance to formulating an overarching theoretical program. Moreover, Herder found a way to justify and to integrate our simultaneous obsession with history and art:

> In poetry's gallery of diverse ways of thinking, diverse aspirations, and diverse desires, we come to know periods and nations far more intimately than we can through the misleading and pathetic method of studying their political and military history. From this latter kind of history, we rarely learn more about a people than

how it was ruled and how it was wiped out. From its poetry, we learn about its way of thinking, its desires and wants, the ways it rejoiced, and the ways it was guided either by its principles or its inclinations.[9]

Poetry, in this account, is not the path to a transhistorical truth, whether psychoanalytic or deconstructive or purely formal, but the key to particular historically embedded social and psychological formations. The first questions to be asked about an art such as drama, Herder writes, are "When? Where? Under what circumstances? From what sources should a people do this?"[10] The deepest sources of art lie not in the skill of the individual maker but in the inner resources of a people in a particular place and time: "A people will wherever possible," Herder writes, with a hostile glance at French neoclassicism, "invent its drama according to its own history, spirit of the times, customs, opinions, language, national biases, traditions, and inclinations."[11] This approach accords well not only with our anthropological and cultural interests, but also with our rather conservative interest in periodization (for each of us had been trained to be a specialist in a given area and to take its geographical and temporal boundaries seriously). More important still, Herder's brilliant vision of the mutual embeddedness of art and history underlies our fascination with the possibility of treating all of the written and visual traces of a particular culture as a mutually intelligible network of signs.

The problem with this vision, as with roughly comparable observations by Schiller, Schlegel, and Schleiermacher, is that we were inclined to argue over each of its key terms, just as we argued over our own attempts to formulate what was roughly the same insight. What is the nature of the "*volk*" that Herder invokes, or the "spirit of the times"? In what sense is any era ever truly finished—who sets the boundaries and how are they patrolled? Do we not have overwhelming evidence, in our own time and in every period we study, of an odd interlayering of cultural perspectives and a mixing of peoples, so that nothing is ever truly complete or unitary?

What are the consequences of treating all of the traces of an era, even if its boundaries could be successfully demarcated, as a single cultural formation? To what extent can bubonic plague, infant mortality, or venereal disease be regarded as cultural? And what is the status, for Herder or for ourselves, of individual makers?

Between Herder's time and our own, historians of culture have answered these questions in a variety of ways, and most recently the hoarier issues, such as the nature/culture distinction or the status of the individual, have, it seems, been rendered obsolete by conceiving of cultures as texts. This conception, too, has a venerable history, but the linguistic turn in the social and humanistic disciplines has heightened its appeal. What becomes newly interesting about the nature/culture distinction, for example, is the very fact that it cannot be fixed because the boundaries between the terms and the significance of those boundaries vary too widely in different contexts. Like other crucial distinctions, the nature/culture divide should be read, in the manner of structural linguistics, as a key binary opposition, loaded with information for deciphering the various social codes one encounters in historical studies. Not that this new textualism solves all of our problems. Are the cultural texts imagined to be coherent? Does it make sense to assimilate visual traces to textual traces? What happens to such phenomena as social rituals and structures of feeling when they are textualized? We found that the harder we pushed on the terms of any prospective programmatic statement for our journal, the further we seemed to get from actually doing the work that drew us together in the first place.

Still, the notion of a distinct culture, particularly a culture distant in time or space, as a text—a notion we got more from Geertz and the structuralists than from the historicists—is powerfully attractive for several reasons. It carries the core hermeneutical presumption that one can occupy a position from which one can discover meanings that those who left traces of themselves could not have articulated. Explication and paraphrase are not enough; we seek something more, something that the authors we study would not have had sufficient distance upon themselves and their own era to grasp.

Does this mean that we have constituted ourselves as, in the words of a detractor, "the School of Resentment"? Not at all: we are, if anything, rather inclined to piety. Nonetheless, any attempt at interpretation, as distinct from worship, bears a certain inescapable tinge of aggression, however much it is qualified by admiration and empathy. Where traditional "close readings" tended to build toward an intensified sense of wondering admiration, linked to the celebration of genius, new historicist readings are more often skeptical, wary, demystifying, critical, and even adversarial. This hermeneutical aggression was initially reinforced for many of us by the ideology critique that played a central role in the Marxist theories in which we were steeped, but, as we were from the beginning uncomfortable with such key concepts as superstructure and base or imputed class consciousness, we have found ourselves, as we will discuss at some length in this book, slowly forced to transform the notion of ideology critique into discourse analysis. Moreover, no matter how thoroughgoing our skepticism, we have never given up or turned our backs on the deep gratification that draws us in the first place to the study of literature and art. Our project has never been about diminishing or belittling the power of artistic representations, even those with the most problematic entailments, but we never believe that our appreciation of this power necessitates either ignoring the cultural matrix out of which the representations emerge or uncritically endorsing the fantasies that the representations articulate.

The notion of culture as text has a further major attraction: it vastly expands the range of objects available to be read and interpreted. Major works of art remain centrally important, but they are jostled now by an array of other texts and images. Some of these alternative objects of attention are literary works regarded as too minor to deserve sustained interest and hence marginalized or excluded entirely from the canon. Others are texts that have been regarded as altogether nonliterary, that is, as lacking the aesthetic polish, the self-conscious use of rhetorical figures, the aura of distance from the everyday world, the marked status as fiction that separately or together characterize belles lettres. There has been in effect a social rebellion in the study of culture, so that figures hitherto kept outside the proper circles of interest—a rabble of half-crazed religious visionaries, semiliterate political agitators, coarse-faced peasants in hobnailed boots, dandies whose writings had been discarded as ephemera, imperial bureaucrats, freed slaves, women novelists dismissed as impudent scribblers, learned women excluded from easy access to the materials of scholarship, scandalmongers, provincial politicians, charlatans, and forgotten academics—have now forced their way in, or rather have been invited in by our generation of critics.

The drastic broadening of the field that results from the consideration of whole cultures as texts leads in several directions:

- Works that have been hitherto denigrated or ignored can be treated as major achievements, claiming space in an already crowded curriculum or diminishing the value of established works in a kind of literary stock market. Shares in Sir John Davies, say, decline, as capital shifts to Aemilia Lanyer and Lady Mary Wroth; John Denham gives way to Lucy Hutchinson and Gerard Winstanley; Wordsworth, Coleridge, and Keats rub shoulders in anthologies and course assignments with the recently revalued Anna Letitia Barbauld, Charlotte Smith, and Mary Robinson.

- The newly recovered authors are of interest in themselves, but they also inevitably change the account of those authors long treated as canonical. Achievements that have seemed like entirely isolated monuments are disclosed to have a more complex interrelation with other texts by "minor" authors. New historicism helps raise questions about originality in art and about the status of "genius" as an explanatory term, along with the status of the distinction between "major" and "minor." The process by which certain works achieved classic status can be reexamined.

- In the analysis of the larger cultural field, canonical works of art are brought into relation not only with works judged as minor, but also with texts that are not by anyone's standard literary. The conjunction can produce almost surrealist wonder at the revelation of an unanticipated aesthetic dimension in objects without pretensions to the aesthetic. It can suggest hidden links between high cultural texts, apparently detached from any direct engagement with their immediate surroundings, and texts very much in and of their world, such as documents of social control or political subversion. It can weaken the primacy of classic works of art in relation to other competing or surrounding textual traces from the past. Or, alternatively, it can highlight the process by which such works achieve both prominence and a certain partial independence.

It is hardly an accident that this broader vision of the field of cultural interpretation, which had been mooted for more than a century, took hold in the United States in the late 1960s and '70s. It reflected in its initial period the recent inclusion of groups that in many colleges and universities had hitherto been marginalized, half hidden, or even entirely excluded from the professional study of literature: Jews, African Americans, Hispanics, Asian Americans, and, most significantly from the point of view of the critical ferment, women. Women's studies, and the feminism that motivated its formation, has served as an important, if little acknowledged, model for new historicism in that it has inspired its adherents to identify new objects for study, bring those objects into the light of critical attention, and insist upon their legitimate place in the curriculum. It has also served to politicize explicitly an academic discourse that had often attempted to avoid or conceal partisan or polemical commitments, and it unsettles familiar aesthetic hierarchies that had been manipulated, consciously or unconsciously, to limit the cultural significance of women.

This unsettling of the hierarchies does not seem revolutionary—we are not inclined to confuse a change in the curriculum with the fall of the state—but it does feel democratizing, in that it refuses to limit creativity to the spectacular achievements of a group of trained specialists. The risk, from a culturally conservative point of view, is that we will lose sight of what is uniquely precious about high art: new historicism, in this account, fosters the weakening of the aesthetic object. There is, we think, some truth to this charge, at least in relation to the extreme claims routinely made by certain literary critics for the uniqueness of literature. Works of art, in the more perfervid moments of celebration, are almost completely detached from semantic necessity and are instead deeply important as signs and embodiments of the freedom of the human imagination. The rest of human life can only gaze longingly at the condition of the art object, which is the manifestation of unalienated labor, the perfect articulation and realization of human energy. The art object, ideally self-enclosed, is freed not only from the necessities of the surrounding world (necessities that it transforms miraculously into play) but also from the intention of the maker. The closest analogy perhaps is the Catholic Eucharist: the miracle of the transubstantiation does not depend, after all, on the intention of the priest; it is not even the consequence of the institution that celebrates the Mass. Rather the institution is itself understood to be the consequence of the miracle of the Sacrament.

When the literary text ceases to be a sacred, self-enclosed, and self-justifying miracle, when in the skeptical mood we foster it begins to lose at least some of the special power ascribed to it, its boundaries begin to seem less secure and it loses exclusive rights to the experience of wonder. The house of the imagination has many mansions, of which art (a relatively late invention as a distinct category) is only one. But the new historicist project is not about "demoting" art or discrediting aesthetic pleasure; rather it is concerned with finding the creative power that shapes literary works *outside* the narrow boundaries in which it had hitherto been located, as well as *within* those boundaries. The risk, from a radical point of view, is a wholesale aestheticizing of culture, and in the formative years of new historicism we often had Walter Benjamin's polemical words quoted at us, as if they were the revelation of a theory crime that we had committed. Fascism, Benjamin writes at the end of his great essay "The Work of Art in the Age of Mechanical Reproduction," has made war the consummation of the principle of art for art's sake: humankind is invited to experience its own destruction as an aesthetic pleasure. "This is the situation of politics which Fascism is rendering aesthetic," he concludes grimly; "Communism responds by politicizing art." Taken out of context and treated as a piece of prescriptive dogma (and a summary judgment), this formula seems to us misguided and absurdly reductive, for our effort is not to aestheticize an entire culture, but to locate inventive energies more deeply interfused within it. To do so is hardly to endorse as aesthetically gratifying every miserable, oppressive structure and every violent action of the past. Rather, it is to imagine that the writers we love did not spring up from nowhere and that their achievements must draw upon a whole life-world and that this life-world has undoubtedly left other traces of itself.

There are, to be sure, specialized skills in writing, as in the other arts, but these linguistic skills, worthy of being admired, are not independent of a much broader expressive power in language, just as skill in drawing is not independent of what Michael Baxandall (in *Painting and Experience in Fifteenth-Century Italy*) calls "the period eye." We are intensely interested in tracking the social energies that circulate very broadly through a culture, flowing back and forth between margins and center, passing from zones designated as art to zones apparently indifferent or hostile to art, pressing up from below to transform exalted spheres and down from on high to colonize the low.

Here is another less visible feature of treating cultures as texts, once again traceable to German romanticism: the triumph of an expressivist and creative notion of language, and with it a fascination with the entire range of diverse expressions by which a culture makes itself manifest. That range is in the abstract virtually limitless, but in any given instance it has a shape, a complex individuality by which we come to identify the peoples who live together in a particular time and place. To wall off for aesthetic appreciation only a tiny portion of the expressive range of a culture is to diminish its individuality and to limit one's understanding even of that tiny portion, since its significance can be fully grasped only in relation to the other expressive possibilities with which it interacts and from which it differentiates itself. Hence even if one's interests were exclusively with high culture, it would be important to cast one's interpretive net broadly, to open the windows to the culture at large. That is at least by implication one of Herder's insights about the relation of an aesthetic form to the life-world of the people from which it arises. As with the aestheticization of culture, there is much to argue with here, since such views could be (and were) the basis for a singularly nasty *volkisch* nationalism, but they also lead to an interest in cultural individuality, a respect for diverse expressive solutions to perennial problems, and a vast broadening of aesthetic interest.

We are trying, in other words, to deepen our sense of both the invisible cohesion and the half-realized conflicts in specific cultures by broadening our view of their significant artifacts. This ambition to specify the intriguing enigmas of particular times and places distinguishes our analyses from the contemporary pan-textualism of the deconstructionists, who have their own version of the proposition that a culture is a text. Stressing the slippages, aporias, and communicative failures at the heart of signifying systems, linguistic or otherwise, their cultural textualism has no historicist ancestry. For them, written language is the paradigmatic form in which the problems of making meaning become manifest, and a culture may be said to be "textual" because its meaningful signs are inherently ambiguous, paradoxical, and undecidable. Deconstructionist literary analyses thus continually turn up textuality itself as the source and structure of all enigmas. Although maintaining that there is nothing outside of the text, no place of simple and transparent meaning where the slipperiness of the sign system can be escaped, deconstructionists nonetheless tend to draw their examples from the literary canon. While we frequently explore other kinds of texts, they urge that literary language uniquely exposes to scrutiny a textuality that operates everywhere and throughout history. Hence, in addition to skipping the levels of analysis that interest us most—the culturally and historically specific—deconstructionism also seems to reerect the hierarchical privileges of the literary.

The deconstructionists have clear methodological directives to stick to the literary despite their putative pan-textualism, but we have no comparable protective regulation. Having impetuously rushed beyond the confines of the canonical garden, we stand facing extraordinary challenges and perplexing questions:

- Out of the vast array of textual traces in a culture, the identification of units suitable for analysis is problematized. If every trace of a culture is part of a massive text, how can one identify the boundaries of these units? What is the appropriate scale? There are, we conclude, no abstract, purely theoretical answers to these questions. To a considerable extent the units are given by the archive itself—that is, we almost always receive works whose boundaries have already been defined by the technology and generic assumptions of the original makers and readers. But new historicism undertakes to call these assumptions into question and treat them as part of the history that needs to be interpreted.

- Similarly, we ask ourselves how we can identify, out of the vast array of textual traces in a culture, which are the significant ones, either for us or for them, the ones most worth pursuing. Again it proves impossible to provide a theoretical answer, an answer that would work reliably in advance of plunging ahead to see what resulted. We have embarked on what Ezra Pound in an early essay calls "the method of Luminous Detail" whereby we attempt to isolate significant or "interpreting detail" from the mass of traces that have survived in the archive, but we can only be certain that the detail is indeed luminous, that it possesses what William Carlos Williams terms "the strange phosphorus of the life,"[12] in the actual practice of teaching and writing.

- If an entire culture is regarded as a text, then everything is at least potentially in play both at the level of representation and at the level of event. Indeed, it becomes increasingly difficult to maintain a clear, unambiguous boundary between what is representation and what is event. At the very least, the drawing or maintaining of that boundary is itself an event.

- In the larger perspective of the cultural text, representations similarly cease to have a settled relationship of symbolic distance from matter and particularly from human bodies. The way bodies are understood to function, the difference between men and women, the nature of the passions, the experience of illness, the border line between life and death are all closely bound up with particular cultural representations, but they cannot simply be reduced to those representations. The body functions as a kind of "spoiler," always baffling or exceeding the ways in which it is represented.

- The unsettling of the relation between imitation and action, between background and foreground, and between representation and bodily reality gives rise to a sense of archival and interpretive inexhaustibility. There is always something further to pursue, always some extra trace, always some leftover, even in the most satisfyingly tight and coherent argument. Moreover, works that are at first adduced only in order to illuminate a particular cultural object develop an odd tendency to insist upon themselves as fascinating interpretive enigmas.

• If a whole culture is regarded as a text—if all the textual traces of an era "count" as both representation and event—then it is increasingly difficult to invoke "history" as censor. That is, for new historicism, history cannot easily exercise that stabilizing and silencing function it possessed in analyses that sought to declare the limits of the sayable and thinkable. Of course, certain things are easier—and certainly safer—to say and to think, at a given time and place, than other things, and it is important to know and to keep in mind the relative ease. But in any culture that has left a complex record of itself—and certainly in any culture that we study—there turn out to be virtually no boundaries that are not transgressed by someone or other (or imagined by those in power to be transgressed in some dark corner). Against the determinism that attempts to insist that certain things in a given period were beyond conception or articulation, new historicism invokes the vastness of the textual archive, and with that vastness an aesthetic appreciation of the individual instance.

Because of this very lack of a given set of objects, new historicism becomes a history of possibilities: while deeply interested in the collective, it remains committed to the value of the single voice, the isolated scandal, the idiosyncratic vision, the transient sketch. From the beginning we thought it was crucially important to have it both ways: we wanted to delve as deeply as possible into the creative matrices of particular historical cultures and at the same time we wanted to understand how certain products of these cultures could seem to possess a certain independence. In our scholarship, the relative positions of text and context often shift, so that what has been the mere background makes a claim for the attention that has hitherto been given only to the foregrounded and privileged work of art, yet we wish to know how the foregrounding came about. We suspect that it occurred through no very peaceful process, and hence we seek to place an emphasis on the tension between certain artifacts (including many of the works that have been regarded as canonical works of art) and their cultures. That is, our work has always been about resistance as well as replication, friction as well as assimilation, subversion as well as orthodoxy. We are fascinated by the ways in which certain texts come to possess some limited immunity

from the policing functions of their society, how they lay claim
to special status, and how they contrive to move from one time
period to another without losing all meaning. Accordingly, we
mine what are sometimes called counterhistories that make apparent the slippages, cracks, fault lines, and surprising absences
in the monumental structures that dominated a more traditional
historicism.

This characteristically double vision of the art of the past—at
once immersed in its time and place and yet somehow pulling
out and away—is deeply related to our understanding of our own
aesthetic experience. We never feel that we can simply put off all
our historically conditioned longings, fears, doubts, and dreams,
along with our accumulated knowledge of the world, and enter
into another conceptual universe. But at the same time we do not
experience works of art—or indeed any significant textual trace
of the past—as confirmation of what we already know. In a
meaningful encounter with a text that reaches us powerfully, we
feel at once pulled out of our own world and plunged back with
redoubled force into it. It seems arrogant to claim such an experience for ourselves as readers and not to grant something similar
to the readers and the authors of the past.

When we began to try to impose some order on the tangled
effects that new historicism has had on the practice of literary
history, we designated four specific transformations that it helped
to bring about: (1) the recasting of discussions about "art" into
discussions of "representations"; (2) the shift from materialist explanations of historical phenomena to investigations of the history of the human body and the human subject; (3) the discovery
of unexpected discursive contexts for literary works by pursuing
their "supplements" rather than their overt thematics; and (4) the
gradual replacement of "ideology critique" with discourse analysis.
Initially, we thought we would address each of these transformations as a team, trading paragraphs back and forth and patiently
reasoning together until we achieved a single voice and a single
vision. But like all utopian voyages, this one foundered on the
sharp rocks of reality. And it deserved to be shipwrecked: for
not only did we recreate in miniature the many small and great
conceptual disagreements that had emerged whenever the larger
group of collaborators sat down together to try to work out a

shared programmatic statement, but also once again (and more happily) we discovered that serious work only got done when each of us became passionately engaged with particular texts, images, archives, and problems. No progress can be made on methodological problems without total immersion in practice, and that immersion is not for us fundamentally collaborative: it is doggedly private, individual, obsessive, lonely. Only when we had drafted the bulk of the core chapters by ourselves—chapters 3 and 5 by Greenblatt, chapters 4 and 6 by Gallagher—could we begin again to exchange work, offer suggestions and counter-arguments, and transform the first-person singular into the first-person plural.

In chapters 3 through 6 we are true, in our fashion, to our original fourfold scheme of new historicist transformations. Chapters 3 and 4 make a contrasting pair that examines how cultures erect collapsible distinctions between representations and what they wish to consider ultimate realities. The first of this pair, "The Wound in the Wall," examines the implicit assumptions about representation embedded in works of art and links these assumptions to institutional strategies. It explains how two Renaissance paintings both bear and efface the marks of the eucharistic doctrine of the Real Presence, especially its anti-representationalism. The second, "The Potato in the Materialist Imagination," jumps forward three and a half centuries to encounter an equally unsettled relation between "the real" and its licensed representations inside nineteenth-century materialism; along the way, it explicates the similarities and differences between historical materialism and the body history that has been new historicism's close intellectual kin. Chapters 5 and 6 form another pair, which juxtaposes two works of literature, *Hamlet* and *Great Expectations,* as well as the pressures to believe or disbelieve that shaped them. The first of this pair, "The Mousetrap," also illustrates the historical uses of supplementarity, since it gets from *Hamlet* to its unacknowledged "context" (the murderous disputes over eucharistic doctrine in England) by tracing God's body through the entrails of a mouse. The second of our literary chapters, "The Novel and Other Discourses of Suspended Disbelief," again fast-forwards into the nineteenth century both to encounter literature's role in normalizing disbelief and to explore the origins and limits of the concept of "ideology."

The chapters route their theoretical and methodological generalizations through dense networks of particulars. As we had not at the outset foreseen that they would take such circuitous ways, we wrote two opening chapters—"The Touch of the Real" and "Counterhistory and the Anecdote"—to try to explain what had emerged as our most consistent commitment: a commitment to particularity. (Even here we had to pull in separate directions—Greenblatt in chapter 1 and Gallagher in chapter 2—before we were able to merge our texts.) Both chapters explore the new historicist attraction to the anecdote, the first by describing the influence of two writers who use anecdotes or fragments to produce the effect of a historical real, and the second by placing the new historicist anecdote inside the historiographical context of other contemporary counterhistorical methods. The book thus took the shape of two chapters *about,* followed by four chapters *of,* new historicism.

Writing the book has convinced us that new historicism is not a repeatable methodology or a literary critical program. Each time we approached that moment in the writing when it might have been appropriate to draw the "theoretical" lesson, to scold another school of criticism, or to point the way toward the paths of virtue, we stopped, not because we're shy of controversy, but because we cannot bear to see the long chains of close analysis go up in a puff of abstraction. So we sincerely hope you will not be able to say what it all adds up to; if you could, we would have failed.

One

T H E   T O U C H   O F   T H E   R E A L

"Analysis," writes Clifford Geertz in the essay "Thick Description" that opens his celebrated book, *The Interpretation of Cultures* (1973), "is sorting out the structures of signification—what Ryle called established codes, a somewhat misleading expression, for it makes the enterprise sound too much like that of the cipher clerk when it is much more like that of the literary critic—and determining their social ground and import."[1] Small wonder then that Geertz's account of the project of social science rebounded with force upon literary critics like us in the mid-1970s: it made sense of something we were already doing, returning our own professional skills to us as more important, more vital and illuminating, than we had ourselves grasped. We perhaps did not wholly appreciate the scientific ambition lurking in the word "determining," but we were excited to find a sophisticated, intellectually powerful, and wonderfully eloquent anthropologist who could make use of the tools in our disciplinary kit and in so doing renew in us a sense of their value.

Within the contentious discipline of anthropology, Geertz has by now been so routinely accused of one or another form of wickedness—such is the cost of academic success—that it is easy to overlook the liberating effect he had on those who came to him, as we did, from the outside and particularly from literary criticism. He did not attempt, of course, to justify the academic analysis of literature, let alone to find in it the radical politics for which we were longing, but he did something that seemed still more important. He argued that our interpretive strategies provided key means for understanding the complex symbolic systems and life patterns that anthropologists studied. The effect was like touching one wire to another: literary criticism made contact with reality. Or rather, as Geertz quickly observed, it made contact, as always, with pieces of writing. But this was writing with a difference: not poetry or fiction but verbal traces less self-consciously detached from the lives real men and women actually live.

The crucial self-defining move in Geertz's essay on "thick description" comes when the anthropologist pulls away from Gilbert Ryle's distinction between a twitch and a wink (and between both of these and a parody of a wink or even the rehearsal of this parodic wink). "Like so many of the little stories Oxford philosophers like to make up for themselves," Geertz remarks, "all this winking, fake-winking, burlesque-fake-winking, rehearsed-burlesque-fake-winking, may seem a bit artificial" (7). What would be the alternative to such artificiality? How could the distinction between "thin description" and "thick description" (the one merely describing the mute act, the other giving the act its place in a network of framing intentions and cultural meanings) be linked, as Geertz puts it, to something "more empirical"? The answer is still, it turns out, a little story—that is, an anecdote; however, now it is not one of the little stories Oxford philosophers make up for themselves, but rather one of the little stories anthropologists record, or are supposed to record, in their notebooks during the great disciplinary rite of passage known as fieldwork. "Let me give," Geertz writes, "deliberately unpreceded by any prior explanatory comment at all, a not untypical excerpt from my own field journal" (7). There follows, set off in a different typeface, a wonderful short account of an episode of sheep stealing, murder, and justice—a series of events that occurred in central Morocco in 1912 and were related to Geertz in 1968 by one of the participants, an old man named Cohen.

"A not untypical excerpt": are such recorded stories typical or not of the contents of the anthropologist's field journal? Geertz's delicate double negative enables the text he quotes to have some representative force without being absorbed into a larger whole. If you understand what it means to interpret this excerpt, you will have some idea of what it means to interpret many roughly comparable excerpts, but you will not thereby possess the entire cultural system. That is, you will not be freed of the obligation to ponder each excerpt individually and (as far as possible) on its own terms, nor will you have comprehended anything like the full range of the materials to be pondered. "Deliberately unpreceded by any prior explanatory comment at all": the excerpt is meant to surprise and to baffle, not to assume a comfortable place in a preexisting analysis of Moroccan culture. It functions then to subvert a programmatic analytical response, a fully systematized methodology, and it helps to call into question, in the midst of a loose allegiance to structuralism, whether either a culture or a method could ever be rendered satisfyingly systematic. The anecdote is, as Geertz puts it, "quoted raw, a note in a bottle." As such, it is meant not only to convey the idea of the "empirical" (as distinct from the philosopher's "artificial" stories) but also to arouse the bafflement, the intense curiosity and interest, that necessitates the interpretation of cultures.

Geertz repeats the image of the note in the bottle twice in the essay on thick description. The image nicely serves to emphasize something at once specific to his sheep-stealing anecdote, since it has bobbed up from 1912 and thus from a Morocco that has by now long vanished over the horizon, and more general, since all cultures that are not one's own are always located beyond one's familiar horizon. It thus underscores the promise, implicit in most ethnographic texts and explicit here, that the excerpt has not been invented by the anthropologist, that it comes from "somewhere else."[2] Moreover, the anecdote has not been carefully cooked up, like Ryle's story of winks and twitches, to exemplify an abstract point; it is not only something found, like a note in a bottle, but also, as Geertz puts it, "raw."

Yet Geertz's link to literary criticism depends upon his immediately qualifying, indeed abandoning, this notion of the "raw." For if it is important for the reader to accept Geertz's claim that he is not making up an exemplary tale but rather quoting something told to him by one of his "informants," it is at least as important for the reader to grasp that the quotation is itself a story, a story that has been written down in the anthropologist's field journal. This insistence on narrative and on textuality helps to justify the appeal to techniques of literary analysis, but it is not quite the same as an insistence that "there is nothing outside the text." Or rather as soon as you collapse everything into something called textuality, you discover that it makes all the difference what kind of text you are talking about. The collapse licenses a certain kind of attention and invites the questions that literary critics characteristically ask, but at the same time it calls for a sharp attention to genre and rhetorical mode, to the text's implicit or explicit reality claims, to the implied link (or distance) between the word and whatever it is—the real, the material, the realm of practice, pain, bodily pleasure, silence, or death—to which the text gestures as that which lies beyond the written word, outside its textual mode of being.

The "raw" excerpt from the field notes makes a stronger claim to reference—it points more directly to a world that has some solidity and resistance—than Ryle's invented example, but the former is no less a textual construction than the latter. The sheep-stealing anecdote has a quality of strangeness or opacity, but not because it is something mute and shapeless, dug up like a potato from an alien soil. What "we" anthropologists call "our data," Geertz writes, "are really our own constructions of other people's constructions of what they and their compatriots are up to." "This little drama" (9), as he calls the passage he quotes from his field notes, is meant to show that there is rather less observation and considerably more explication—*explication de texte*—than anthropologists generally admit to.

Thick description, as Ryle uses the term in his essays on thinking, entails an account of the intentions, expectations, circumstances, settings, and purposes that give actions their meanings.[3] The distinction between a twitch and a wink is secured by the element of volition that is not itself visibly manifest in the contraction of the eyelid; a thin description would miss it altogether. So too with the other layers of framing intentions that Ryle piles on: fake twitches, rehearsals of fake twitches, and so forth. Many of these framing intentions seem to introduce an explicitly aesthetic or representational quality, but such a quality is not essential to the notion of thick description. A thin description of what you are doing when you are pumping up bicycle tires, to cite another of Ryle's examples, would be an account of a series of repetitive physical motions that produce a certain effect. A thick description of those same motions would involve a fuller sense of the significance of what you are doing. If you are pumping up your bicycle tires because you are preparing to go for a bike ride, a thick description of your pumping requires a reference to your intended ride, whether that ride actually occurs or not; if, on the other hand, you are pumping up your bicycle tires because you want to strengthen the muscles of your arms so that bullies will no longer kick sand at you at the beach, the thick description of your pumping would differ accordingly.

Ryle is fascinated by receding planes, a fascination that repeatedly draws him to the game of inventing chains of further complications around what initially seems a simple action: winking (or twitching), clearing your throat, hitting golf balls, playing tennis, cooking, jumping over flower beds. The mental game is not difficult to play: you are not actually intending to go on a bike ride (to continue in Ryle's vein) but only pretending that you are, in order to deceive an observer; or you are rehearsing for a drama in which you will play the part of someone who deceives an observer by pumping up bicycle tires as if in anticipation of a bike ride that your character never really intends to take. And so on. The difficulty lies in accounting persuasively for the relation between these surrounding circumstances and the action as thinly described. Thick description, in Ryle's account, involves two major features: intention-parasitism (the intention with which a person undertakes to pump up bicycle tires is ancillary to and hence parasitical upon his intention to take a bike ride) and circumstance-detachment (the actor rehearsing the part of the tire pumper need not actually have a pump or a bike on hand—a stick and a table will do just fine for the purpose of rehearsal—but the act of rehearsing only makes sense in reference to the intended performance).

For Ryle, thick description is manifestly a quality of the explication rather than of the action or text that is explicated: it is not the object that is thick or thin, but only the description of it. A thick description thus could be exceedingly straightforward or, alternatively, exceedingly complex, depending on the length of the chain of parasitical intentions and circumstantial detachments. A thin description need not be brief or schematic; it could be quite lengthy and complicated—an adequate account of the physiology and pneumatics involved in pumping tires would take many pages—but it would not concern itself with the agent's framing intentions or the culture within which those intentions acquire their significance. Thickness is not in the object; it is in the narrative surroundings, the add-ons, the nested frames.

As Geertz's famous essay deploys the term, however, thickness begins to slide almost imperceptibly from the description to the thing described. For, though Geertz may wish to imply that his excerpt was chosen virtually at random and that one fragment would have been as good as another, some texts seem far more amenable to thick description than others, and consequently some texts seem "thicker" than others. Thickness no longer seems extrinsic to the object, a function solely of the way it is framed. The sheep-stealing narrative is supposed to be nothing more than the ethnographic equivalent of Ryle's winks and twitches, but in fact they seem profoundly different: Ryle's is a purpose-built illustration of a carefully delimited philosophical point; Geertz's supposedly "raw" excerpt from his field notes is a complex narrative in which the motivating intentions seem intrinsic. That is, neither of Ryle's key terms, intention-parasitism and circumstance-detachment, is remotely relevant to Geertz's anecdote, precisely because the intentions and circumstances are not securely situated on the outside of the actions reported.

This slide is not a theoretical proposition, nor is it, in its divergence from Ryle, a mistake; rather, it is part of the disciplinary interest of anthropology. The shift from the philosopher's tale to the "native informant's" tale is for Geertz a shift from the "artificial" toward the "empirical"—that is, toward textual constructions, presented as "raw" data or "evidence," that seem less purpose-built, more resistant to simple appropriation, and hence more nearly autonomous. As the anthropologist interprets his exemplary texts, these texts seem to be increasingly embedded in the cultures from which they come and to possess within themselves more and more of the culture's linked intentions. In practice (that is, in Geertz's interpretive practice), certain constructions of cultural reality appear compressed and hence expandable: "From this simple incident," Geertz remarks about the sheep-stealing anecdote, "one can widen out into enormous complexities of social experience" (19).

Are these complexities actually inscribed in the textual fragments, or are they brought to bear upon them from the outside in the course of interpretation? Part of Geertz's power was his ability to suggest that the multilayered cultural meanings by which he was fascinated were present in the fragments themselves, just as the literary criticism of William Empson or Kenneth Burke managed to suggest that the dense ambiguities and ironies were present in the literary texts themselves and not only in the acts of interpretation.[4] Those acts of interpretation were not completely supplementary—they helped to create as well as to disclose the effect of compression—but the dense networks of meaning charted in an effective thick description had to be traceable back to the anecdote initially held up for scrutiny.

What we are calling the effect of compression enabled a literary historian like Erich Auerbach to move convincingly from a tiny passage to a sprawling, complex text (and, finally, to "Western Literature"). Drawing on literary criticism—Auerbach is cited, along with Samuel Taylor Coleridge, T. S. Eliot, Burke, Empson, R. P. Blackmur, and Cleanth Brooks[5]—Geertz did something similar with cultural fragments, small bits of symbolic behavior from which he could "widen out" into larger social worlds. The techniques of literary analysis thus helped to make possible for Geertzian anthropology something akin to what in optics is called "foveation," the ability to keep an object (here a tiny textualized piece of social behavior) within the high-resolution area of perception. Foveation in cultural interpretation is rather difficult because of problems of both scale and focus. The interpreter must be able to select or to fashion, out of the confused continuum of social existence, units of social action small enough to hold within the fairly narrow boundaries of full analytical attention, and this attention must be unusually intense, nuanced, and sustained.

Geertz grasped that, along with analytic philosophy, literary criticism had for years been honing useful foveation skills. Hence the terms that he uses to describe his piece of thick description not only emphasize its own textuality (in keeping with his insistence that ethnographers are writers), but also repeatedly extend that textuality to the object described: "our sheep story—an assortment of remarks and anecdotes," "a not untypical excerpt from my own field journal," "a note in a bottle," a "passage," "this little drama," "our text," a "social farce," "our pastoral drama," "the rigmarole," a "social discourse"—and moving away from the excerpt and toward what the excerpt is meant to exemplify: "a manuscript—foreign, faded, full of ellipses, incoherencies, suspicious emendations, and tendentious commentaries, but written not in conventionalized graphs of sound but in transient examples of shaped behavior" (10). That is, culture is itself an "acted document," whether it takes the form of "a burlesqued wink or a mock sheep raid" (10). The point is that to understand what people are up to in any culture—and, "leaving our winks and sheep behind for the moment," Geertz takes a Beethoven quartet as his example—you need to be acquainted "with the imaginative universe within which their acts are signs" (11).

For the purposes of literary criticism, "imaginative," "drama," "manuscript," and "signs" were reassuringly familiar terms, as was the whole emphasis on symbolic behavior, but the specific force of Geertz's work for new historicism resided in the expansion of these terms to a much broader and less familiar range of texts than literary critics had permitted themselves to analyze. For Geertz this expansion reflected an empowering appropriation of analytical tools, an appropriation that conferred the prestige accorded to the supreme achievements of Western high culture, such as Beethoven quartets, on the flotsam and jetsam in an anthropologist's field notes. At issue was not only prestige—what Pierre Bourdieu famously analyzed as cultural capital—but a transference of the kind of attention paid to canonical works of art to the ordinary and extraordinary behavior of the subjects of anthropology. To construct descriptions, Geertz notes, "of the involvements of a Berber chieftain, a Jewish merchant, and a French soldier with one another in 1912 Morocco is clearly an imaginative act, not all that different from constructing similar descriptions of, say, the involvements with one another of a provincial French doctor, his silly, adulterous wife, and her feckless lover in nineteenth century France" (15–16). If it is not altogether clear at this moment in Geertz's essay whether it is the anthropologist himself or the anthropologist's informant Cohen who is being likened to Gustave Flaubert, this is because both the informant's discourse and the anthropologist's discourse about that discourse (and, for that matter, the series of actions from 1912) are alike fictions, in the root sense of things *made, composed, fashioned.*

Our goal in response to Geertz was not exactly to reverse the disciplinary appropriation, that is, to apply to literary analysis the terms and concepts developed by anthropologists. (Such an application, of course, was in fact occurring, especially in literary structuralism's use of Claude Lévi-Strauss.) What we wanted was not social science but ethnographic realism, and we wanted it principally for literary purposes. That is, we had no interest in decisively leaving works of literature behind and turning our attention elsewhere; instead, we sought to put literature and literary criticism in touch with that elsewhere. It is a tribute to Geertz that it was not his method that seemed powerful to us (after all, that method was in part borrowed from literary criticism), but rather the lived life that he managed so well to narrate, describe, and clarify. That lived life, at once raw and subtle, coarse and complex, was the thing that had been progressively refined out of the most sophisticated literary studies, or so it seemed to us at the time. By embracing and displacing literary studies, *The Interpretation of Cultures* provided an impetus for recovering what had been lost. Literary criticism could venture out to unfamiliar cultural texts, and these texts—often marginal, odd, fragmentary, unexpected, and crude—in turn could begin to interact in interesting ways with the intimately familiar works of the literary canon.

To Auerbach's powerful ability to conjure up complex life-worlds from tiny fragments, Geertz added the anthropologist's strong claim to a hold on the world. That is, it was crucial, as part of the pleasure and interest of reading Geertz, to believe that he had not made up his Mr. Cohen and that Cohen too had not simply made up his story. To be sure, Geertz encourages the reader to grasp that his informant's version of the story is not identical to one that would have been produced by any of the other principals in it and that he may have considerably enhanced the story for rhetorical effect; but Cohen was a real person recounting actual experiences, and his story was *his* story and not the ethnographer's.

"I can call spirits from the vasty deep," claims Owain Glyndwr, the strange Welsh magus in Shakespeare's *1 Henry IV*. "Why, so can I, or so can any man" is Hotspur's sardonic reply, "But will they come when you do call for them?"[6] So too an anecdote may conjure up reality, but will reality come when it is called? If it is only a matter of rhetoric—the effect of what the ancient rhetoricians called *enargeia*, or vividness—then only a reality-effect is conjured and nothing more. But something more is at stake. Geertz gestures toward that something when he acknowledges that there are important problems of verification or, as he prefers to term it, appraisal. This process of appraisal is largely internal to a particular discipline—we obviously had no way of testing Geertz's interpretation of Moroccan culture nor could we confirm the authenticity of his field notes—but it is in principle significant for the value anthropology could have for literary studies. For the interest was never to collapse anthropology and literary criticism into each other but to draw upon their particular strengths, strengths that depended at least as much upon the differences between their characteristic texts as upon their surprising similarities. Indeed it is an awareness of how those differences are constituted and what they mean—an understanding of the emergence of the literary and the imaginative force of the nonliterary—that has virtually obsessed not only our own work but that of new historicism in general.

What then should we make of Geertz's claim that an anecdote from the field journal is "not all that different," as an imaginative construction, from *Madame Bovary*? Very little beyond the critical incentive, or rather the imperative, to interpret. To be sure, if it turned out that Geertz's Cohen had taken it upon himself to be the Flaubert of the Maghreb and had made up his entire story, we might still have concluded that we possessed something of ethnographic value: a glimpse of the fantasies of an old man who had been steeped in the symbolic systems of colonial Morocco.[7] If, however, it turned out that Geertz had made up Cohen, we at least would have concluded that as an ethnographer Geertz was not to be trusted, and his work would have immediately lost much of its value. For it is precisely not as a fiction or as a little philosopher's tale that Geertz invites us to read his anecdote; it is as a "raw" sample of his field notes. The frame is crucial, since in this case it helps us to conjure up a "real" as opposed to an "imaginary" world.

Geertz's conjuring of the real seemed to us useful for literary studies not because it insisted upon the primacy of interpretation—that was already the norm in literary criticism—but because it helped to widen the range of imaginative constructions to be interpreted. His thick descriptions of cultural texts strengthened the insistence that the things that draw us to literature are often found in the nonliterary, that the concept of literariness is deeply unstable, that the boundaries between different types of narratives are subject to interrogation and revision. We wanted to argue that human creativity, including narrative and linguistic creativity, only makes sense in the long run because it is a widespread, indeed democratic, possession—a possession that is almost impossible to contain within a small elite or sequester from the sweet, familiar light of the everyday. We wanted also to use the anecdote to show in compressed form the ways in which elements of lived experience enter into literature, the ways in which everyday institutions and bodies get recorded. And we wanted, conversely, to show in compressed form the ways in which poetry, drama, and prose fiction play themselves out in the everyday world, since men and women repeatedly find themselves in effect speaking the language of the literary not only in their public performances, but also in their most intimate or passionate moments.

We sought something beyond this: we wanted to find in the past real bodies and living voices, and if we knew that we could not find these—the bodies having long moldered away and the voices fallen silent—we could at least seize upon those traces that seemed to be close to actual experience. Literature seemed to us, as to many others, almost infinitely precious because its creators had invented techniques for representing this experience with uncanny vividness; but there were other techniques and other texts, outside the conventional boundaries of the literary, that possessed a nearly comparable power. The greatest challenge lay not simply in exploring these other texts—an agreeably imperial expansion of literary criticism beyond its borders—but in making the literary and the nonliterary seem to be each other's thick description. That both the literary work and the anthropological (or historical) anecdote are texts, that both are fictions in the sense of things made, that both are shaped by the imagination and by the available resources of narration and description helped make it possible to conjoin them; but their ineradicable differences—the fact that neither is purpose-built for the other, that they make sharply different claims upon the actual, that they are incommensurable and virtually impossible to foveate simultaneously—made the conjunction powerful and compelling.

We wanted to recover in our literary criticism a confident conviction of reality, without giving up the power of literature to sidestep or evade the quotidian and without giving up a minimally sophisticated understanding that any text depends upon the absence of the bodies and voices that it represents. We wanted the touch of the real in the way that in an earlier period people wanted the touch of the transcendent.

*"Readers of the *Odyssey* will remember the well-prepared and touching scene in book 19, when Odysseus has at last come home, the scene in which the old housekeeper Euryclea, who had been his nurse, recognizes him by a scar on his thigh."[8] This is how the text of Erich Auerbach's great book *Mimesis*, both in the German-language original and the English translation, begins: no pages of acknowledgments, no methodological foreword, no theoretical introduction. Between the title (*Mimesis: Dargestellte Wirklichkeit in der Abendländischen Literatur*) and the table of contents, there is only an epigraph in English, to which we will return, from Marvell's "To His Coy Mistress": "Had we but world enough and time. . . ." In the first edition, published in Switzerland by A. Francke AG. Verlag in 1946, there is also along with the copyright information, in very small letters, the words "Mai 1942 bis April 1945." Then we plunge immediately into a close reading of the episode of Odysseus's scar, an analysis meant to

bring out "the genius of the Homeric style." This genius, Auerbach writes, "becomes even more apparent when it is compared
with an equally ancient and equally epic style from a different
world of forms" (7), and thus he moves to an analysis of the biblical account of the sacrifice of Isaac. By the chapter's close, Auerbach has sketched two styles that

> represent basic types: on the one hand fully externalized descrip-
> tion, uniform illumination, uninterrupted connection, free expres-
> sion, all events in the foreground, displaying unmistakable mean-
> ings, few elements of historical development and of psychological
> perspective; on the other hand, certain parts brought into high
> relief, others left obscure, abruptness, suggestive influence of the
> unexpressed, "background" quality, multiplicity of meanings and
> the need for interpretation, universal-historical claims, develop-
> ment of the concept of historically becoming, and preoccupation
> with the problematic. (23)

What is going on here? In some twenty pages, Auerbach has
moved from pointillist textual detail—"To the word scar (v. 393)
there is first attached a relative clause ('which once long ago a
boar . . .'), which enlarges into a voluminous syntactical parenthe-
sis. . . ." (7)—to a huge vista, an overview of the foundational
modes for the representation of reality in European culture. It is
the literary critical equivalent of one of those canvases—Altdorfer's *Battle of Issus* is the supreme example—where the eye moves
from the tiny but legible design on the soldier's button to the
curvature of the earth at the horizon. Or rather in *Mimesis* the
button, as it were, is made to reveal the shape of the whole wide
earth: such is the power of the concept of "representation" in
Auerbach's skillful hands. His textual fragments represent the
enormous multiauthored texts from which they are drawn—the
Odyssey and the Bible—and the styles disclosed in those fragments represent historically determined and determining methods by which the world is apprehended, imitated, and reproduced.
    The subsequent nineteen chapters of Auerbach's *Mimesis* all
begin with short excerpts from a text—a few pages, quoted first
in the original and then in translation.[9] Each chapter then proceeds to unpack its excerpt, sometimes in the light of other briefer

passages from the same author's work or from that of contemporaries, but more often by intense close reading, that is, by examining very carefully modulations in the level of style, resonances of
diction, nuances of tone, rhetorical strategies, latent philosophical
and sociological assumptions. *Mimesis* does, it emerges, have a
grand overarching theme—what Auerbach calls, late in the book,
"the history of the literary conquest of modern reality" (331)—
along with a series of recurrent preoccupations and motifs, but
there is no programmatic statement of purpose, and each of the
chapters is discrete and self-contained. Throughout these chapters there is a profound sense of historical process and a rich
awareness of complex intertextual relations, but Auerbach makes
almost no gestures toward a wholly integrated and sequential
account, a history of causes and effects. Even the "basic types"
adumbrated in the opening chapter, though they remain available
as powerful points of reference, are not insisted upon rigorously,
nor is Auerbach's book a sustained history of their rivalry or
intertwining.

An immensely ambitious book without a purpose, or at least
without a declared purpose: with a lesser book we might assume
that this conjunction was a sign that its author took for granted,
perhaps fatuously, the importance of his enterprise; or that his
ambition lacked an adequate end; or that an elaborate display of
learning and interpretive power was, among the community for
whom the book was written, an end in itself. But none of these
assumptions is correct. Auerbach had been expelled from the academic community for which he had been trained; he writes with
a profoundly melancholy sense that the centuries-long project he
lovingly chronicles is close to exhaustion, disintegration, or irrelevance; and at the same time his book carries the conviction that
it possesses a supremely adequate object. This conviction, never
made explicit but pervasive nonetheless, has about it something
of an implied religious faith, a faith that seems almost to become
manifest in the chapter on the *Divine Comedy*, "Farinata and
Cavalcante."[10] Dante wrote, Auerbach observes, in a supremely
elevated style, a style that owed everything to his acknowledged
master Virgil and to the sublime gravitas of the classical epic, and
yet his great work constantly violates the central principle by

which classical writers achieved sublimity, the principle of the separation of styles. Paradoxically, the elevated style of the *Comedy* "consists precisely in integrating what is characteristically individual and at times horrible, ugly, grotesque, and vulgar with the dignity of God's judgment—a dignity which transcends the ultimate limits of our earthly conception of the sublime" (194). For all its magnificent gravity and seriousness and gigantic reach, Dante's style is still, in his own words, a *sermo remissus et humilis.* Hence, in Auerbach's account, Dante's Christianity triumphantly fused the two basic types of represented reality, classical and biblical.

Dante's mixing of styles and his insistence upon the everyday even in the midst of the sacred is linked, Auerbach argues, to figural realism, a mode Auerbach had analyzed at length in a crucially important essay, "Figura," published two years before *Mimesis.* Figura, a concept by which each earthly thing has its fulfillment in the world beyond, allows both for the overarching divine order in which everything that exists is ultimately fulfilled and for the historical specificity of each particular event, phenomenon, and personality. Nothing, no matter how vulgar or grotesque, need be discarded for fear of undermining the elevated style, for the weightiness of Christian representation depends upon the intense apprehension of an earthly drama whose meaning is fully realized in a timeless eternity. "Conceiving all earthly occurrences through the medium of a mixed style—without aesthetic restriction in either subject matter or form—as an entity sublimely figural, is Christian in spirit and Christian in origin" (198).

The sublime Christian realism of the *Comedy*, its capacity through the figural power of the *sermo humilis* to integrate the classical and biblical modes of representation, stands at the very center of *Mimesis.* Auerbach's opening chapter posed a riddle—how was it possible for the representation of reality in Western literature to progress from two antithetical and incompatible modes?—that Dante brilliantly solved, plunging "the living world of human action and endurance and more especially of individual deeds and destinies" into the "changeless existence" of life after death. The phrases we have just quoted are not from Auerbach but from Hegel, and they suggest the extent to which *Mimesis* has a buried Hegelian plot.

Yet, as we have already suggested, the plot is not finally realized. To be sure, in Auerbach's vision, Dante's synthesis has its own inherent forward-driving dynamic of a kind we might expect in a Hegelian analysis. The intensity of Dante's realism, its immensely powerful representation of human passions and irreducible individuality, broke the theological scheme from which it derived: "Dante's work made man's Christian-figural being a reality, and destroyed it in the very process of realizing it" (202). But, though Auerbach is fascinated by the secularized representations of human destiny that ensue upon this destruction, he entirely lacks Hegel's confidence in a grand design, a meaningful higher order. Instead, each of the textual worlds that he enters by means of the excerpt has a way of seeming complete in itself, a complex, compelling whole. If there is a hint of a direction in the succession of these isolated representations, it is toward dissolution, but this melancholy intimation of the end of the world as we know it only intensifies Auerbach's commitment to the existential claim of individual, autonomous literary visions.

Those of us who began writing literary history in the 1970s had a strong affinity both with Auerbach's existential pessimism and with his method, a method by which many of us were, from the beginning, influenced and that we self-consciously emulated. The influence is most striking in the adaptation of Auerbach's characteristic opening gambit: the isolation of a resonant textual fragment that is revealed, under the pressure of analysis, to represent the work from which it is drawn and the particular culture in which that work was produced and consumed. That culture in turn renders the fragment explicable, both as something that could have only been written in a moment characterized by a particular set of circumstances, structures, and assumptions and as something that conveys the life-world of that moment. The new historicist anecdote as many of us deployed it is an Auerbachian device. Of course, we typically moved outside of canonical works of art for our anecdotes; we frequently sought an effect of surprise by selecting passages from what looked, in the context of literary criticism, like oddly marginal or eccentric works; and we allowed the analysis of the anecdote to pull away from or alternatively to swamp the explication of the canonical work of art to which it was at least nominally conjoined. We will return to the significance of these differences, but it is important to grasp what was so appealing about Auerbach's strategy.

Its principal appeal is that it enabled critics to illuminate extremely complex and—quite simply but not inconsequentially—long works without exhausting themselves or their readers, without making their audience feel that the task of reading was futile or intolerably boring and repetitive, and without stepping back to a detached distance, a level of generality in which the issues became banal and predictable. Here the epigraph from Marvell finds its meaning: "Had we but world enough and time," Auerbach could examine the entire vast storehouse of Western literary representations of reality, he could grapple with complex questions of periodization, and he could probe every detail of the works on which he has chosen to focus his attention. Above all, he could attempt to explore the concept "realism" around which his whole book turns and that nonetheless he steadfastly refuses to define. But time's wingèd chariot is hurrying near, and here the anecdotal, fragmentary method, which rests on the principle of representation, rescues him. "I could never have written anything in the nature of a history of European realism," Auerbach writes at the close of *Mimesis;* "the material would have swamped me" (548). Moreover, as he explains in the epilogue, he wrote his book in Istanbul, where there was no library suitable for European studies. Auerbach had gone to teach at the Turkish State University after his dismissal in 1935 on racist grounds from his teaching position at Marburg, and after the outbreak of the war there was no possibility of consulting other libraries: hence in part the significance of the dates in the small print at the beginning. So he faced the problem of too few texts as well as too many, and here again he was rescued by the anecdote. Auerbach can say convincing and fresh things about texts like the Bible, the *Odyssey,* the *Inferno, Don Quixote,* Montaigne's *Essays,* and Balzac's *Comédie humaine* because he has liberated himself from the task of writing a full "history," because his analyses have the kind of intensity and detail more typically associated with readings of Shakespeare sonnets or Donne lyrics, and because the fragmentary passages he chooses to analyze seem to represent not only whole works but whole ages.

Auerbach knows perfectly well, of course, that an entire epoch cannot be adequately represented in a single text, let alone in a small textual fragment, but in his work we repeatedly glimpse what we regard as a quasi-magical effect: the conjuring of a complex, dynamic, historically specific spirit of representation out of a few paragraphs. The spirit of representation sometimes corresponds to the boundaries of nation or class or religion or language, but is not consistently linked with any of these, for Auerbach does not assent fully to any of the categories that governed the principal literary histories of the nineteenth and twentieth centuries. He is above all allergic to the nationalism, often racially inflected, that generated most of these histories. National self-consciousness is occasionally granted considerable importance, of course, but *Mimesis* repeatedly absorbs it into the larger project of "Western" literature, where "Western" functions as an antidote to the exclusive claims of a territorial or racial group. (This strategy, we might note in passing, draws Auerbach into the familiar paradox of positing the origins of the "Western" in works from Asia Minor and the Middle East.) The organizational principle, after the opening chapter, is sequentiality, though here too Auerbach is careful to restrict the significance of the chronological order he observes; it is not the link between one age and another that interests him, but rather what we might call a sequence of specters, the specters of mimetic genius.

We suspect that Auerbach would have disliked this characterization of his work. He writes not in the manner of a conjurer but in the sober, solemn manner of a learned literary historian. Nonetheless, in *Mimesis* he does what Francis Bacon in a strange passage from *The Advancement of Learning* (1623) counseled the historian of literature to do:

> For the *manner* of compiling such a history, I particularly advise
> that the manner and provision of it be not drawn from histories

and commentaries alone, but that the principal books written in each century, or perhaps in shorter periods, proceeding in regular order from the earliest ages, be themselves taken into consideration, that so (I do not say by a complete perusal, for that would be an endless labour, but) by tasting them here and there and observing their argument, style, and method, the Literary Spirit [*genius literarius*] of each age may be charmed as it were from the dead.

It is this *genius literarius*—the creative, generative power of language in a particular historical period—that Auerbach repeatedly charms from his fragmentary passages, a conjuring trick that is enhanced, as *Mimesis* proceeds, by what seems to be the increasing arbitrariness with which the passages are chosen. The episode of Odysseus's scar is highly charged, and still more the sacrifice of Isaac: these are fables of identity, to borrow Northrop Frye's phrase, resonant, momentous, and exquisitely shaped. But Alcofribas's brief sojourn in Gargantua's mouth and Prince Hal's expression of weariness to his boon companion Poins are not conspicuously great moments in the works of Rabelais and Shakespeare; and by the time we reach the chapters on the realist classics of the nineteenth century, the passages seem chosen almost by chance, and they begin to proliferate, as if a single resonant anecdote were no longer sufficient. Indeed at moments, in a modern, demystified version of the Virgilian *sortilegium*, Auerbach appears simply to be opening a book—*The Red and the Black* or *Madame Bovary*—at random and starting his analysis wherever his eyes happen to fall. Yet it is precisely in these later chapters, with their analyses of bits of text that no longer tell meaningful stories, that Auerbach's conjuring trick is most striking, and it is here too that Auerbach comes closest to acknowledging that it *is* a conjuring trick.

From Balzac's *Père Goriot,* a novel replete with melodramatic incident, Auerbach selects an almost negligible detail, a passage describing the appearance in the dilapidated pension dining room of its shabby owner, Madame Vauquer. Nothing about this particular appearance of the pension mistress is momentous; on the contrary, Balzac is describing her daily routine, one in keeping with the petty, fetid, claustrophobic triviality of the entire milieu over which she presides. This very ordinariness linking the repulsive, vulgar woman to every corner of her repulsive, vulgar pension fascinates Auerbach, for it perfectly exemplifies the "atmospheric realism" that he finds in Balzac. The hallmark of this kind of realism, he suggests, is the organic unity of the moral, physical, social, and historical environment, so that virtually all details, even those apparently idiosyncratic or marginal or jumbled together in disorder, are clues to the true nature of the whole to which they are structurally bound. Thus there is no need for anecdotes that take the form of miniature narratives, with beginning, middle, and end; the description of a chair, a pair of slippers, or a tablecloth will do.

This atmospheric realism and the disordered, hasty jumble of features through which it is constituted do not bespeak a cool demystification of the world—the leaching out of its narrative glamour—but rather a quality Auerbach proposes to call "demonic." In part the term seems to be elicited by certain details in the text: the arrival of the hideous Madame Vauquer is preceded by that of her cat, the dining room's walls "ooze misfortune," and so forth. But Auerbach characteristically employs these local details as a platform on which to construct a far larger structure. The demonic impression does not finally depend upon invocations of witchcraft or the spectral; it is implicit in the organic unity of what Balzac was the first to term the *milieu,* a unity that is "not established rationally but is presented as a striking and immediately apprehended state of things, purely suggestively, without any proof" (471). That is, there is something eerie in the pervasiveness of the moral and physical atmosphere of the dreary lower-bourgeois Parisian pension, impregnating the room, the furniture, the clothing, along with the faces, ideas, dreams, and fates of its inhabitants. And, similarly, there is something eerie in the pervasiveness of the very different atmospheres described in *Père Goriot*'s other milieux, as well as in the unity of the "total atmosphere" that envelops all of them taken together.

Auerbach's close reading of the brief anecdote from Balzac helps us understand how strange the familiar notion of "organic" unity actually is, as if random and apparently autonomous units were revealed to be mysteriously interlinked cells in a monstrous living body. Balzac advanced zoological and sociological theories to explicate his work, but the deepest affinities of his atmospheric realism, Auerbach shows, are to "atmospheric Historism": "his people and his atmospheres, contemporary as they may be, are always represented as phenomena sprung from historical events and forces" (480). The power of these historical forces is manifested equally in a tulle bonnet and in a revolution, in a particular style of petticoat and in a stock market crash.

This "historism" that, in Auerbach's view, unifies the fictive worlds of the great French realists, Stendhal and Balzac, also gives Auerbach his own critical method. For the anecdotal technique of *Mimesis* rests on the conviction that tiny details can be made to represent the nature of larger and larger wholes. It is possible for Auerbach to unpack long works and even entire cultures out of a close encounter with a tiny fragment because he is less concerned with sequence and form than he is with "the representation of reality." Hence he does not need to say something about the origin and internal structure of the work so much as he needs to address and explicate its characteristic practice of referring to the world. The paradox here is that it is easier for him to address the representation of reality than it is to address the inner organization of a finite text, an organization resistant to the analysis of short excerpts. The literary work is interesting to Auerbach not for its swerve away from reality—as if reality were something monumental, unchanging, and assured, and as if the literary work needed to make a space for itself, apart from the world—but rather for its claim on the world, its ability to give the reader access to the very condition for perception and action, along with the very condition for textuality, at a given place and time, in a given culture. For Auerbach, textuality—in its specificity, its local knowledge, its buried network of assumptions—is not a system distinct from lived experience but an imitation of it, and "imitation" (that is, representation) is the principal way human beings come to understand their existence and share it with others.

Auerbach thus does not look for textual traces—anecdotes—that reveal some gap between the work and the world, some sense of tension between life experience and the description of that experience. He is not interested in the ineffable or inexpressible, though he is cannily alert to the significance of silence—for example, all that is unsaid in the account in Genesis of the sacrifice of Isaac. For Auerbach what is unsaid in Genesis is not a sign of tension, a crisis or breakdown in representation, but rather one of the great resources of this particular mode of representation (distinct, as he claims, from the very different resources of Homeric narration). Similarly, Auerbach does not seize on textual traces that disclose some anomaly in the work, something that is not assimilable to the larger conscious design of the author or the dominant values of the period. What principally interests Auerbach, what draws him and what he is brilliant at locating, are moments of representational plenitude: moments in which a culture's apprehension of reality, its experience of reality, and its representation of reality converge.

Auerbach does not believe that there was a single ideal form for this convergence.[11] Rather, *Mimesis* begins with two distinct models, equally prestigious, capacious, brilliant. To be sure, as we have seen, Dante's *Comedy* draws upon Christian figural faith to integrate the two, but the integration collapses, in Auerbach's view, under the very weight of its success, and even Dante's genius could not disclose a stable common ground where the classical and biblical modes could meet. On the contrary, Auerbach observes, for example, that the jealousy over election and the promise of blessing that undermines the peace of daily life in the house, in the fields, and among the flocks in the Bible "would be utterly incomprehensible to the Homeric heroes" (22), while we may assume that the patriarchs would be comparably baffled by Odysseus's "reality."

What does it mean that Auerbach and his readers are not similarly baffled and that they do not have to choose one or the other type? It must in some sense mean a loss of the worlds in which these works were originally created: neither the *Odyssey* nor the Bible can make the claim upon us that they must have made on their earliest readers and hearers. But though Auerbach treats texts as integrally bound up with the cultures in which they were produced—that is the nature of his own "atmospheric Historism"—he does not assume that these texts could only be read, in the fullest and richest sense, when they were first written.[12] An awareness that there are alternative modes for the representation of reality actually works to heighten the richness of our understanding: we can see features of the Bible that would be virtually impossible to detect did we not know the *Odyssey.* Moreover, *Mimesis* is written with something like figural faith, faith that these great texts are in effect addressed to us and that it is at once our obligation and our pleasure to open and read them. In a dark time Petrarch in desperation wrote letters to the great figures of the past. Auerbach was writing in a still darker time: with a war raging whose outcome was by no means certain and an enemy that would have consigned him to the gas chambers. For Auerbach to read the Western literary canon as a series of letters that the past had sent to him was an act of civility in a vicious world. And his informed appreciation of multiple styles bespeaks a kind of cultural catholicity, an openness to alternative ways of responding to the world.

At the same time, there are distinct limits to what Auerbach could comfortably accept. Ironically, perhaps, it was the texts of his own contemporaries, the letters sent from closest to home, that seemed to him difficult to incorporate in the great capacious vision of literary representation. He responded with some dismay to the modernist attack on representation, to the fascination with distortion, brokenness, failure, and the void. He could find in masterpieces by Proust, Joyce, and Woolf a version of what shaped his study: "confidence that in any random fragment plucked from the course of a life at any time the totality of its fate is contained and can be portrayed" (547). But this confidence was now turned away from the solid exterior world—the material existence that always seemed to him essential to a robust realism—and toward the inward reaches of the psyche. Similarly, he could find in literary modernism the wide range of alternate motifs for the representation of reality that his own philological studies had embraced and illuminated, but these motifs were now intertwined uneasily within single works. That is, Auerbach discovered in the literature of his own time the very "multiple consciousness" that his own work as a critic had brilliantly cultivated, but his encounter with this consciousness was deeply unnerving. *Mimesis* is one of the great literary critical exhibitions in our century of one mind's capacity to grasp "multiple and multivalent reflections of consciousness" (551). How better to describe the power to respond with the deepest sympathetic intelligence to the *Odyssey* and the Bible, Arthurian romance and Shakespearean history, the *Decameron* and *Manon Lescaut*? But the grasp is sequential, a museum effect in which one passes serenely from room to room, each organized neatly by period. Faced with Joyce or Woolf, Auerbach senses in the modern artist's simultaneous grasp of conflicting and/or noncontiguous representation systems something close to nihilistic despair: "We not infrequently find a turning away from the practical will to live," he writes about modern fiction, "or delight in portraying it under its most brutal forms" or "a vague and hopeless sadness" (551).

Mimesis closes with a poignant blend of personal melancholy and impersonal, curiously sour hope. Auerbach sees the murderous violence unleashed in his world as the expression of what he calls, in almost comic understatement, "a crisis of adjustment" to the terrifying acceleration of change in modern existence. This change has forced together into close conjunction peoples, ideas, and forms of existence that had never before been compelled to acknowledge one other's existence, let alone interact. One obvious consequence is armed conflict; less obvious, but crucial in relation to Auerbach's study, is the damage, probably fatal, to the "clearly formulable and recognized community of thought and feeling" upon which any given literary representation of reality had over the centuries been constructed. It is easy to assimilate such a reflection to our own widespread sense of the homogenizing power of certain international technologies and corporate symbols, but in fact Auerbach was thinking about what looked rather like nativist movements, movements that at first glance seemed to appeal to an all too "clearly formulable and recognized community of thought and feeling." But it is precisely here, in what appear to be strident celebrations of cultural particularity, that Auerbach in the late 1930s finds a devastating loss of the individuality, the subtle particularity, of the spirit of representation. In a letter sent from Istanbul to Walter Benjamin, Auerbach reflects on what he calls the "fanatically anti-traditional nationalism" of Kemal Atatürk, "nationalism in the extreme accompanied by the simultaneous destruction of the historical national character."[13] What he witnessed in Turkey seemed to Auerbach a particularly vivid example of what was happening, partially disguised, in countries like Germany, Italy, and Russia: "It is becoming increasingly clear to me," he writes, "that the present international situation is nothing but a ruse of providence, designed to lead us along a bloody and tortuous path to an International of triviality and a culture of Esperanto" (82).

It was to this "ruse of providence" that modern writers, Auerbach understands, are responding. The randomness, the dissolution, the fragmenting of consciousness, the multiplicity of perspectives in modern fiction are, in Auerbach's view, direct expressions of contemporary reality. They are also, he suggests, attempts—by embracing the random, the quotidian, the inward, and the common—to get beyond "the controversial and unstable orders over which men fight and despair" (552). Auerbach had every reason to hope passionately for the resolution of conflict through the lessening of differences between distinct ways of life and forms of thought. But the simple solution toward which he thought the world was tending—"a common life of mankind on earth"—gave him pause: "Perhaps it will be too simple," he writes at the close of his book, "to please those who, despite all its dangers and catastrophes, admire and love our epoch for the sake of its abundance of life and the incomparable historical vantage point which it affords." But, he concludes with a shrug, "they are few in number, and probably they will not live to see much more than the first forewarnings of the approaching unification and simplification" (553).

For Auerbach, surveying European literature from his "incomparable historical vantage point," there was a succession of living monuments to the power of representation, each bound up in the conditions of its time and place, each existentially exigent. The new historicists who adopted his method did not necessarily embrace his vision: they were less inclined to share his distaste for leveling, less suspicious of modernism, and less convinced that the world was tending toward the erasure of difference. If they

were also for the most part vastly less learned than Auerbach—
he seems indeed from this distance like one of the philological
giants who lived before the Flood—they were at the same time
grappling with texts that *Mimesis* had confidently ignored or consigned to the margins. We refer not only to works by women—
it is notable that Virginia Woolf is virtually the only female author
accorded sustained attention in Auerbach's book, and then as an
emblem of dissolution and decadence—but also to texts that did
not seem to qualify for inclusion in the category of "literature,"
a category that, like "realism," Auerbach carefully avoided defining. It is clear that the term "literature" functions in part as an
honorific; new historicists did not so much doubt the splendors
of the monuments as suspect the exclusiveness of the honor roll.
For what was the point of claiming, as Auerbach did, the cultural
significance of a particular representational practice if that significance did not extend beyond the work in question, that is,
if one could not find comparable texts elsewhere? Was not the
representation of reality a crucial social and political phenomenon, as well as an aesthetic one? Why did the imagination seem
to belong, in Auerbach's view, to such a small community of makers? And why (after the Bible) were the texts almost entirely literary, or, rather, why was the category of the literary left so undisturbed by a text on "the representation of reality"? Auerbach
would appeal to a particular ideology to explicate the representational strategies manifested in one of his textual fragments—
Christian creaturalism for Montaigne, for example—but what
was the relation between Montaigne's unique talent and the surrounding culture that he represented and upon which he drew?
Where was the historical reality in which Montaigne was so
deeply engaged? Where were the violent struggles that gave his
tragic sense of the human condition its specificity?

The point for new historicists was not to assemble a large number of comparable texts, as if to prove statistically the rightness
of Auerbach's canon. If anything, the urge Auerbach aroused was
something else: to see a vast social process, a life-world, through
the lens afforded by a particular passage, a few paragraphs apprehended with sufficient passion, alertness, and sympathetic intelligence. In a sense, as Auerbach said of Dante, the very success of

Mimesis, the extent to which each chapter seemed not merely a piece of literary history but a conjuring of spirits, fractured the very ethos, the tragic, existential weightiness, that the book was meant to uphold. To be sure, we could continue to acknowledge the special character of each author, and yet the individual author's achievement seemed less monumental, less unique, precisely to the extent that this achievement led to the uncovering of a dense textual and material field. And that field no longer seemed to fit securely within traditional period boundaries.

The spectral effect rather was like that so teasingly depicted in Borges's cunning essay "Precursors of Kafka," where texts that otherwise have nothing to do with one another and were written quite independent of one another are revealed, but only after the fact (which is to say, only after Kafka), to be "precursors." But the Borges example is precisely something that would not be allowed by Auerbach—for he wished to assert something about the fundamental coherence and historical integration of the culture that the literary work represented, the integration assumed by traditional schemes of periodization.

But even on these terms—that is, accepting the premise of periodization that Auerbach assumes and that provides the cultural frame for his individual readings—new historicists writing in his wake felt eager to expand the field, to open criticism to a vast number of texts that needed to be "read," to register conflict and dissent. The fact that Auerbach did not feel obliged to read every moment in his text, that he could concentrate on an anecdote and pressure it to reveal a whole system, in principle liberated the critic to look for fragments scattered across a period's entire textual production.

Nonetheless, how would the choice of any particular text be justified? Auerbach could in effect count on canonicity—that, and the limits placed upon him by his wartime isolation as a Jewish exile in Istanbul. If one abandoned canonicity, what was there beyond a completely arbitrary cut? Arbitrariness, the randomness Auerbach noted in modernist novels, was indeed built into the new anecdotal practice: one made good on one's choice by an act of will, or rather by an act of writing, an act of interpretation whose power was measured by its success in captivating readers. If

the attention—one's own and that demanded of one's readers—
seemed justified, then it was a successful intervention. But that
is not the whole truth: for how would the sense of justification
be achieved? The answer seems to be by a sense of resonance for
other texts, other readings. In large part—at least in the earliest
essays of new historicism—the other texts were canonical literary
texts: the anecdote worked if it illuminated a major literary work.
There is an obvious problem with this procedure: one chose an
anecdote—out of the hundreds of thousands of possibilities—
because it "sounded like" a passage in Marlowe or Shakespeare,
and then achieved a spurious effect of surprise and confirmation
when it turned out to sound like Marlowe or Shakespeare.

Why would you not simply bypass the problem and turn directly to Marlowe or Shakespeare? There were several reasons.
In part, it was because the canonical authors had begun to seem
exhausted, at least for the close readings that Auerbach performed
so brilliantly. One could turn away to other, less heavily worked
authors—Thomas Middleton or Elizabeth Carew or Mary Sidney (women authors, long neglected, being particularly ripe for
new attention). But the trouble is that the procedure itself—pick
a passage from a literary text, examine it closely, and show how
an entire representational system is disclosed in its narrow compass—had begun to lose some of its force precisely because it
assumed the stability of the literary and because it assumed as well
a concept of totality or wholeness that had come into question. It
was not the canonical authors then that had begun to seem exhausted but the approach to them and the notion of the boundaries of their achievement. What had promised a new access to
the real—Auerbach wrote of represented *Wirklichkeit*—had come
to seem curiously detached from anything real, absorbed in the
formal identification of modes of literary, high-cultural representation organized by traditional period.

The turn to the historical anecdote in literary study promised
both an escape from conventional canonicity and a revival of the
canon, both a transgression against the domestic and a safe return
to it. The anecdote was not merely background: it demanded attention; it threatened indeed to take over the whole enterprise.
But it could somehow be turned toward a revivification of a ca-

nonical work, provided that the canonical work lent some of its prestige, its self-justifying importance, to the marginal anecdote. And the anecdote satisfied the desire for something outside the literary, something indeed that would challenge the boundaries of the literary. It offered access to the everyday, the place where things are actually done, the sphere of practice that even in its most awkward and inept articulations makes a claim on the truth that is denied to the most eloquent of literary texts. Or rather the anecdote was a way into the "contact zone," the charmed space where the *genius literarius* could be conjured into existence.

Two

COUNTERHISTORY AND
THE ANECDOTE

B ut to most mainstream historians, anecdotes are no-account items: tolerable, perhaps, as rhetorical embellishments, illustrations, or moments of relief from analytical generalization, but methodologically nugatory. When modern historians write about individual lives or small events, they usually stress their broad historical significance or generalizable typicality. Such people and events usually come into view historically only at a distance from the trivialities and intricacies of daily life, in a cognitive retreat where the reliability of the data of experience can be weighed and proportional significance assigned. Certainly there are notable exceptions to the rule—we will examine several in this chapter—but historians have generally been more interested in making an epistemological break with the past to create the protocol of objectivity than in producing "the touch of the real." It might, therefore, seem odd that literary critics would invoke "history" through anecdotes.

Indeed, the anecdote as a form has often been counterpoised against more ambitiously comprehensive historical narratives.[1] Our late colleague Joel Fineman, for example, claimed that *any petit récit* would puncture the historical *grand récit* into which it was inserted. All anecdotes, simply as complete little stories unto themselves, perforate the context of narrative explanation:

> The anecdote produces the effect of the real, the occurrence of
> contingency, by establishing an event as an event within and yet
> without the framing context of historical successivity. . . . [T]he

opening of history that is effected by the anecdote, the hole and rim—using psychoanalytic language, the orifice—traced out by the anecdote within the totalizing whole of history, is something that is characteristically and ahistorically plugged up by a teleological narration that, though larger than the anecdote itself, is still constitutively inspired by the seductive opening of anecdotal form—thereby once again opening up the possibility . . . that this new narration, now complete within itself, and thereby rendered formally small—capable, therefore of being anecdotalized—will itself be opened up by a further anecdotal operation, thereby calling forth some yet larger circumcising circumscription, and so, so on and so forth.[2]

In Fineman's view, the miniature completeness of the anecdote necessarily interrupts the continuous flow of larger histories; at the anecdote's rim, one encounters a difference in the texture of the narrative, an interruption that lets one sense that there is something—the "real"—outside of the historical narrative. The anecdote thereby exposes history. He goes on to explain that these openings provoke their own contextualizations inside new teleological narratives, which strive for completeness, themselves becoming summarizable ("formally small") and therefore once again separable from the unending sequence of events. Each explanatory narrative can be summed up in a further anecdote, which makes a new tear and provokes yet another contextualization. Ultimately, then, history perpetuates itself through these punctures, but only because the anecdote is irritatingly antithetical to historical discourse. Fineman here gives a formal explanation of the anecdote's repercussions: its compact wholeness has always, independently of time, place, or the intentions of the storyteller, impeded the progress of more comprehensive historical narratives and prompted new surrounding sequences.

Roland Barthes had described a slightly different antagonistic relation between history and the anecdote in the late 1960s. He defined "the discourse of history" in modern times as one that constantly tries to efface the difference between the signified and the referent by presenting its own narrative sequence (the signified) as identical to a sequence of past events (the referent). But this elision of signified and referent is exposed when some mere "notation," often an anecdote incompletely digested by the larger narrative, divulges a different reality, which is behind or beside the narrative surface and composed of things that historians cannot assimilate into typicality or coherent significance.[3] This "effect of the real" momentarily betrays the incompleteness and formality of historical narrative—which is only to say its discursive nature—and so, as in Fineman's account, notational anecdotes work against the historical grain.

Like Fineman and Barthes, new historicists linked anecdotes to the disruption of history as usual, not to its practice: the undisciplined anecdote appealed to those of us who wanted to interrupt the Big Stories. We sought the very thing that made anecdotes ciphers to many historians: a vehement and cryptic particularity that would make one pause or even stumble on the threshold of history. But for this purpose, it seemed that only certain *kinds* of anecdotes would do: outlandish and irregular ones held out the best hope for preserving the radical strangeness of the past by gathering heterogeneous elements—seemingly ephemeral details, overlooked anomalies, suppressed anachronisms—into an ensemble where ground and figure, "history" and "text" continually shifted. The desired anecdotes would not, as in the old historicism, epitomize epochal truths, but would instead undermine them. The anecdotes would open history, or place it askew, so that literary texts could find new points of insertion. Perhaps texts would even shed their singular categorical identities, their division into "literary" and "historical"; at the very least, "history" could be imagined as part of their contingency, a component of their time-bound materiality, an element of their unpredictability. Approached sideways, through the eccentric anecdote, "history" would cease to be a way of stabilizing texts; it would instead become part of their enigmatic being.

Unlike the anecdotes described by Fineman and Barthes, then, these were to puncture on purpose, relying as much on their offbeat content as on their formal incisiveness. Moreover, they were designed not merely to disrupt and tantalize with flashes of an always inaccessible "real." Anecdotes consciously motivated by an attempt to pry the usual sequences apart from their referents, to use Barthes's terms, might also point toward phenomena that were lying outside the contemporary borders of the discipline of history and yet were not altogether beyond the possibility of knowledge per se. New historicists deliberately departed from the literary-historical practice of creating embrasures for holding texts inside of established accounts of change and continuity; we used anecdotes instead to chip away at the familiar edifices and make plastered-over cracks appear. However, because we also hoped to learn something about the past, the cracks themselves were taken to be recovered matter. Or, adjusting our metaphor slightly, the anecdote could be conceived as a tool with which to rub literary texts against the grain of received notions about their determinants, revealing the fingerprints of the accidental, suppressed, defeated, uncanny, abjected, or exotic—in short, the nonsurviving—even if only fleetingly. New historicist anecdotes might, as Fineman's analysis proclaims, provoke new explanations, but these were not taken to be exclusive, uniform, or inevitable. The histories one wanted to pursue through the anecdote might, therefore, be called "counterhistories," which it would be all the more exhilarating to launch if their destinations were as yet undetermined and their trajectories lay athwart the best traveled routes.

We'll be using the term "counterhistory"[4] to name a spectrum of assaults on the *grands récits* inherited from the last century. We take the term from Amos Funkenstein, who finds its earliest instances in rabbinical polemics against the Gospels, but who applies it to the early stages of secular history as well. Counterhistory opposes itself not only to dominant narratives, but also to prevailing modes of historical thought and methods of research; hence, when successful, it ceases to be "counter." The *grands récits* of the nineteenth century themselves began as counterhistories, and Funkenstein claims that history as a discipline has its roots in rebellion against the convenient, self-justifying, official stories of priests and rulers.[5] Counterhistory and history, in this view, are moments in a continuous conflictual process rather than substantial opposing activities with independently distinguishing characteristics.

Nevertheless, there are times when, even among professional historians, the impulse to discredit the old narratives and methods seems stronger than the impulse to synthesize new ones, and the 1960s and 1970s were such a time. The various facets of the counterhistorical project in those decades were too self-conscious and determined, too programmatically opposed to the established orthodoxies, to be easily assimilated into the processes of history as usual. The counterhistorical spirit was, moreover, very widespread, inspiring poststructuralists with a Nietzschean contempt for history's normal epistemological assumptions, but also touching many whose faith in the possibility of historical knowledge remained quite undisturbed, even as they took up a rhetorical stance in opposition to history's dominant narrative discourse: for example, the practitioners of anti-narrative, structural, *Annales*-style history, as well as those who emphasized the study of daily life, following the lead of Norbert Elias and Michel de Certeau. Less resolutely structuralist was the host of feminist, anti-racist, working-class, and other radically revisionist historians, practitioners of "history from below" who professed to counter the history of the victors with that of the vanquished. Also bearing the pressure of counterhistory were some studies that had nothing to do with structuralism, postmodernism, or radical politics, but that instead made use of new statistical techniques to develop "counterfactual" arguments in social and economic history.[6] Counterfactuals were, in turn, near neighbors to one of the most popular genres of postwar fiction, "alternate histories" like Philip K. Dick's *The Man in the High Castle*. Both counterfactual and alternate histories are thought experiments starting from fictional suppositions—"Suppose the American economy had developed without the railroads" or "Suppose the Axis powers had won World War II"—and the latter had a powerful impact even on mainstream fiction writers who were experimenting with non-linear chronologies and multiple universes in various attempts at translating Einsteinian and post-Einsteinian physics into meaningful human terms.

Along this counterhistorical continuum—from poststructuralist negativity, through the recovery of the *longue durée* and the history of the losers, to the envisioning of counterfactuals and provisional historical worlds—our sense of delayed and alternative chronologies, of the resistances to change, its unevenness, and the unexpectedness of its sources, grew more complete and assured. The reality of unrealized possibilities became fuller and more engrossing, while deterministic and unilinear explanations became correspondingly unappealing and unsatisfying.

The new historicist anecdote was a conduit for carrying these counterhistorical insights and ambitions into the field of literary history. It might, indeed, be said to have carried too many of them in ill-assorted bunches, for the anecdotes often seem to combine desires for maintaining enigmas and for recovering lost worlds, for anachronizing events and for historicizing texts. The anecdotal impulse in new historicism, that is, drew from different and not always strictly reconcilable parts of the counterhistorical spectrum. But these very inconsistencies may account for some of the anecdotes' appeal; instead of making choices, they combined theoretically paradoxical elements, letting one have one's Nietzschean skepticism along with a desire to make contact with the "real," or driving one to divulge the suppressed unofficial, authentic story as well as to imagine what might have, but did not, actually happen.

New historicism's counterhistorical affiliations are thus a tangle of crossing lines, and in this chapter we can sort out only two: British radical history and French Foucauldianism. At the time, these seemed the most historically ambitious and energetically rebellious, and in hindsight we can see that they were also given to anecdotes. Although all of the writers we're about to discuss were influential, we are not exactly claiming that they were models; instead, they formed an environment: a large, unmapped, and inviting disciplinary borderland.

⚓

The anecdote was a hallmark of humanist or "culturalist" British left-wing history, with its strong emphasis on experience, social consciousness, and world-making. The anecdotal methods of radical culturalists counterpoised themselves against the continuous, unidirectional movement of change posited by both liberal academic history and determinist Marxism. When the historian E. P. Thompson,[7] for example, interspersed his prose with the putatively unprocessed "voices" of the lower classes, he was striving to present previously disregarded historical subjects, who could give access to a multiplicity of pasts. Thompson strove to grant even the most "mistaken" of his historical subjects the dignity of a full hearing: "I am seeking to rescue the poor stockinger, the Luddite cropper, the 'obsolete' hand-loom weaver, the 'utopian' artisan, and even the deluded follower of Joanna Southcott, from the enormous condescension of posterity."[8] As Thompson moved from the study of the English working class, within a fairly ordinary Marxist framework, to the study of more unconventional subjects (food rioters, Muggletonians, William Blake), the rescue increasingly entailed both a suspension of previous theoretical presuppositions about the essential determinants of historical processes and an openness to the historical documents, a willingness to dwell in history's dead-ends and keep one's ears open: "If you want a generalization I would have to say that the historian has got to be listening all the time. . . . The material itself has got to speak through him."[9]

Paraphrase could never have given Thompson the effect he sought, which was to force the reader to take in the past "in its own terms," without the "abstraction" of translation into standard twentieth-century prose. Since estrangement of the reader, the creation of surprise and conceptual dissonance, was the key to his method, he particularly relished marginal language that was dense, specific, misspelled, and ideologically irretrievable, such as the threatening letters that found their way into the *London Gazette* of the eighteenth century alongside the proclamations of the king and Privy Council and other news of the court:

> Sr: Your Baily or Steward proper is a black gard sort of fellow to the Workmen and if you dont discharge him You may Look to Your House being sett on fire if Stones will not Burn You damned Son of a hoare You shall have Your throat cutt from Ear to Ear except You Lay L50 under the Second tree of Staple Nashes from his house at the frunt of the Great Gates near the Rabbit Warrin on Wesdy Morn next. . . .[10]

The "voice," as Thompson no doubt realized, has a paradoxical effect: its immediacy is only felt through its strangeness. In fact, the deviant textuality of the above passage—the quaint spelling and lack of punctuation—is what makes the voice "audible." Deprived of certain orthographic conventions, the reader must subvocalize, supplying stops and producing a meaning in an extraordinarily active manner, so that the language seems intimately "inside" the reader and unusually palpable in strict proportion to its foreignness, its violations of the reader's linguistic and social conventions. Beginning by requesting the redress of grievances against the addressee's steward, the voice quickly moves to insults and threats against the landlord himself and concludes with rather businesslike directions about where to leave blackmail money. The less predictable the voice is, the less recognizable as a voice from "our" past, the more it produces "the effect of the real." For all of Thompson's faith in sympathetic identification, therefore, the "speaking through" of this radically unfamiliar subject opens a thrilling gulf between "them" and "us": "But they lived through these times of acute social disturbance, and we do not."[11]

Thompson's paradoxical "effect of the real"–via-the-strange is a far cry from the usual rhetoric of objectivity that divides the historian from his object. To be sure, Thompson subscribed to the prevailing standards of historical practice, and in that sense his objectivity is not at issue; but his rhetoric and methods were unabashedly partisan in favor of those who had been slighted and excluded by most historians, and he produced the shock of unfamiliarity to emphasize our ignorance rather than his subjects' availability as objects. He happily violated a methodological taboo by thus determining, not to judge the behavior of common Britons by the putatively objective standards of later historical developments, but instead to retrieve their own rationales, their understandings in the moment, and to present them in the most favorable possible light.

One could read Thompson as a methodologically traditional historian, exercising his sympathetic imagination to fill in the blanks left by other historians and painstakingly building his own grand story of the lower orders. He certainly clung to a humanist faith in historical understanding throughout his career, and he does not seem to have doubted his capacity to construct an accurate account of the past. Nevertheless, the very nature of his enterprise required him to reconstruct not only what happened, but also what might have happened. For example, consider Thompson's essays on the food riots of the 1790s,[12] riots that looked futile and self-destructive in the hindsight of most late-twentieth-century economic historians, who traced the inevitable breakdown of local markets, the standardization of grain prices, and the capitalization of agriculture. In this activity of charting the necessary sequence of social and economic history, Marxists and non-Marxists were equally zealous. In contrast, Thompson attempted to stop the action at the moment of the riots themselves in order to fill out—not the linear dynamic of the only possible economy—but the structure of an alternative, competing economy, with different rules and the potential for another, albeit unrealized, future. Where other historians saw merely the blind reactions of hungry bodies, Thompson saw the as yet undetermined struggle for survival of another cultural formation. In analyses like this, when Thompson imagines the "moral economy" half lived and half dreamt by the rioters, his counterhistory from below of the bread riots shades into alternate history: the history, to paraphrase Isaac D'Israeli, of things that did not happen.[13] The methodological implications of this sort of counterhistory were several: first, that the present is not necessarily a superior objective vantage point, but is often, instead, a reductive one; second, that social realities are often not singular or even reciprocal, but multiple and incommensurable; and third, that the historian must be able to push beyond understanding a past social reality into imagining the social imaginary. It's little wonder that Thompson sought the history of the unrealized in the visionary poetry of William Blake.

Thompson's rhetoric and method countered that of most historians in another way, as well: he was always remarkably ready to see himself not only as the champion of previously unheeded historical voices, but also as a speaker just like them, struggling to be heard against the chorus of establishment historians. His function as a class-conscious aeolian harp by no means deprived him of his own voice and the drama of his own conflict. By surrounding the voices of the dispossessed with relentlessly self-regarding polemics against both "Cambridge historians," with their faith in "Namier's England," and Althusserian Marxists, with their condescension toward an ideologically controlled working class, Thompson's own voice became as singular and pugnacious as those he quoted. His powerful authorial persona—his defiant, anti-professional, charismatic will-to-represent—shunned all pretense to value-free objectivity and became a model of heroic history-making for a generation of New Left historians.

The use of the anecdote as a badge of the counterhistorian became even more marked in the next generation. The historians who immediately followed Thompson and launched the radical history movement—which promoted feminist, family, racial, and ethnic histories in the United States, as well as village and workplace histories in the United Kingdom—personalized the anecdote even further. Many of them prized continuities of experience between themselves and their historical subjects, so they stressed their individual qualifications in autobiographical stories. These often highlighted the historian's hostile professional environment; feminists like Sally Alexander, for example, reported facing not only the common enemies of left-wing culturalism—Marxist economism, bourgeois elitism, academic quantitative history, and Althusserian scientism—but also male derision in the "peoples' history" movement itself:

> It is difficult to remember now how there could have been such a gust of masculine laughter at the 1969 Ruskin History Workshop when a number of us women asked for a meeting of those present who might be interested in working on "Women's History." . . . "A history of our own," "a language of our own," "the right to determine our own sexuality," these were the distinctive themes of rebellion for the Women's Liberation Movement in the early 1970s. . . . As a feminist I was (and still am) under the spell of those wishes, while as a historian writing and thinking in the shadow of a labour history which silences them.[14]

The maverick historian and her subjects are not analogues for each other, as in Thompson's rhetoric, but are, rather, people who experience the *same* oppression.

This autobiographical turn toward historical subjects who were intuitively grasped as similar stressed continuity over historical rupture, shifting the emphasis of counterhistory toward aspects of daily life that seemed to change slowly, if at all. Instead of shocking us with the radical alterity of the past, Alexander's anecdote reminds us of the dogged persistence of derisory male behavior toward women. But that stagnant backwater of social relations also proved to be fertile ground for the counterhistorian. To mainstream historians, gender relations had appeared too stable and universal for historical analysis; if they were not natural and therefore utterly impervious to historical analysis, they seemed at least to belong in that archaic region of culture where anachronistic survivals abound. The feminist historian who asserted her identification with her subjects, indeed, relied on the relative stability of women's condition even as she denied its naturalness by subjecting it to historical analysis. These analyses, which in many ways resembled *Annales*-school histories of the *longue durée,* generally had two aims: (1) to reveal the unfamiliar in the seemingly identical (for example, to show that gender relations, despite the endurance of male domination, only appear to stand outside of historical processes); and (2) to show the relation between a culture's obviously dynamic elements and its seemingly static ones.

Feminists attempted not only to fill in the history of things that hadn't changed much or to exploit the novelty of their having changed at all, but also to demonstrate that change in some aspects of life depends on a sense of relative stability in others. Rapid alterations in working conditions, for example, might seem more bearable if family relations appear to remain unmodified. In general, all kinds of social, political, and economic innovations might be tolerated as long as certain "cultural" continuities are preserved. "Culture"—designated as a realm of customary behavior, which needn't answer to utilitarian considerations and was better suited to the analytical skills of ethnographers than to those of historians—might be counted on to maintain the substrata of enduring national and gender identities, over which truly historical forces could play. By making this very division of labor between the changeful and the stable an object of historical scrutiny, feminist counterhistorians raised a metahistorical question: What was it that made phenomena "historical," and why did so much "culture" fail to qualify?

Although those questions may now seem obvious, at the time

they were highly controversial. Referring to one's own experienced oppression openly as a reason for questioning the boundaries of the discipline and insisting that there were no topics
intrinsically unsuited to historical analysis, radical counterhistorians offended orthodox Marxists perhaps even more than they an-
noyed historians further to the right on the political spectrum.
In response to the proliferation of previously ignored histories of
such phenomena as childhood, the family, sexuality, criminality,
food, and death, then-Althusserian Paul Hirst, for example, com-
plained in 1972 that "crime and deviance are no more a scientific
field for Marxism than education, the family or sport. The objects
of Marxist theory are specified by its own concepts, the mode
of production, the class struggle, the state, ideology etc."[15] Such
pronouncements did little to stem the flow of radical counterhistory, for the movement was too large and vital to stop, but they
might have augmented the belief that all the *grands récits,* including Marxism's, were stifling.

If one person can be said to have epitomized the renegade
tendencies of the British "culturalist" left in those years, it was
Raymond Williams. The various streams of what we've been calling "counterhistory" met in his work: an attention to those forces
resisting the processes of modernization; the exploration of the
cul-de-sacs where unrealized possibilities were stranded; a determination to chart the dynamic interaction between history's usual
object of study—the myriad relations constituting "society"—and
the "culture" normally assigned to anthropologists and literary
critics; as well as an overriding interest in the making of such
concepts as "society" and "culture." Because Williams's disciplinary hybridity gave him a much wider readership than that of the
radical historians, especially in countries like ours where the literature of Britain is more frequently studied than its history, he not
only diffused the counterhistorical mentality throughout literary
and cultural studies, but also gave it a peculiarly literary spin.

One implication of Williams's work is that literature itself can
be read as counterhistory, but first one would have to abandon
or drastically modify the kind of "ideology critique" that had
formed the standard fare of literary critics on the Left. And just
as Althusserian Marxists objected to historians taking an interest

in "crime and deviance . . . education, the family, or sport," they also resisted scrapping the base-superstructure model for separating "determinant" social phenomena from cultural epiphenomena. Witness, for example, this conversation between Williams and interviewers from the *New Left Review*, who were quizzing him in the late 1970s about passages in his books that are "in frontal contradiction with [the] central tenet of historical materialism."[16] The interview neatly captures a moment when critics such as Williams were simultaneously praised for nonreductionist analyses and browbeaten into giving properly "historical materialist" formulations of their ideas. The interviewers aggressively press for such a formula, asking the same question a dozen times:

> It is true that historical materialism does not possess any worked-out theory, even for one epoch, let alone trans-epochally, of the exact connections between the economic and political and cultural or ideological orders. But to dwell at exclusive length on this point can be a way of burking and evading the central fact that we can in a perfectly reasonable and empirically verifiable way assert that the processes of physical production have till now exerted an ultimate power of constraint over all others. . . . Would you accept that?[17]

Williams never does wholeheartedly accept it; he points out that the various "systems" of the social totality are inseparable, that the primacy of economic production may be a mirage of capitalism itself, that "culture" is just as "material" and economically significant as any other social activity, and that "the processes of physical production" are certainly not the "ultimate power" in late capitalism. In other words, his objections tend to come from inside what he called "Marxism's alternative tradition"[18] of cultural criticism (which included primarily the work of Lukács, Gramsci, and Goldmann) that had taken "consciousness" as a primary object of analysis. And yet the "central tenet of historical materialism" must still be conceded, the interviewers insist, and Williams only obliquely denies it. The "structuralist" Althusserianism of his interlocutors appeared to Williams as the ghost of the base-superstructure models of Christopher Caudwell and other orthodox Marxists of the 1930s; perhaps thinking that he had fought these battles before, he seems anxious to change the subject. He does not, for example, point out that we can hardly claim to have "empirically verifiable" knowledge of the economy's "ultimate power of constraint" if we have no understanding (as the interviewer has tortuously admitted) of *how* it constrains. With Althusser's words resonating in the background—"The economy is determinant in the last instance, but the last instance never comes"—the exchange seems less a discussion of methods than an attempt to elicit a profession of faith regarding an otherwise inconsequential metaphysical point.

Normally the pleasure of reading Williams lay in the absence of such seemingly stale and futile doctrinal controversies. His insistence that theory had an obligation to meet concrete "experience" or "the lived" may, on first hearing, sound naive,[19] but it led him beyond the history of ideology, where many left-wing critics were stuck, into a more counterhistorical inquiry, where literary texts half disclose the roads not taken. Williams, however, did not read literature as the direct expression of otherwise forgotten mentalities, but rather as the record of submerged, semiconscious structures. He read literature as the history of what hadn't quite been said.

Williams felt the limitations of ideology critique most keenly when it posited a seamless, coherent, and articulable worldview as an adequate frame for historical consciousness. Like other counterhistorians, he haunted the borderlands where dissonance and incoherence are registered, and stressed that modern social experience is replete with cognitive and affective discrepancies, which rarely find direct expression. For Williams, though, the discrepancies became legible mainly between the lines of literary works, where "hegemony" collided with what he called "experience." Reading for the not-quite-said, Williams turned literature itself into a form of counterhistory.

Normal histories would have had to leave out the "experiences" encountered there, for those elusive and enigmatic episodes could never be explicitly recorded. "Experiences," Williams claimed, were clashes between hegemonic "articulations" and "the lived." Ideology critique alone was powerless to grasp them, but they could be understood as "structures of feeling":

The peculiar location of a structure of feeling is the endless comparison that must occur in the process of consciousness between the articulated and the lived. . . . For all that is not fully articulated, all that comes through as disturbance, tension, blockage, emotional trouble seems to me precisely a source of major changes in the relation between the signifier and the signified, whether in literary language or conventions. We have to postulate at least the possibility of comparison in this process.[20]

But "comparison" isn't exactly the right word here, for Williams denies that "the articulated" and "the lived" are a pair of equal and opposite entities. "The lived," in Williams's work, tends to remain unspecified, leaving a descriptive vacuum at the heart of his writing. He frequently relies on a form of quasi anecdotalism in which experiences are alluded to but not told. Unspecified things have happened that have resulted in psychic dissonance, which in turn motivates the writing: "There are times . . . when there is so high a tension between experience and description that we are forced to examine the descriptions, and to seek beyond them for new descriptions, not so much as a matter of theory but as literally a problem of behaviour."[21] Williams counts on introspection to provide evidence of a countercurrent to the normal, ideologically guided course of thought, and yet at the same time the countercurrent cannot be described because it is the opposite of "descriptions." If the experience and description were to coincide, one would be aware of a decrease in "tension" and thus "a problem of behaviour" would be solved, but then "the lived" as opposed to "the articulated" would have evaporated. "Experience," in other words, seems to be defined by its unavailability to language. Hence it cannot be "found" in documentary evidence. Only traces or symptoms appear at the superficial level of "articulation," and these can only be read as evidence of the clash between ideology and its opposite by generalizing from one's own experience. This "lived" material cannot have an explicit content; it not only appears at the level of consciousness and language as inchoate disturbance, but also *feels* like pure "trouble."

Experience, therefore, cannot speak through the historian like Thompson's voices or be narrated in even the most enigmatic little stories, and its occulted status might explain why Williams is one counterhistorian who seldom uses anecdotes. His references to experience tend to be vague and formless, as if to emphasize that "the touch of the real" normally is not felt. His quasi anecdotes, in contrast, with their abstract and halting allusions to muffled uneasiness, seem to preserve the place of experience in its absence. They have, nevertheless, a distinct literary pedigree. These appeals to an "experience" that cannot be described derive from a tradition of thought stretching back to English romanticism and defining the modern as a state of experiential lack or repression. That tradition is well suited to counterhistory, since both imply that a knowledge of modern times requires constant reference to, and imagination of, all that modernity leaves unregistered in consciousness. Placing himself squarely in this tradition, Williams paradoxically writes of experience as that which modern society disallows, not only at the level of ideology, but also at the level of experience: "There are major features in the social structure which are barring intense experiences. . . . They lie very deep within the whole cast of the civilization which is, for its own deepest reasons and often while denying that it is doing so, repressing intensely realized experiences of any kind."[22] One has, therefore, mainly experiences of not experiencing. As in Wordsworth, Arnold, Lawrence, and Leavis, "intense experience" is an occulted thing, a "buried life." The "trouble" that reaches our consciousness is not this interdicted "experience" but rather its blockage. The "structures of feeling" that Williams analyzes are, for this reason, invariably structures of repression. Elizabeth Gaskell's industrial fiction, for example, "embodies," rather than displays, the author's blocked sympathy for the workers; the "structure" of her novels is that of sympathy not being realized and of a ghostly would-have-been sympathy troubling the ideological discourse. The study of literature, therefore, allows us to extrapolate the unthought, the unfelt, from the tensions in the constraining structures of feeling.

This attempt to go beyond ideology critique by exploring the history of what might have been felt and written—and yet was not—verges, like much counterhistory, on counterfactual speculation. And in Williams's work, the counterfactual creation—that which *might* have been *but* for hegemonic restraints—too often seems a transhistorical notion of natural humanity in retreat from an inhospitable modern world. One might, therefore, protest that this creation is at least as unavailable to historical analysis as Althusser's elusive economic "last instance" that never arrives. Moreover, when Williams complains about our modern lack of a vivid fullness of being, about our privation of "life," he seems captivated by the modern literary sensibility and unable to subject its rhetoric of experiential crisis to critical scrutiny. It's no wonder that he frustrated the Althusserians, with their antipathy to the humanist subject, for he transcribed the most typical form of literary subjectivity—the alienated self who carries around a deep, inaccessible life, the emergence of which is constantly thwarted—into an analytical concept. Althusserians pointed out that the rhetoric of a fugitive "true" self was part of the "ideological apparatus" through which subjects are "interpellated." Foucauldians might similarly have expostulated that the mighty flood of language about the inarticulable and the inaccessible creates a desirable, half-submerged object for the disciplines of the human sciences to pursue.

Williams's insouciance on these points is undeniable; he did not register the force of such criticisms because they seemed to him to emanate from dogmatic, deterministic, and unicausal analytic schemes, which he was predisposed to reject. The conflict that developed on the British Left between "culturalists," like Thompson and Williams, and poststructuralist Althusserians certainly carried an excess of political baggage. Although it often concentrated on the prevailing theoretical issues of subjectivity and agency, underneath one always heard the rumblings of a much older and more practically consequential debate about whether common people were capable of knowing their own situations or instead needed a scientific leadership (a vanguard party) to enlighten them. Rightly or wrongly, Thompson and Williams heard the familiar strains of Communist Party elitism in structuralism and were, as a result, deaf to its more powerful arguments. Exacerbating this political antipathy—the suspicion that Althusserianism was Stalinism redux—was the threat of a return to monolithic history, without side shadows, alternatives, or

countercurrents. For "the critique of the subject" seemed a reduc-
tion of the complexity of human history: subjects who were merely
epiphenomena of specific interpellations of dominant ideological
structures could never have alternate historical realities to rescue;
they would not even possess organs for sensing the dissonance so
important to Williams's idea of "experience." In short, they would
seem to be devoid of all of those countervailing cultural, psychological, and political traits that make the stuff of counterhistory.

So (to indulge in a counterfactual of our own) even if the British
culturalists had modified their "humanism," their counterhistorical impulses might nevertheless have required them to imagine
an "other" of history's determinations: if not a repressed natural
man, then at least some discernible locus of alternative possibilities. Michel Foucault was one counterhistorian who consciously
tried to root sentimental nostalgia for such beings out of his work
and yet confessed in the late 1970s that encounters with those who
remained unassimilated into the narratives of power had always
animated his studies. A little-read text from 1979 is perhaps the
best expression of Foucault's counterhistorical ardor: "This is in
no way a history book," begins the introduction to "The Life of
Infamous Men,"[23] and it continues:

> This is an anthology of existences. Lives of a few lines or of a few
> pages, countless misfortunes and adventures, gathered together
> in a handful of words. Brief lives, chanced upon in books and
> documents. . . . Singular lives, those which have become, through
> I know not what accidents, strange poems: that is what I wanted
> to gather together in a sort of herbarium.

"The Life of Infamous Men" was to be composed entirely of anecdotes of the obscure and atypical, chosen unsystematically for
their emotional force: "The selection that shall be found in it has
conformed to nothing more important than my taste, my pleasure, an emotion, laughter, surprise, a certain fright or some other
feeling, whose intensity perhaps I would have difficulty justifying
now that the first flush of discovery is past." The introduction
delivers one of the fullest and liveliest expressions of the peri-

od's counterhistorical impulse. Declaring his fascination with the ephemerality and the visceral effectiveness of these fragmented and miniature stories, Foucault articulates even the contradiction between anecdotes and their incorporation into his own historical texts:

> A long time ago, I utilised similar documents for a book. If I did so then, it is doubtless on account of that vibration which I feel even today when I happen to run across these lowly lives reduced to ashes in a few phrases that have destroyed them. The dream would have been to restore their intensity in an analysis. For want of the necessary talent, I therefore brooded for a long time over analysis alone; . . . I sought the reason for which the poor spirits had been so zealously prevented from walking upon unknown paths. But the primary intensities which had motivated me remained outside. And since there was a risk that they might not pass into the order of reasons . . . wasn't it best to leave them in the same form which had made me experience them? (77)

The frisson of the anecdotal rupture, the flash of the undiscernible real, the use of historical analysis to arrest and know what made that fleeting effect, the disappointing realization that the original intensity of the anecdote's effect has thus been lost, and the hope that reproducing the anecdote shorn of analysis and surrounding narrative would restore its pristine effect: the whole conflictual dynamic of counterhistory and history is summed up in this paragraph.

It seems obvious that Foucault spoke directly to those issues that British "culturalists" had clustered around the anecdote. His early work especially had an undeniable appeal for those who wanted to break the continuities of the *grands récits*, to hear the voices of history's excluded, to escape from lingering economism and the constraints of orthodox Marxist chronology, to reflect on their own investments in the past, to study the shaping power of discursive activity, and to attend to the unsaid. Without minimizing the equally obvious differences between British culturalism and Foucault's more skeptical Nietzschean brand of counterhistory, we should recognize that they converged in significant ways. In reading Foucault, however, one additionally felt the attraction—indeed, the relief—of encountering an author who could acknowledge and reflect on the *pathos* of anecdotalism: the strong desire to preserve the energies of the anecdote by channeling them into historical explanation, which is followed by frustration and disappointment when the historical project stills and stifles the very energies that provoked it. Foucault was not just doing counterhistory; he seemed to be living its paradoxes as an intense drama that all of us shared whenever we set out, as we constantly did, to capture the animation, the dynamism, of things that were bound to become inert and passive under our disciplinary gaze.

This combined personal and disciplinary self-reflectiveness, to be sure, had advantages other than dramatic pathos as well. For one thing, it seemed to provide an alternative to the starkly posed choice between "culturalist" or "humanist" and "structuralist" viewpoints. Instead of either marshaling anecdotes to represent freestanding, alternative social subjects or systematizing them into a set of ideological templates for interpellated subjectivities, Foucault presented the anecdotes in the historical archives as residues of the struggle between unruly persons and the power that would subjugate or expel them. He thus focused theoretical attention on the archive—the source of the anecdotes—to explain how those elements that were putatively outside of history could become most visible precisely at the moment of their expulsion. The anecdotes were, therefore, produced by the workings of power, but they also demonstrated that power relied on those who resisted it. The anecdote binds structures and what exceeds them, history and counterhistory, into a knot of conflicted interdependence.

This paradox of the anecdote corresponds inversely to the pathos of the anecdotalist: the structures of power preserve the errant subjects in the very act of apprehending and destroying them; conversely, the (counter)historian clutches the life of the anecdote, but it expires in his or her grasp. "The Life of Infamous Men" is concerned with both dynamics; it is both an effort at resurrecting the lives "outside" and an argument that reanimation can only be achieved by the éclat of rereading the death sentences. Foucault's own desire to pass along his sensation of "terror and awe," on the one hand, and his desire to normalize it by explaining its social function, on the other, remain irreconcilable. Neither impulse wins out: the anecdote is not ultimately in the service of the explanation, nor is the explanation just an excuse for repeating the anecdote. In Joel Fineman's terms, neither the activity of tearing nor that of repairing is allowed to dominate. The anecdotes were to be drawn from "archives of confinement, police, petitions to the king, and *lettres de cachet*" of Foucault's "classical" age (1660–1760); moreover, to heighten their paradoxical drama, Foucault also imposed a performative condition for inclusion. The passages had to be not only the records of encounters between power and obscurity, but also the very instruments of the encounters themselves:

> I haven't sought to unite texts which would be more faithful to reality than others, which would merit selection for their representative value, but texts which played a role in this real of which they speak, and which in return find themselves, whatever their inexactitude, their turgidity or their hypocrisy may be, traversed by it: fragments of discourse trailing the fragments of a reality in which they take part. What shall be read here is not a collection of portraits. they are snares, weapons, cries, gestures, attitudes, ruses, intrigues for which the words have been the instruments. . . . These existences have effectively been risked and lost in these words. (78–79)

He does not deny that, apart from these words, there were lives, but he doubts that we could hear such loud echoes of them in any less tumultuous record: "The most intense point of lives, the one where their energy is concentrated, is precisely there where they clash with power, struggle with it, endeavour to utilise its forces or to escape its traps. . . . These words are what gives to them, in order to travel through time, the brief flash of sound and fury which carries them even to us" (80).

Of course, there has to be a medium through which the sound carries, and the archive itself is an insufficient echo chamber. The anecdotalist, in the attempt to wake the dead, must know where to find them and how to publicize them, and this knowledge, it turns out, is provided by the historical continuities between the sovereign power that overcame those lives and the discipline he or she practices. Here is yet another knot binding the desire to resurrect life and the power to end it. Anecdotalists are implicated, it seems, in the annihilating force, indebted to "the lightning flash of power," because it makes the only illumination by which we can see what counterhistorians want to see: that which is thrown out of official history, the "other" of power, and the means by which it was discarded. Moreover, we are further involved because we are the linear heirs of the methods of infamy that those disposers of the lives of the obscure employed. Of course, those who dealt out the punishments were not yet creating the languages of the human sciences; but, for all of their bombast and invective, they are establishing a new relation "between power, discourse and the everyday, quite a different way of regulating the latter and formulating it" (84). And without the introduction of everyday life into discourse, where would the counterhistorian be?

Surely there was overdramatization in imagining one's research to be implicated in the life-and-death struggles of even these unsung offenders. One cannot deny that an exaggerated sense of immediate moral brinkmanship featured prominently among Foucault's attractions, and it bears separate consideration here, as we approach the conclusion of our discussion, for it discloses a final dimension of the counterhistorical project.

Foucault's rhetoric of personal involvement stood out from that of other counterhistorians, first, by the sheer complexity of his account of the relation between himself and his anecdotes, and, second, because of the impossibility of that relation ever seeming satisfying or reassuring. He seemed frequently to be warning himself against any complacent separation between his desire to hear the voice of the other and his desire for disciplinary and institutional power. The very documents preserving the beguiling voices were, after all, the products of disciplinary ambition. His insistence on this complicity with the dirty business of power contributed to his success in jolting his readers out of the contemplative or analytical frame of mind in which history is normally read. The wish of the anecdotalist may always have been to revivify, to bring something back to life that had been buried deep in oblivion, and Foucault often underlined the macabre implications of that wish: the revived creature comes back in the agony of its death throes. This sensationalism, this striving after "terror and awe," produced a heightened sense of being on the extremities of the historically knowable, at the very edge of what we could know, cognitively, about the past.

Even the famous anecdote that opens *The Order of Things*, which is neither lurid nor macabre, records and tries to induce this effect. Foucault reports that, upon reading a passage of Borges that purports to describe a Chinese encyclopedia's categorization of animals—"animals are divided into: (a) belonging to the Emperor, (b) embalmed, (c) tame, (d) sucking pigs, (e) sirens, (f) fabulous, (g) stray dogs, (h) included in the present classification, (i) frenzied, (j) innumerable, (k) drawn with a very fine camelhair brush, (l) *et cetera*, (m) having just broken the water pitcher, (n) that from a long way off look like flies"—he broke into a

> laughter that shattered . . . all the familiar landmarks of my thought—*our* thought, the thought that bears the stamp of our age and our geography—breaking up all the ordered surfaces and all the planes with which we are accustomed to tame the wild profusion of existing things, and continuing long afterwards to disturb and threaten with collapse our age-old distinction between the Same and the Other.[24]

This is an anecdote about experiencing, rather than thinking, the limits of our thought:[25] "In the wonderment of this taxonomy, the thing we apprehend in one great leap, the thing that, by means of the fable, is demonstrated as the exotic charm of another system of thought, is the limitation of our own, the stark impossibility of thinking *that*." Like Williams's semi-reports on quasi experiences, this autobiographical anecdote gives us almost nothing in the way of positive knowledge (neither Foucault nor the reader learns anything about China from Borges's completely fictitious passage); rather it reports an exaggerated, shattering, and demonically comic instance of what Williams called "trouble."

As the laughter subsides, though, Foucault comments on the sense of uneasiness that replaces it:

> There arose in its wake the suspicion that there is a worse kind
> of disorder than that of the *incongruous,* the linking together of
> things that are inappropriate; I mean the disorder in which frag-
> ments of a large number of possible orders glitter separately in
> the dimension, without law or geometry, of the *heteroclite.* (xvii)

This image of the collapse of any succession of ordering principles
is the underside of the counterhistorical anecdotalism we've been
examining. Separate orders, those that have been as well as those
that might have been, show their fragments in a dimension that
is neither spatial nor temporal. No analytic pattern appears; no
narrative arises that would identify the causal links between them,
distinguish the realized from the potential, account for their differences or similarities. There is no order to these disparate orders. This is a nightmarish counterhistory, in which everything
is present, all possible orders, with no chronological sequence or
ontological hierarchy.

One is tempted to say that this is an anecdote to end all anecdotes because in it the counterhistorian's utopia turns out to be
madness; the desire to avoid ordering the historical diversity of
orders (real and imaged) places him or her on the brink of thought
itself. Everything is in shreds, and there is no possibility of repair.
And yet, this queasy encounter with ultimate disorder, this thinking *in extremis,* turns out to be the dread that often drives disciplines toward the discovery of new orders, which are always apprehended, or intuited, in the interstices of the given cognitive
grid. This is not simply to say, once again, that history and counterhistory are inseparable; it is additionally to claim that the truly
sensational anecdote, by emitting flashes of a horrific outside to
any conceivable historical order, puts one beside oneself, momentarily beyond a merely cognitive relation to one's task.

The possibility of the experience of the heteroclite, what we
might call the limit experience of counterhistory, motivates the
more routine sensationalism of disciplinary activity described in
The Order of Things. There Foucault (rather like Williams) outlines a three-tiered cultural configuration. Two tiers, the "lowest"
and the "highest" respectively, are (1) the mental grid, or code,
according to which people process information and live their lives

and (2) the fully articulated justification for that code. Foucault describes them as: "The fundamental codes of culture . . . [that] establish for every man, from the very first, the empirical orders with which he will be dealing and within which he will be at home"; and "the scientific theories or the philosophical interpretations which explain . . . why this particular order has been established and not some other." But the disciplines that interest Foucault originate in neither of these realms; they grow up in a wild space between, a space "more confused, more obscure, and probably less easy to analyze": "between the already 'encoded' eye and reflexive knowledge there is a middle region which liberates order" (xxi). Allowing "imperceptible" deviations from the primary codes, this middle ground is a place where "culture finds itself faced with the stark fact that there exists [*sic*], below the level of its primary orders, things that are in themselves capable of being ordered, that belong to a certain unspoken order; the fact, in short, that order *exists*" (xx). The impulses to find the unseen order and to criticize the culture's codes, which are the founding impulses of the disciplines Foucault investigates, arise from "the pure *experience* of order and of its modes of being." Eventually such experiences themselves might found "general theories as to the ordering of things" and thus become "reflective knowledge," but "the experience of order in its pure primary state always plays a critical role"; it always obtrudes between "the already 'encoded' eye and reflexive knowledge" (xxi).

Foucault's experience of the possible nonexistence of order recorded in his anecdote and this more quotidian experience of order in its "pure, primary state" are certainly opposites: the first is a vague and sickening encounter with thought in ruins, while the second is an impression of grounding, of touching behind the cultural grid a reality that is "anterior to words, perceptions, and gestures . . . ; more solid, more archaic, less dubious, always more 'true' than the theories" (xxi). We are, of course, to understand that this solidity is partly illusory, for *The Order of Things* takes shifts in the seemingly intransigent "unspoken order" as its subject, but those shifts take place when a group—a profession, a discipline, a sect—believes it has encountered, beneath the conventional codes, an order that can serve as the basis for judging the codes themselves as "more or less exact, more or less happy, expressions of it" (xxi). As experiences, therefore, the aftermath of the Borges reading and the confrontation with "order in its primary state" are as different as sensing an absence and sensing a presence.

Nevertheless, they both estrange us from "our thought, the thought of our time." They both bring the mind up against the given empirical codes as limitations, causing them "to lose their original transparency" and introducing the notion that "these orders are perhaps not the only possible ones" (xx). They are both, therefore, liminal experiences, confused encounters on the edge of thought with something that can be sensed but not fully grasped. Like *The Order of Things* itself, the disciplines spring "from the limit-experience of the Other" (xxiv), and they cannot entirely exorcise the alterity within.

⚊

Counterhistories have tried instead to revive that alterity, fostering disciplinary eccentricity; and it was that eccentricity that the anecdote carried into literary criticism as well. The force field of the anecdote pulled even the most canonical works off to the border of history and into the company of nearly forgotten and unfamiliar existences. There literature's own dormant counterhistorical life might be reanimated: possibilities cut short, imaginings left unrealized, projects half formulated, ambitions squelched, doubts, dissatisfactions, and longings half felt, might all be detected there. They were buried beneath the surface, no doubt, but would stir, one hoped, at "the touch of the real."

Three

THE WOUND IN THE WALL

In the Palazzo Ducale in Urbino there is a very large altarpiece by the Flemish painter Joos van Gent of the *Communion of the Apostles*. In a subject relatively common in Byzantine art but unusual in Western painting, Jesus himself administers the holy bread to his kneeling disciples. Though executed on a grand scale, the altarpiece is not likely to strike modern viewers as a particularly memorable work of art. The figures are rather stiff, in the manner of Joos van Gent's teacher, Hugo van der Goes, but without van der Goes's intensity: nothing in the dutiful attitude of the disciples suggests passionate love or awe, while Jesus keeps an oddly formal distance even as he reaches out with his right hand to place the wafer, held delicately between thumb and forefinger, in the mouth of the first communicant. This distance extends to the viewer, who has full access to the scene, without the illusion of being drawn into it or bearing witness to it.[1] Instead of engendering either emotional intensity or mystical remoteness, charismatic presence or sacred awe, the painting makes a doctrinal statement: the narrative of the Last Supper has been almost entirely absorbed into institutional ritual. A table, covered with a white cloth, must allude to the meal Jesus shared with the disciples, but the dishes and food have all but disappeared, leaving only a jeweled chalice and a small heap of holy wafers on the left and, on the right, two pieces of risen bread, a saltcellar, and a bottle of water. The domestic space in which the meal must have taken place has likewise vanished; the table is located in a Romanesque church. Holding a paten in one hand and a wafer of

Figure 1   Joos van Gent (ca. 1460/80). *Communion of the Apostles.* Galleria
Nazionale delle Marche, Urbino, Italy. Photograph: Alinari/Art Resource,
New York.

unleavened bread in the other, Jesus stands rather woodenly in
front of the table, which has in effect been transformed into an
altar, with the spotless tablecloth serving as the "corporale," the
cloth spread for the wafers, or any fragments of wafers, to rest
on. Augustine believed that when Jesus said, "This is my body,"
he carried himself in his own hands.[2] Joos van Gent's representation of this unutterably strange moment transforms it into a formal religious service. Assisted by Saint John, who serves as altar
boy, Jesus is a priest standing in the crossing of the transept, with
the apse behind him, celebrating the Mass.

This institutionalization of the sacred story is linked, it would
appear, with the group of five figures toward the back right, be-

hind the kneeling disciples and the table. Immediately identifiable in this group is the hawk-nosed profile of Federico da Montefeltro, duke of Urbino and patron of the Confraternity of Corpus Domini that commissioned the altarpiece. More than thirty years ago, in an article in *Art Bulletin,* the art historian Marilyn Lavin argued that the turbaned, bearded figure toward whom the duke is gesturing is an ambassador from the Persian court, a Jewish doctor named Isaac, who had come to Italy in 1472 to negotiate on behalf of his master, Uzun Hasan, an alliance against the rival Muslim power, the Turks. Unexpectedly, when in Rome, the ambassador Isaac had been converted to the Catholic faith and had taken the name Sixtus, after the reigning pope, Sixtus IV.[3] If Lavin is correct, this extraordinary event—the conversion of the Jewish representative of a Muslim potentate—is commemorated in Joos van Gent's painting, which may allude to a visit by the ambassador to the court of Urbino. The risen bread and salt on the table in front of Sixtus né Isaac would allude to the Jewish sacrificial meal in which they are essential elements (see Leviticus 2:13 and 24:5–9). This meal has been at once fulfilled and displaced by the Lord's Supper, the sacrificial mystery in which the converted Jew, no longer the enemy of the faith, can now participate.

But the Jew's participation is more implied than represented, more potential than event. The ambassador, the duke, and the others grouped around them are not depicted as waiting with the disciples to receive the Host directly from Jesus. They are witnesses, privileged onlookers of the sacred scene. If the story of the ambassador's conversion is part of the altarpiece's background and occasion, it is not in any sense narrated. Narrative of any kind has been stilled, even the so-called institution narrative— the story of the origin of the Eucharist—that is ostensibly commemorated. For the Gospel recounting of Jesus' Last Supper, a story about particular people at a particular place and time, is of course historically incompatible with the painting's ecclesiastical setting. The confounding of temporal logic is a central element in Christian thought and representation, closely bound up with the way in which Christianity had understood its relation to the Judaism it appropriated and hoped to supplant.[4] "Abraham and other holy fathers did eat" Christ, writes archbishop Cranmer, echoing centuries of typological speculation, "many years before he was incarnated and born."[5] Similarly, in Joos van Gent's panel, time is twisted back upon itself, so that in this case, end and origin meet and touch, with Jesus depicted as a priest performing an institutional ritual not fully established until the thirteenth century when the Feast of Corpus Domini became an official part of the Church calendar. There is, Lavin observes, "an allusion to a narrative dining scene, the straw-covered flask on the floor in the left foreground" (13), but it leans at the extreme margin of the painting's world, an isolated, humble trace of an unrepresented event. The altarpiece has no interest in imagining or dramatizing the supper described in the synoptic Gospels; it wishes to represent not History but Truth.

Joos van Gent's altarpiece is art in the service of faith, the faith of a community that built and maintained magnificent churches of the kind depicted on his panel; established cults to honor local saints; housed precious relics; sponsored Corpus Christi processions adorned with banners, garlands, and lights; created confraternities to carry the Eucharist to the sick and dying. And it is at the same time art in the service of doctrine. Its point is theological: the Roman Catholic Mass is not an institutional interpretation or ritualized recollection of the Last Supper; it *is* the Last Supper, constantly renewed through the Christlike offices of the priesthood. The painting's representational mode is doctrinal formalism; that is, it expresses in structural rather than narrative terms the ideological consensus of a dominant institution, a ruling class, or a hegemonic elite. Doctrinal formalism rarely eschews narrative altogether. Thus somewhere "behind" the figures at the rear of the painting are histories that can be reconstructed. These histories could conceivably extend into the distant past, to the figure of a Jew in Palestine who may or may not have sat at a Passover Seder and likened himself to the matzoth. For the original viewers of Joos van Gent's altarpiece, they would have certainly included not only the spectacular conversion of Uzun Hasan's emissary, but also, as Lavin observes, a wave of anti-Semitic agitation in Italy in the 1460s largely motivated by the increasing power and success of Jewish moneylenders, who posed, or were thought to pose, an economic threat to local merchants. The agitation was instigated or at the least greatly fanned by the Franciscans. The Minorite friars' impassioned preaching against Jewish usury and indeed against the very existence of Jews was a key element in their campaign for religious renewal. This renewal in turn was linked with the Monte di Pietà, an institutional strategy for combating the power of Jewish bankers. The no-interest loans offered by the Monte di Pietà were associated with the Confraternity of the Corpus Domini, which, let us recall, commissioned the altarpiece.[6] In the wake of Franciscan sermons, Jews were in extreme danger; many were beaten and killed by mobs, while others were protected by papal officials and civic leaders anxious to avoid popular riots and disorder.[7]

But Joos van Gent does not directly narrate any of these dramatic events. Rather, insofar as it figures in the painting at all, the history at which we have briefly glanced is very indirectly evoked by placing the ambassador Isaac, if that indeed is whom the bearded figure depicts, near the symbols of the old Jewish sacrifice and by setting him against the figure of Judas, wrapped in a prayer shawl and clutching his bag of silver at the left. The figures may thus be responding indirectly to contemporary debates about the fate of the Jews by suggesting that at least some Jews may be saved through conversion, but the response, if it is one, does not assume the form of a story. Narrative presses closer to representation in the painting's principal subject, Jesus feeding his disciples. The scene alludes to the Gospel story: "And as they were eating, Jesus took bread, and blessed it, and brake it, and gave it to the disciples, and said, 'Take, eat; this is my body.' And he took the cup, and gave thanks, and gave it to them, saying, 'Drink ye all of it; For this is my blood of the new testament, which is shed for many for the remission of sins'" (Matthew 26: 26–28).[8] But, as we have remarked, the placement of this scene in a church and the representation of the supper as a Mass moves the image away from narrative and toward theology. The temporal unfolding of an action, with a beginning, middle, and end, is absorbed into the representation of a timeless ritual that makes manifest what Paul in the Epistle to the Hebrews formulated as "the Eternal Priesthood of Christ."[9]

Doctrinal formalism then reduces the presence and weight of the stories to which it alludes, as if it had something to lose by history, as if any determinate location and time would invalidate its claim to eternal efficacy, as if any record of struggle and process and change would necessarily threaten its universal validity. The allusions, however, offer a standing invitation to the viewer to recover and interpret those narratives that are not directly represented but are half hidden in the "background," and for centuries connoisseurs, art historians, and literary critics encountering doctrinal forms have accepted this invitation. They have turned the elements of synchronic structure back into diachronic history, translating representations of eternal truth into a tangle of likely stories: the humble flask can be made to conjure up the supper recounted in the Gospel; there is "every possibility" that the turbaned, bearded figure is Sixtus né Isaac, who might well have visited Urbino on his way from Rome to Venice ("roughly after September 12, 1472 and before January 28, 1473"[10]); Federico da Montefeltro touches the convert's arm in order to give him personal encouragement to persevere in his new faith; the courtier to Federico's side who seems to be counting on his fingers is enumerating arguments for Christianity's superiority to Judaism; the bread and the salt on the table probably refer to the Jewish sacrificial meal; and so forth.[11]

We assume, perhaps incorrectly, that contemporaries read such ceremonial symbols effortlessly—what is laborious research for us, the argument goes, was life experience for them—but even they would have viewed certain figures, such as the man with the turban and beard, through a veil of rumor, speculation, and uncertainty. (There is no probability of an actual portrait likeness, since Joos van Gent's time in Urbino did not correspond to the time of the ambassador Isaac's presumed visit, and the figure he depicts is borrowed, as Lavin shows, from a painting by Dirk Bouts.) Nor was sacred history a secure and uncontested possession. After all, the Gospel accounts of the Last Supper are themselves various, and the more knowledgeable the viewers, the more mindful they would have been of the long history of doctrinal dispute over their meaning. That dispute, centering on the interpretation of Jesus' words "This is my body," is not directly figured in the panel, but it lurks behind any representation of the Eucharist, all the more one that includes the figure of a Jewish convert. If Joos van Gent's panel works to contain the potentially disruptive energies of history—*excluding* conflict, *relegating* contemporary events to its background, and *marginalizing* narrative—it cannot and does not eliminate history altogether. Indeed its very exclusions, relegations, and marginalizations constitute, as we have seen, a network of allusions that stimulate a rich variety of historical speculations.

Confronted by doctrinal formalism in objects and texts, cultural historians have eagerly tracked down the allusions, but they have seldom reflected on the fact that their own activity is both stimulated by the exclusions that structure the works they study and in tension with these exclusions. Interpretive practice should, we believe, keep this paradoxical relationship to the work in mind, acknowledging the strange blend of identification and aggression, "reading with" and "reading against," that motivates historical analysis. If Joos van Gent's painting relegates its contemporary figures (Federico da Montefeltro, Sixtus né Isaac, et al.) to the background, interpretation pulls them toward the front and center; if it makes those contemporaries witnesses to a sacred ritual in which they do not themselves participate, interpretation insists that they are in fact the crucial participants; if the altarpiece strives to represent doctrinal order by lifting recognizable individuals into a realm of timeless communion, where their historical particularity no longer counts and is, like the wafer's materiality, a mere appearance and accident, then interpretation sets itself against this striving and pulls them back toward the time-bound and material world. The interpreter behaves in this regard like Castiglione's Emilia Pia—to recall another great work from Renaissance Urbino—who listens with mingled delight and skepticism to Cardinal Bembo's ecstatic hymn to the transcendent power of divine love. "Take care, messer Pietro," she replies, tugging at the hem of his robe, "that with these thoughts your soul, too, does not forsake your body."[12]

This is not the place for a full-scale interpretation of Joos van Gent's painting, nor are we equipped to attempt one. But we can use our response as a model for the interpretive practice to which we aspire. Thus, in looking at the painting, we observe that it is the site of a struggle between doctrinal and historical impulses, a struggle in which our own interpretive choices will be implicated. We do not, therefore, take either doctrinal formalism or historical narrative on its own terms. We tend to pull away from the exposition of abstract doctrine, from the explication of beliefs or the analysis of institutional structures—though some attempt at exposition, explication, and institutional analysis is necessary—and attempt to recover repressed, subordinated, or forgotten narratives. We ask not only what stories were occluded, but also how they have been concealed from view in order to facilitate the elaboration of a closed system. But we also tend to pull away from straightforward retelling of the story and toward the recovery of occulted or implicit doctrine. Here the implication is that the story, however pleasurable or absorbing, is shoring up ideological propositions or confirming the legitimacy of institutional arrangements. What is the doctrinal point, for example, of including the image of Sixtus né Isaac among the observers of the *Communion of the Apostles* and what institutional need does his marginalized presence meet? By insisting on the claims or the ruses of doctrine, we attempt to break the spell of historical narration—its "once upon a time" siren song—even as we attempt to reconstruct a half-effaced history.

But our interpretation should acknowledge more than the tension between doctrine and story both in the painting and in our own account of it. We must also recognize that the tension in Joos van Gent's altarpiece involves the status of likenesses, of icons, themselves. That status is most clearly at issue in the figures of the young woman and child that may be glimpsed between the heads of Federico and the ambassador. In part, but only in part, because of some deterioration in the condition of the painting, the nature of these figures is unclear: are they people standing in a niche, or polychrome sculptures, or figures on a painted panel? Since the child is crowned and the woman, tenderly declining her head toward his, is depicted only to the waist, they give the initial appearance of the Virgin and child in a painting, an icon whose familiar unreality in this ecclesiastical setting would confirm by contrast the implicit assertion that the other figures—including

Jesus and the apostles as well as the duke of Urbino and his en-
tourage—are present, as it were, in the flesh. But if this is an
icon, painting, or statue, there is no devotional apparatus, no altar,
no frame, no formal setting-off of this image from its surroundings. The woman and child appear rather to be figures like the
others, only half hidden in the background. Once again, art historians—responsive to allusion, inclined to pull background figures
into the foreground, and determined to reintroduce history onto
the scene of doctrine—have proposed that the child is Prince
Guidobaldo, the cherished son given to Federico da Montefeltro
by his wife Battista Sforza after eight daughters. Poor Battista
had offered her life in exchange for divine assistance in producing
a male heir; six months after his birth, she was dead, aged twenty-
six. Since Battista died the year before the altarpiece was painted,
the simply dressed woman holding the child has been identified
in several studies as a nursemaid, but Lavin suggests plausibly
enough that she is Battista Sforza herself, her modest dress reflecting the Franciscan robes in which at her request she was buried. She is present then not in the flesh but in the spirit, for painting has the power to represent what no longer exists or what never
existed at all—and in the spirit mother and child can be reunited.
The pair, so charged with hope and loss and sacrifice, can in turn
be assimilated to the Virgin and child. The figures then are at
once portrait and memorial, sacred icon and secular representation, consoling sign of presence and mournful acknowledgment
of absence.

The complex issues that gather around these figures are related
to the larger questions about the status of memorial representation and presence that inhere in the doctrine of the Eucharist.
The *painting* of this particular doctrine is in tension with its doctrinal point—that one should learn to look with the eyes of faith
past appearances to a reality invisible to the senses—because it
is, after all, a painting, an image that appeals to the senses even
as it tries to limit the authority of their testimony. Thus there is
a fundamental difference between the painting's other figures—
including the woman and child—and the Host that Jesus administers. Despite their stiffness, the figures are recognizable as likenesses, but the Host, far from looking like the body of Christ,

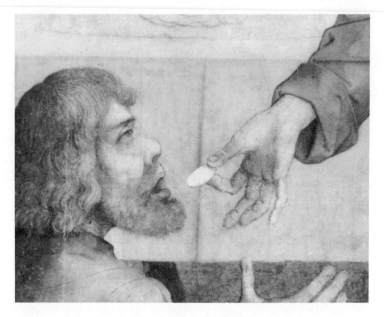

Figure 2   The Host, Jesus' body, between the fingers of Jesus. Joos van Gent (ca. 1460/80). *Communion of the Apostles* (detail). Galleria Nazionale delle Marche, Urbino, Italy. Photograph: Alinari/Art Resource, New York.

which the doctrine affirms it *is,* does not even look like the bread of the Gospel story or, for that matter, the bread in the small loaves on the table. Rather, the painting's representation of the specially prepared and consecrated wheaten disc under whose accidents that body supposedly exists and is eaten is a small blank in the center of the composition. Indeed, though its elliptical shape signifies by the logic of perspective a foreshortened disc, this blank, this dab of white in the space between the thumb and index finger of the painted Savior, is by doctrinal logic less a representation than a space where visual representation is emphatically refusing to happen.

To be sure, Joos van Gent's painting is atypical in this regard; most doctrine is not necessarily or essentially at war with iconicity, and hence the visual representation of doctrine is not always so

deeply paradoxical. Nevertheless, even representations that signify within systems of thought far more amenable to the idea of
representation demonstrate the impossibility of a complete con-
gruence between instantiation and idea. We must be alert to this
incongruity, bringing to light the complex tension in traditional
societies between doctrine and historical narrative and the still
more widespread tension between representation and meaning.
Disclosing and analyzing these tensions not only reveals ideological contradictions, but also traces the paths along which representational energies and historical motivations flow. The tension
between doctrine and iconicity, tenor and vehicle, signified and
signifier is not the consummation of new historicist analysis but
its starting point.

In the *Communion of the Apostles*, the portion of the Urbino
altarpiece we have discussed thus far, both narrative and image
are tautly controlled by doctrine. Their energies, however, do not
seem similarly constrained in the altarpiece's separate predella,
the long rectangular panel situated beneath the main panel. Those
things at the margins of doctrine in Joos van Gent's conception—the pleasures of story and vividness—have been accommo-
dated directly beneath it. A predella often differs in style as well
as scale from the panel beneath which it is placed, though this
is an extreme case both because Joos van Gent's painting is huge,
its figures just under life-size, and because the predella is by a
different artist from a different culture, the Italian Paolo Uccello.
We do not know why the altarpiece, begun by Uccello, was finished by Joos van Gent,[13] but it is at least possible that the features
in the main panel on which we have been concentrating are responses—answers or solutions—to problems raised by the extraordinary but deeply disturbing predella. Far from attempting
to arrest or constrain narrative energy, Uccello's predella tells a
story in six episodes, proceeding from left to right and divided
by painted columns. In the first, a woman in a shop stands at a
counter and holds out a small white round object, vividly highlighted against a black background, to a shopkeeper. In the second, the shopkeeper, standing with his wife and two children,
looks with astonishment at a shallow pan that is cooking over
a fire in the fireplace toward the back of the room. The pan is

Figure 3   Jewish shopkeeper purchases the consecrated Host. Paolo
Uccello (1397–1475). *Profanation of the Host*. Palazzo Ducale, Urbino, Italy.
Photograph: Alinari/Art Resource, New York.

overflowing with a red liquid that runs along the floor. Outside,
a group of soldiers are beating at the door and trying to enter.
The third scene shows a procession in which a figure in a papal
tiara, with priests and citizens, is walking toward the altar of a
church. In the fourth scene, the woman from the first episode is
about to be hanged by soldiers. She and the soldiers look up and
see an angel making a gesture above her head. In the fifth scene
the shopkeeper, his wife, and children are tied to a single stake
in what appears to be a cauldron and burned to death. Finally,
in the sixth scene, the woman, now clad in a red robe and dead
or near death, is lying on a litter. Two angels are at her head;
two devils are pulling at her feet.

    These scenes evidently recount one of the legends of miracu-
lous Hosts, legends that circulated in substantial numbers from

Figure 4 The miracle of the bleeding Host. Paolo Uccello (1397–1475). *Profanation of the Host.* Palazzo Ducale, Urbino, Italy. Photograph: Alinari/Art Resource, New York.

the thirteenth century onward. Typically, a desecration of the Host by an enemy of the faith is followed by spectacular, incontrovertible proof of the Real Presence of Christ under the accidents of bread and wine. The most famous of these eucharistic miracles was one that supposedly occurred in Paris in 1290, and it is to this that Uccello's panel seems to refer. The story, circulated in sermons, chronicles, miracle plays, and visual images, is of a Jew who purchases a consecrated Host in order at once to profane it and to expose the fraudulence of the doctrine—"Are not these Christians fools to believe in this Host?"[14] But when he stabs the wafer and then attempts to boil it, it bleeds and returns to the form of flesh, whereupon (depending on the version) the Jew either converts or is burned to death.

Obviously, the predella's story is relevant to the main panel:

Figure 5   The Host is returned to the altar. Paolo Uccello (1397–1475). *Profanation of the Host.* Palazzo Ducale, Urbino, Italy. Photograph: Alinari/Art Resource, New York.

both are concerned with the mystery of the Eucharist, both allude to the doctrine of the Real Presence—the actual body and blood of Christ in the ritual of the Mass—and both establish the meaning of the Christian symbol in relation to the figure of the Jew. But if Joos van Gent's panel is in the mode of doctrinal formalism, Uccello's predella is in the very different mode of legendary narrative. There is doctrine "behind" Uccello's represented actions, as there is story "behind" Joos van Gent's represented ritual, but the predella's concern is with events unfolding in time—with actions and their consequences—rather than with eternal structures and the formal rituals consecrated to the manifestations of these structures. The predella does not relate any of the histories, recondite or common, biblical or contemporary, alluded to and marginalized in the main panel; rather it tells a miraculous legend of the

Figure 6 Angel intervenes in hanging of guilty woman. Paolo Uccello (1397–1475). *Profanation of the Host.* Palazzo Ducale, Urbino, Italy. Photograph: Alinari/Art Resource, New York

sort that mediated between everyday understanding and abstruse doctrine. The doctrine of the Eternal Priesthood of Christ is esoteric; as we have remarked, though representations of the Last Supper are common, the scene of Christ holding the wafer in which he himself is bodily present is relatively rare in Western art,[15] probably because it brings uncomfortably close to the surface certain recurrent objections to orthodox eucharistic theology. Those objections are more commonsensical than esoteric: their characteristic substance and tone are conveyed by the English Protestant John Frith, burned at the stake for heresy in 1533. Christ's body, Frith writes,

> was natural and not phantasticall, but had the qualyties of an other body in all thynges saue synne, nether was it more possible for

Figure 7   Execution of Jewish family. Paolo Uccello (1397–1475). *Profanation of the Host.* Palazzo Ducale, Urbino, Italy. Photograph: Alinari/Art Resource, New York.

that naturall body so beyng mortal and not gloryfied to be in dyuers places at once, then for myne. So that when we heare these wordes spoken, this is my body, and se that they were spoken before his body was gloryfied, knowyng also that a natural body vngloryfied can not be in many places at once, and that yf these wordes were vnderstanden as they sounde he shuld haue ben at ye least in .xii. or .xiii. places at once in his Disciples mouthes, and syttyng at the table with them, It causeth vs to loke better vpon it, and so to search out the pure vnderstandyng.[16]

Catholic theologians had subtle answers to these objections, of course, but they were answers whose sophisticated intellectual acrobatics tended to confirm the wisdom of avoiding the frequent depiction of a scene whose full doctrinal meaning could only have been the possession of the clerical elite and that could inadver-

Figure 8 Angels and devils fight over body of woman. Paolo Uccello (1397–1475). *Profanation of the Host*. Palazzo Ducale, Urbino, Italy. Photograph: Alinari/Art Resource, New York.

tently raise doubts about the flesh-and-blood presence of Christ in the baked wafer.[17] The story in the predella, by contrast, concretized doctrine (this is what the Real Presence means; this is ocular proof of the mystery; this is the resolution of all doubt) and set people in motion. The teaching must have seemed effective: certain elements of the elite made a substantial effort to ensure the story's wide diffusion, particularly in the service of heightening piety and of inciting popular hatred, beating, and massacres of the Jews.

Distinct representational modes thus organize the major and minor panels of the altarpiece. The upper panel's mode is primarily doctrinal. It is principally interested not in telling a story but in expressing a set of abstract ideas and relations. It pulls away from the particular and the time-bound and toward the institutional and the structural. It is associated with high culture, with intellectual and administrative elites, and with the institutional apparatuses in which these elites participate. The lower panel's mode is legendary narrative. Such narrative is by no means innocent of doctrine, but it can pass more readily—and in both directions—between high culture and low, elite and popular. It is concerned with events that take place in a particular sequence. Where the doctrinal image focuses on a single central figure around whom the others are grouped in a circle, the narrative is broken into discrete units, a succession of episodes conspicuously detached from one another and arranged in a set order. Meaning does not radiate out from a sacred center but is established though a linear visual progress.

The doctrinal mode does not insist that the represented action took place as depicted; on the contrary, it collapses the future into the past, so that the Communion of the apostles can be celebrated in the cathedral that could not yet exist at the time of the historical Jesus. This seeing of the future in the past resembles what in grammar is called the future perfect tense—the future is conceived as having already happened—but it is still closer to what we might call the present perfect tense: when this happened long ago, the future was already present, and that future is now. Hence Joos van Gent can introduce Federico da Montefeltro and his contemporaries as witnesses to the sacred scene. The episodes in the narrative mode by contrast lay claim to the representation of actual events, events involving a particular set of agents at a given place and time (though the details—the names, the dates, and so forth—may be given with greater or lesser specificity). The legend lays emphasis on event rather than institution, on process rather than structure.

But the modal energies that characterize the separate works also circulate between them. As we have already noted, Joos van Gent's panel has traces of many stories. And there are signs of the institutional in Uccello's predella: in one of the episodes the papal procession moves toward an altar situated in a domed apse; in another, the body of the Christian woman is laid out in front of a similar structure. But these are more allusions than full representations: in both instances, only the apse is present; where the rest of the church should be, we see a landscape. Institutional containment, so dominant in the main panel, gives way to movement through space and (by way of the flowering of the trees in the successive glimpses of the landscape) time. What matters most are the temporally unfolding events, not the structures in which those events transpire. Indeed, as we will see, the narrative progress depends upon a literal tear or rupture in one of these structures.

As the idea of circulation implies, there is no fixed relation between doctrine and legend, no set order and hence no a priori determination of precedence or causality. Uccello's Urbino predella was commissioned and painted before Joos van Gent's main panel: in this case, then, the narrative sequence preceded the doctrinal representation, a representation that seems to have been designed to correspond with it. The mystical, timeless *Communion of the Apostles* sits on top of the story of Jewish profanation, just as some bleeding Host shrines of the Middle Ages were built on the sites where Jews had allegedly desecrated the Eucharist.[18] But the story of the profanation is itself built upon doctrine, unless, that is, one were actually inclined to *believe* that a Parisian Jew bought a Host in order to put it to the test—a perilous submission to narrative charm that would altogether collapse the distinction between history and legend. And even if one were so inclined, one would nevertheless be drawn to concede, if not that the doctrine *produced* the events, then that the events as depicted fulfilled and manifested a doctrinal design. The point here is not only that in some cases narrative precedes doctrine and in other cases doctrine precedes narrative, but also that any determination of precedence is necessarily local and limited.

Our discussion of Joos van Gent's painting deployed a set of opposed terms:

doctrinal formalism	historical narrative
synchrony	diachrony
universal truth	local contingency
structure	process
substantial identity	accidental likeness

These oppositions are obviously closely connected to the relation between the main panel and the predella, a relation we have characterized as that between doctrinal formalism and legendary narrative. It is important to emphasize that history and legend are not the same, that they have distinct structures, functions, institutional affiliations, ways of establishing authenticity, and long-term trajectories.[19] But the narrative mode that they share—that links the historical figure of Sixtus né Isaac above and the legendary Jewish violator of the Host below—unsettles and destabilizes this distinction, as indeed the complex thematic circulation between main panel and predella destabilizes all of the binary oppositions. It is not that the distinctions are useless: on the contrary, it is impossible to get an analytical purchase without them. But they are always contingent, and if we treat them as stable givens, we risk missing the actual work of cultural objects. We know that the subject of Joos van Gent's panel is rare in Western art and that the story depicted in Uccello's predella is repeated in sermons, miracle plays, poems, stained-glass windows, woodcuts, and the like. Hence it is perfectly reasonable to characterize them in terms of elite and popular spheres of culture. But eucharistic piety is at the heart not only of abstruse theological doctrine but also of popular religion in the fifteenth century. It is misleading to treat the subject of the altarpiece, however rare, as divorced from a community whose solidarity was to a considerable extent built around the ritual of the Mass. And if there is ample evidence in Italy and elsewhere of popular anti-Semitism in the period, it nonetheless is misleading to suggest that anti-Semitism welled up from the people, as if it only found its origin and expression among the unlettered.[20] Anti-Semitism was repeatedly instigated and manipulated from above and could be used to make complex doctrinal points: we need look no further than the connection between the perfidious Jewish merchant in Uccello's predella and the figure of Judas lurking at the left of Joos van Gent's *Communion of the Apostles*.

The connection should not obscure an important difference in the conception of Jews in the main panel and in the predella. In Uccello's scenes, the fate of the soul of the Christian woman who sells the Host is ambiguous. Angels and devils seem to be struggling over her on her deathbed, and the outcome was evidently sufficiently unclear to drive an early viewer to attempt to intervene on her behalf: someone has carefully scratched the paint off the devils, as if in the hope of driving them away. But there is no ambiguity about the fate of the Jews. Though the desecration legends often ended in the conversion to Christianity of the wife and children of the wicked Jew who was executed, Uccello makes no such distinction: in his vision, not only the merchant but also his wife and children are burned at the stake. In the *Communion of the Apostles,* by contrast, Judas is set over against the figure of the converted Jew. We have in effect contrasting visions of Jewishness: in Uccello's narration it seems inseparable from the bodies of the Jews, so that they must all be destroyed; in Joos van Gent's doctrinal image, Jewishness can be discarded as an accident, and the substance—the soul—of the Jew redeemed. Though the latter was the Church's official policy, both positions were voiced in Christian communities of the fifteenth century and are in effect debating with one another in the Urbino altarpiece.[21]

The account we have given thus far establishes a dynamic interchange between the main panel and the predella, an interchange set in motion by the exclusions and allusions that each representational mode practices. This interchange, we suggest, allows the complete altarpiece to function as a critical relay point in circuits not only between formal categories, but also between social levels and even degrees of coercive and violent action. And yet the circuitry, we would now like to argue, does not function smoothly. Both paintings contain sites of resistance and disruption, sites that increase the dynamic flow between them but also undermine the complementarity on which their cooperation depends.

We have already looked at one point of trouble, the Host in Joos van Gent's panel, the circle of white that serves as a representational challenge to representation itself, the emblem of a doctrine that points beyond iconicity by commanding the believer to regard appearances as accidents. To view the painting from this doctrinal perspective is to derealize its other figures, to notice their illusionistic quality. Focusing on the anti-iconicity of the doctrine interferes with the suspension of disbelief on which paintings such as this rely. Challenged at the main panel's center, we might say, the suspended disbelief seems to travel, as did the

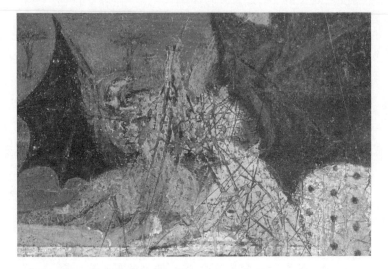

Figure 9　Detail of devils. Paolo Uccello (1397–1475). *Profanation of the Host* (detail). Palazzo Ducale, Urbino, Italy. Photograph: Alinari/Art Resource, New York.

narrative impulse generated at the panel's margins, to the predella. In the predella, which we should remember was painted first, iconicity and narrative seem equally indulged. We are given a story that not only supports eucharistic doctrine but also asks us to believe our eyes. At precisely the place, however, where the legendary and visual come together most emphatically, the predella also seems to expose its own iconicity to critical scrutiny, to strain the conventionality of its representation to the breaking point, and to provide an aporia like the Host in Joos van Gent's panel. In the predella, this place is a wound in the wall.

Uccello's second scene depicts the Jewish family in their house, boiling the Host in a frying pan over a brazier. We can see into the house because the fourth wall has been removed entirely, exposing the interior to our view. The interior does not occupy the entire panel; it is painted at an angle, enabling us to see the outside as well, by the front door, where the soldiers are hammering for entrance.[22] We can look into the secret recesses of the Jews' chamber—recesses elegantly intensified by the perspectival depiction of the tile floor—but, as in a theater, we cannot be seen and are not implicated in the acts we are watching. But how have the soldiers—who do not, after all, have the privileged vantage point afforded to us by the excision of the fourth wall—been alerted to the profanation of the Host? No window is depicted through which someone might have glimpsed the crime.[23] If Uccello had not bothered to provide an explanation, we might not have given the matter a thought. But evidently he felt that his representation called for a link between inside and outside, a clue that would alert the Christian community. The narrative link he depicts is at the same time an elegant and witty aesthetic device: the blood that overflows from the pan spreads out on the tile floor. According to the rules of perspective by which Uccello was so deeply fascinated, that floor is tilted up, in order to suggest distance, and it is as if the blood felt the tilt. For it gathers together into a narrow stream, runs down across the tiles, and seeps out of the house through a passage resembling a bruise or wound, the size of a mouse hole in a cartoon, in the front wall near the door.

The wound in the wall is at once an important structural element in the aesthetic representation and a tear in the fabric of that representation. Narratively it works as a way of explaining how the secret Jewish profanation was discovered by the surrounding community; aesthetically it works as a way of concentrating and focusing the threads of red paint, paint that stands for the blood that courses from the dab of white paint that stands for the wafer that for believers is the body of Christ. Abstractly, the little dab of white in this panel may be just as problematic as the represented Host in Joos van Gent's painting, but since we are being asked to see the red paint as blood, just as the Real Presence supposedly manifested itself miraculously to the eyes, believing in this legend is homologous (rather than antagonistic) to practicing the aesthetic suspension of disbelief. At first glance, the Real Presence in this instance seems to have been rendered unproblematically visible. On closer inspection, however, we notice that its visibility to the Christian community in the painting relies on the wound in the wall.

To understand why the question of visibility should reappear

Figure 10   The Wound in the Wall. Paolo Uccello (1397–1475).
Profanation of the Host (detail). Palazzo Ducale, Urbino, Italy.
Photograph: Alinari/Art Resource, New York.

just where it seemed most likely to be mooted, in the panel de-
picting the miracle of the bleeding Host, we should look more
closely at the structure of these miraculous narratives in the early
Renaissance. They provided a vivid image of the ocular proof that
tantalized Christianity in the wake of the elaboration of eucharistic orthodoxy. Orthodoxy obliged the faithful to believe that what
they saw (and, at least once a year, tasted and swallowed) was not
what it manifestly appeared to be; that their direct experience
was at the utmost remove from the truth. The distance between
sense experience and higher reality could be transcended by the
faith that bound individual and community to God, but, judging from the widespread stories of miraculously bleeding Hosts,
this transcendence left an intense residual desire for confirmation. Such confirmation was on rare occasions given, as if in reward for exceptional piety, to the blessed: hence, for example,
Colette of Corbie received a vision of "a dish completely filled

with carved-up flesh like that of a child."[24] But it came more frequently and disturbingly to those who showed, even inadver-
tently, some doubt: a story, related in an anti-Protestant tract by
an English Jesuit of the late sixteenth century, tells of one such
person, an English gentlewoman who traveled to Rome for the
Jubilee Year. Upon her arrival, the woman went

> to Father Parsons, who was her Confessor: and he administring
> vnto her the blessed Sacrament (which in the forme of a little
> Wafer, hee put into her mouth) obserued shee was long chewing,
> and could not swallow the same: whereupon he asked her, whether
> shee knew what it was shee receiued? She answered, Yes, a Wafer.
> At which answer of hers, Father Parsons beeing much offended,
> he thrust his finger into her mouth, and thence drew out a piece
> of red flesh, which after was nailed vp against a post in a Vespery
> or priuate Chappell within our Lady-Church: and though this
> were done about some twenty yeeres since or more, yet doth that
> piece of flesh there remaine to bee seene, very fresh and red as
> euer it was.[25]

The proof of the Real Presence here comes not as a reward for
perfect faith, but as a rebuke to imperfect faith, a polemical version of Jesus' words to "doubting Thomas": "Thomas, because
thou hast seen me, thou hast believed: blessed are they that have
not seen, and yet have believed" (John 20:29).

Theologians argued that the fact that one could not ordinarily
see God's flesh and blood in the Host was a sign of God's grace,
since it would be horrible to experience in the senses what one
was actually eating. This is why it so often falls to unbelievers,
heretics, and Jews, caught in the act of profanation, to encounter
the true nature of the Eucharist. In Uccello's painting, when the
rescued Host is brought back into the church and placed on
the altar, it is no longer bleeding: it has returned mercifully to
the form of bread. It is the Jewish merchant and his family who
are the prime witnesses of the sacred blood, blood that Christian
believers know is present but need not see or taste. For a Jew
to attack the Host seems strange, since there would appear to be
no reason to attack something you believe to be a mere piece
of bread, particularly if the assault, conducted in a windowless,

barred room, can serve no public polemical purpose. From a Christian point of view, to be sure, the Jew is not attacking a piece of bread but directly reenacting the Crucifixion: indeed this is a crime worse than the alleged Jewish murders of Christian children to make matzoth, for here the violence is directed at the very body of God.[26] But only a believer could know that the wafer is God's body; the unbeliever would have to think that he was dealing with common baked bread—until, that is, the blood began to flow.

Church officials were at least sporadically aware of the problems of verification associated with bleeding wafers, and particularly with any wafer that had been removed from the altar: How could it be proved that the wafer had been consecrated? What if the priest's finger happened to be bleeding when he touched the Host?[27] How could counterfeit wafers be distinguished from authentic ones? What was to prevent someone, eager to cause trouble, from putting a wafer on which he had smeared some blood on the doorstep of a Jew's house? Beyond such concerns, the icon of the holy blood—even in a case that the Catholic Church accepted, such as the "miracle" depicted by Uccello purports to be—raises three related problems. First, the Jewish unbeliever has to behave as if he were instead a doubter, determined to test the validity of the doctrine by seeking direct corporeal evidence of its truth or falsehood.[28] Second, since the Host bleeds in response to doubt, unbelief, or desecration, the viewer's pleasure in its appearance indicates a barely submerged lack of faith, the stubborn persistence of reliance on the senses, even when one is trying to acknowledge and comprehend their inadequacy. And third, because the painting is an icon, a representation of the miracle, it seems to reintroduce imagination and illusion precisely where they are meant to be excluded. The miracle, after all, supposedly defeated representation in the name of reality, but representation comes back in the substitution of paint for blood. The miracle itself was already disturbingly dependent on doubt, and the icon increases the disturbance by confounding the conquest over doubt with the mere suspension of disbelief. Faith, that elusive gift of God so ardently prayed for, then moves into uncomfortable proximity with the aesthetic experience of "seeing" the pigment as blood, an easy, pleasurable make-believe.

Faced with these problems, the best Uccello's painting can do is to externalize the doubt by implying that it is Jewish. It is the Jews who doubt that the consecrated bread has literally become body, just as their ancestors doubted that Jesus was the Messiah; and it is the Jews—imagining perhaps that the wafer is only a version of the unleavened bread that they eat at Passover in commemoration of the Exodus—who perversely put the Host to the test and discover that it bleeds. Having burdened the Jews with the Christian community's doubt and need for verification, the painting then allows believers the ocular gratification of the represented blood and punishes the Jews for the desire, confounding them and showing the fate of the doubter and his whole family. Thus the problem of doubt is finessed; but the problem of representation remains.

Let us return to the wound or bruise in the wall, for it is both the crucial agent of the terrible fate of the Jews and the emblem of the representational dilemma. The passing of the blood through the wall, we have said, works as both a narrative and as an aesthetic device. It is thus different from the panel's preeminent aesthetic device: the removal of the wall that enables us to look into the locked and windowless house of the Jewish merchant and his family. The removal is strictly detached from the represented world of the painting; to allow it to contaminate that world would be to make a mockery of the soldiers beating at the door or of the Jewish merchant, who has withdrawn into the privacy of his house in order to conduct the secret profanation. The missing wall is a convention, just as the side of the cave is missing in a quattrocento Florentine panel now in the Fogg Art Museum, so that we can see into the darkness where Christ frees Adam and Eve from Limbo. In the case of the cave, the convention has been complicated—we might say muddied—by the artist's attempt to naturalize the opening by rusticating the edges: the effect is to make one wonder why on earth the poor prisoners did not simply walk out or why Christ had to break the door down to gain entry.

Figure 11 Christ frees Adam and Eve from Limbo. Master of the Osservanza (1425–1450). *The Descent into Limbo* (ca. 1440–1444). Courtesy of the Fogg Art Museum, Harvard University Art Museums, Gift of Paul J. Sachs, "A testimonial to my friend Edward W. Forbes." Photograph: Photographic Services. © President and Fellows of Harvard College, Harvard University.

Uccello is too sophisticated to attempt anything comparable: the wall is neatly, one might say surgically, cut away, enabling us to see the image of the blood streaming across the floor. We observe an interior space marked "Jewish," the space of doubt, while we remain safely outside. The phantom wall acts, therefore, as an invisible shield against identification with the need for ocular proof; it is another device of disavowal. But it is also a reminder that the painting achieves its effects only because the viewer is willing to go along with certain representational conventions; it emphasizes the gap between aesthetic illusion and the Real Presence. A salutary admission of the distinction between paintings and miracles, representation and sacrament, the wall's transparency does not require faith, only the suspension of disbelief. Its patent conventionality, that is, sorts out the ontological layers.

The surgical cut, however, is complicated, one might say infected, by the passage through which the blood seeps into the street. This passage is supposed to stand on a different plane of reality; it is, as it were, in the picture, a crucial element in the miracle itself. Some unexpected escape route for the blood is necessary for the discovery of the secret profanation—a wicked act in a windowless room, with the door bolted—as well as for the demonstration of the truth of transubstantiation. But what are we to make of the escape route? Or rather what are we to make of its relation to its world? Are we to think that the sacred blood possessed some mystical quality that enabled it to pass through the wall (as the Glorified Body of Christ was said to be able to do)? But what, in this case, are we to make of the impression of a stain or bruise in the wall—an impression that the Glorified Body would certainly not leave? Are we to think rather that its passage is strictly natural? But how is it possible to construct a coherent natural explanation for a stream of blood to pass through a wall of this represented thickness? Should we imagine, despite appearances, that there is a hole in the wall, through which the blood is passing?[29] But if so, how can we account for such a hole? Are we to think that Italian houses of the period had holes cut in the front walls for drainage—that is, that the hole is an architectural feature? Are we to imagine that it is there quite by accident—that is, that the husband might have said to his wife, "My dear, one of these days we've got to do something about that hole"? Are we to conjure up a providential story to account for it, to think, for example, that a divinely driven mouse made the hole unbeknownst to the inhabitants? Are we to believe that the sacred blood, like a corrosive, burned its way through the wall? And, of course, there is something absurd about any of these desperate explanatory measures, since the blood is flowing before our eyes from a tiny Host, a Host in which miraculously is found the crucified flesh from whose wounds the blood once flowed and flows even now. The wound in the wall—as if displaced from Jesus' own buffeted and pierced body—is there for one overwhelming reason: to gather the streaming blood into a satisfying narrow ribbon, which runs through it and thereby awakens the community to the crime within.

The uncertainty about the origin and logic of the wound in the wall is the inescapable consequence of the panel's attempt to conjoin aesthetic, narrative, and doctrinal functions in a single visible sign. Uccello's very brilliance as a painter, his ability to satisfy the craving to see what cannot be seen, thereby threatens to expose the conspiracy, as it were, behind the represented conspiracy, the crime hidden within the represented crime: the Jewish family has been framed, both literally and figuratively. In the desecration stories that circulated after 1290, whether in popular legends and sermons or in formal legal investigations held in the wake of an accusation or a murderous riot or a precipitous execution, there was always some way or other in which secret Jewish guilt was exposed. In one version it was one of the merchant's children who casually remarked to a Christian woman of his acquaintance that she did not have to seek her god in church since he was being tortured at this very moment by his father; in other versions the threatened Host itself emitted a strange light or noise; and in testimony taken from witnesses, it sometimes turned out that the Host—or, in any case, a small piece of bread rumored to be a consecrated Host—was found on the threshold outside the Jews' door.

The Jews are inevitably guilty in such stories because they do not believe and because at the same time they are made to act out, to embody, the doubt aroused among the Christian faithful by eucharistic doctrine. In Uccello the doubt projected onto them has to run through the wall of their enclosure in order to call up the soldiers who will burn them at the stake, killing not only the merchant but also his wife and children—for their crime is not strictly limited to the merchant's act but is bound up with the very existence of Jews. Here too Uccello's genius has the odd effect of at once intensifying and undermining the legend he paints. For in most versions there is a kind of Jewish residue, in the form of the children who are taken away from their guilty parents and converted to the true faith. In Uccello's predella, by contrast, the Christian community triumphs altogether over Jewish doubt, but

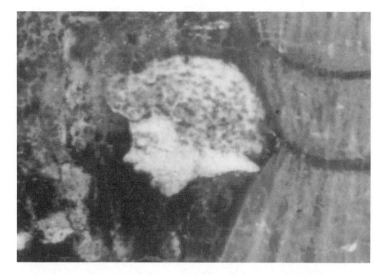

Figure 12 Child screaming. Paolo Uccello (1397–1475). *Profanation of the Host* (detail). Palazzo Ducale, Urbino, Italy. Photograph: Alinari/Art Resource, New York.

the narrative vividness, the *enargeia*, that characterizes the scene of the flowing blood also manifests itself in the execution scene. Once again Uccello has removed an obstacle to our sight—here half of the metal cauldron or fire screen—and once again the effect is profoundly unsettling. What we see is not a doctrinal emblem of doubt but a family in flames. One of the children, his face in profile, is screaming.[30]

To proceed further with an analysis of the altarpiece, we would need to follow and, if possible, extend Marilyn Lavin's investigation of the status of Jews in fifteenth-century Urbino, along with the cultural politics of confraternities, the shifting theological and diplomatic currents in Italy, the social history and devotional uses of altarpieces, as well as their formal resources and constraints.[31] Following recent work on the distinction between the natural and the preternatural and between both of these and the supernatural, we would want to explore the complex aesthetic and philosophical dimensions of wonder. We would hope to use recent scholarship—we think particularly of Caroline Walker Bynum's *Holy Feast and Holy Fast,* Miri Rubin's *Corpus Christi,* and R. Po-chia Hsia's *The Myth of Ritual Murder*—to bring into sharper focus the gender concerns at which we have only briefly glanced. Above all, we would want to return with redoubled attention to the formal design of the paintings,[32] attention not only to the internal structures of the individual works but also to the formal relations that would have been established in the original setting and that are now difficult to perceive. The two panels are currently displayed side by side on the bare whitewashed walls of the Ducal Palace; but if, as seems likely, they were actually set together in a single altarpiece within an ecclesiastical setting, then their full significance must have derived to a very considerable degree from the implications of this placement and from the ritual in which the altarpiece participated. We have already alluded several times to the possibility that Joos van Gent's panel is a response to Uccello's predella, but a thorough exploration of this response would require a slow, patient, detailed analysis of the complex echoes and tensions that would have been more completely manifest when the two pieces were placed in the aesthetic and institutional structure for which they were intended. That structure would have included the altar itself upon which the sacrifice of the Mass was performed and toward which the blood that flows out through the wound in the wall was tending. There would have been a complex movement then, at once formal, representational, and institutional, from the painted figure of Christ standing before an altar and holding the wafer between his fingers, to the predella narrative of the bleeding wafer restored to the altar, to the actual altar on which the holy wafers and the other elements and implements of the sacrifice would be placed, and thence to the priest who would stand at Mass and take up a consecrated Host between his fingers, exactly as the painted figure of Christ as priest was shown to be doing.

But for the moment we must be content simply to acknowledge the incompleteness of our discussion and to stop with a few closing observations. First, we have spoken of doubt as a Christian *projection* on the Jews, but of course Jews did (and do) deny the truth of eucharistic doctrine.[33] The reality of that disbelief hardly licenses persecution, but it does mean that the altarpiece participates in a historical encounter that includes but is not limited to the representation of Christian faith and Christian doubt. Christian doubt is projected upon Jewish disbelief, while at the same time Christian doctrine draws upon certain aspects of the sacrificial logic of Jewish faith. The boundary line between Jews and Christians was crucial—it could be, and frequently was, a matter of life and death—but it was porous and unstable, subject to holes and wounds. Second, even on the evidence of the altarpiece alone, Christian attitudes toward Jews were ambiguous and complex. Analysis of an aesthetic representation must not be a way of containing or closing off this complexity but rather of intensifying it. The boundary line between the attitude toward Jews expressed in the main panel and the attitude expressed in the predella is crucial—again, it could, when transformed into actions, be a matter of life and death—but here too it is, as we have already seen, porous and unstable. Third, we have spoken of the legendary narratives of Host desecration as the expression of doubt, but the narratives, and the doctrinal claims that they represent, are also manifestly the expression of an intensified faith across the Christian community in the mystical truth of transubstantiation. The boundary line between faith and doubt is crucial—it was a matter of eternal life and death—but once again it is porous and unstable. Doubt is the consequence of the heightened claims of faith, and faith is tested and renewed on the dangerous shoals of doubt.

Fourth, and finally, we are deeply concerned with the tension between beliefs and their representations. The altarpiece at which we have been looking is an especially fraught case, since it makes its doctrinal point about the irrelevance of visible appearances to the eyes of faith through the vehicle of those very appearances and then further stigmatizes the craving for ocular proof as wicked unbelief. The doctrine of the Real Presence might be said to exceed all representational claims—the Host *is* the body and blood of Christ—while the painting relies on the representational efficacy of the icon, which ensures that we will embrace the make-believe and recognize, for example, the redness of blood in the redness of paint. The painting also, however, relies on several non-iconic representational conventions—such as the cutaway fourth wall—that require a different and still greater act of make-believe. Here the pleasure the altarpiece offers you depends not on a resemblance between what you see and what you are willing to imagine that you see, but rather on a violation of the normal perceptual world, a transfiguration of vision as if by magic, miracle, or (in our own cultural terms) technology.

We have focused on two places in the altarpiece that strain these representational conventions to the breaking point and confound the different modes of make-believe. The represented Host between Christ's fingers, an object whose centrality and minimalism seem to render its very iconicity problematic, pulls representation toward its opposite, toward the blank spot where what is visible is a mere insignificant accident. The blankness of the Host is the "point" of the doctrine. The second of these places, the wound in the wall, is the consequence of Uccello's attempt to negotiate not between Real Presence and representation, but between visual likeness and self-conscious conventionality. This attempt is at once a formal solution and the solution to a narrative problem, a forensic question: How did the Christian community discover the secret Jewish crime? But because the wound so thoroughly confounds any distinction between an illusionistic detail and a formal convenience, it also calls iconicity into question, putting pressure, as we have seen, on the partition between perfidious Jews and pious Christians who long to see the Host bleed. The Host reminds us that if we truly believe, we should not need paintings; the wound reminds us that paintings require us to acquiesce, for the sake of ocular satisfaction, in many things we do not necessarily believe.

If the altarpiece seems overloaded with riddles and with the peculiar paradoxes of eucharistic faith, it nevertheless only exaggerates a tendency in all representation, for, whether doctrinal or legendary, any representation is distinct from that which it purports to exemplify. The pleasure of representation is bound up with this distinction, with perceived differences that mark the gap, in Elaine Scarry's terms, between the made-up and the

made-real. We contend that these differences are not what remove representations from ordinary reality, but rather what con-
nect them to reality's collaborations, tensions, and murderous
conflicts. Aporia are not places where forms refer only to themselves, but are rather the tears where energies, desires, and repres-
sions flow out into the world.

Four

THE POTATO IN THE
MATERIALIST IMAGINATION

When Vice President Dan Quayle was being ridiculed for misspelling "potato" by putting an "e" at the end, President Bush defended him by claiming that Chaucer had spelled the word that way. Bush thus revealed that he knew something about the history of the English language and its orthography but nothing about the history of the potato, which was not introduced into Europe until the seventeenth century. The English word derives from the Spanish pronunciation of the Haitian name for what we call the sweet potato, "batata." It was first used in English in 1597. Bush, though, is not the only American who assumes there were medieval potatoes: a medieval theme park in the Midwest advertises that it makes its potato pancakes from an authentic fourteenth-century recipe.

Belief in the medieval potato is not really surprising, given the strong association in the modern mind between potatoes and peasants, on the one hand, and peasants and medieval Europe, on the other. Indeed, despite its very late arrival on the scene, the potato represents something like an Ur-food even in the northern European imagination. We don't wish to make excuses for George Bush in this chapter, though; we intend, rather, to unearth the long-neglected British potato debate of the late eighteenth and early nineteenth centuries,[1] with the hope of exploring simultaneously the relation between the body history[2] that has deeply influenced new historicism and older forms of materialist thought.

The potato debate was basically a controversy over the relative merits of potatoes and grain as the staple food of the working poor. It raged with peculiar intensity during the 1790s and then again in the 1830s, both eras of dispute over poor-law policy. Most conceded that a unit of land producing potatoes would feed three times as many people as the same land bearing wheat, but they disagreed over the desirability of such an arrangement. Several issues were involved, such as the proper level of wages, the effect on population growth, the danger of setting wages according to the cheapest possible staple food, and the social consequences of having two standard foods, wheat bread for the middle classes and potatoes for the poor.

This list of abstract issues, however, gives little sense of the passion suffusing the potato debate, the vehemence with which the opposing parties predicted that either misery or abundance would accompany the spread of the tuber. The very idea of a potato debate seems mildly ridiculous because we've forgotten what the debaters knew—that the vast majority of people would live primarily on one food and that this food would cost the majority of their income. The cost of labor, most political economists agreed, was determined fundamentally by the cost of grain, and the supply of grain largely controlled the supply of laboring people. In the debaters' minds, therefore, bushels of the staple food became almost interchangeable with people themselves, and many insisted that potato people were radically different from grain people. If we take a look at the rhetoric of this debate, we can see that potato eaters often undergo a peculiarly quick transition from plant to person, as if they were literalizing the political economists' equations. In this debate, anxieties about the tuber generally sprout from this quick transition, from a perception of the potato's primeval, archaic power to conjure people right out of the ground. But this same, at times disturbingly close, link between soil and people led others to extol the plant as "the root of plenty." The potato, to put it briefly, became an icon of the autochthonous body for certain late-eighteenth- and early-nineteenth-century writers, and hence it seems an appropriate topic for launching a discussion of the modern materialist imagination.

The potato also gives us an opportunity to assert that representation knows no natural limits. That vegetable's very significance as a peculiarly primitive food, a thing representing mere subsistence and (in some minds) the virtual end of culture, gave it tremendous symbolic weight. But the potato did not restrict itself to one meaning; it was as ambivalent, arbitrary, historically overdetermined, unstable, and opaque as any other signifier. Like all signifiers, it spoils the distinction between matter and idea, but its placement in the imagined ground of existence especially unsettles attempts to distinguish a physical material base from an ideological superstructure or a bodily need from a cultural exigency. When, for example, Raymond Williams tries to devise a scale on which phenomena could be ranged from the "less cultural" to the "more," he claims that food would be down at the "less cultural" end because any symbolic function it might have would be submerged in its primary purpose of sustaining life. Food, he admits, has "signifying" moments; one can analyze it semiotically, demonstrating the various social meanings of how and what people prepare and consume. Nevertheless, its nonsignifying, merely physiological utility takes precedence over its ideational meaning.[3] If Williams were right, the more an edible item was merely food to a people, the more it seemed simply to satisfy a bodily need, the less it would "signify" and the less "cultural" it would be. But the potato debate demonstrates that "mere food" is not only already a cultural category, but also an extremely potent and disturbing one. It was precisely by being *only food* that the potato became symbolically resonant.

The potato in the materialist imagination thus enjoys a certain uncanny resemblance to the elusive object of the previous chapter: the consecrated Host in the doctrine of the Real Presence. Both attempt to mark the limits of representation, to define the outer reaches of the realm of human signification. Just as the Host, by *being* rather than *meaning* the literal presence of Christ's body and blood, is placed beyond artistic representation, the potato conducts us to the nineteenth-century materialists' beyond, where the Real is the physical ground of our existence, as harsh and unremitting in its determinism as it is generally indifferent to our constructions of its import. Like the Host, the potato is a threshold phenomenon: the former gives access to the divine, independently of the intentions or control of the participants in the sacrament; the latter threatens to turn culture into nature or to overwhelm meaning with matter. Believing Catholics and nineteenth-century materialists alike seem to have needed a sign for the end of signification, and each found it in a bit of matter that could be thought of as a literal body.

To be sure, the literal body of Christ and the autochthonous body of the potato would occupy opposite extremes on the sort of spectrum imagined by Raymond Williams. In Williams's terms, the potato would have an excess of matter and the Eucharist an excess of signification: in its primal materiality, its lumpish absence of standard form, the potato seems the antithesis of the eucharistic Host, whose matter has been sublimated almost out of existence. And, indeed, a similar contrast is implied in the potato debate when potatoes are compared and contrasted to bread, just as the Eucharist had been. The common comparative term only strengthens the case for their diametrical difference. The Host is infinitely more than the physical accidents of the bread, whereas the potato is ever so much less. Indeed, compared to potatoes, bread is anything but accidental. The possibility of subsisting on the potato is what made it comparable to bread rather than to other roots (like carrots and parsnips).[4] It was understood, therefore, as a substitute for the very food that most commonly stood as a signifier for all food. Although bread has this general synechdochal function in European culture (even in Ireland people don't ask God to "Give us this day our daily potatoes"), the potato, introduced much later, is imagined to be the more *primitive* contender because it comes right out of the earth, haphazardly shaped, like a clot of dirt, but virtually ready to eat. If the eucharistic Host was the body made transcendent and immortal, the potato was rhetorically associated by its opponents with physical wretchedness, filth, and infirmity. Those who compared bread and potatoes frequently stressed that bread partook of several elements and required many differentiated stages of production. Wheat, which bears its grains aboveground, ripens all golden in the sunlit air, while potato tubers expand unseen in occulted darkness. Passing through few stages of civilized productive mediation, the potato makes a startlingly abrupt transition from ground to human being. The whole satisfyingly social and symbolic cycle of planting, germination, sprouting, growing, ripening, harvesting, thrashing, milling, mixing, kneading, and baking, which makes wheat into bread, is bypassed in tuber culture. Without being formed by human hands, baked in man-made ovens, passing through a differentiated society, or circulating in an economy, the very root of the potato plant itself becomes something like a hard, knobby little loaf of bread, a point succinctly made by one of the earliest words for the potato in English—"bread-root." Just as the Eucharist enacts Christ's continued dwelling among his communicants, bread represents the cooperation of the elements in human endeavors and the cooperation of people with one another in a society where the division of labor has been achieved but people nevertheless share the same food. In short, whereas the Eucharist partakes of divinity and bread of culture, the potato represented a presocial state of isolation in which the poor were cut off from civilization and undifferentiated both from each other and from nature.

The English had a word for this state: Ireland. Ireland was a place without bread, a land of spurious substitutes: potatoes and Communion wafers believed to be the literal body and blood of Christ, the one a cause of degrading carnality, the other a focus of mass delusion. Of course the believers didn't see it that way, but to them as well the potato and Host were on opposite sides of that rare commodity, bread. To the believer, the Host is spiritual, as opposed to bodily, nourishment. It gathers up the symbolic meanings of bread—including human community, mutual nurturance, and reliance on natural cycles of death and resurrection—saturates them with transcendent spirituality, and lets the physical gravity of bread—for example, bulk and nutrition—drop away like dross. Only a hint of bread remains in the Host, whose papery thinness and stamped impression recall a text or a coin (despite the anti-representationalism of the doctrine of the Real Presence) far more than they do any kind of food. Thus even for the believer, the Communion wafer and the potato, as spiritual and physical food, even as antimatter and matter, would have seemed an obvious pair of opposites.

But for those who feared what Ireland represented, the potato and the Host might seem destructively complementary opposites that canceled their mutual term of comparison: bread. The potato was often imagined to be the root of mere materiality, whereas the Host was the symbol of chimerical spirituality; together they might trick a people into thinking that they had no need for the middle term represented by bread—culture—because they were gathered by their religion into a transcendent mystical body. By believing the bizarre claim of the transubstantiation, that the consecrated Host *is* the body and blood of Christ, the Irish became victims of a misplaced concreteness that eradicated culture, the realm of transformation through labor and of exchanges that were recognizably symbolic. Perhaps it was because the Irish peasantry was in the grip of superstition, because they thought they could eat God's body, that they uncomplainingly lived on a hog's diet.

To our knowledge, no nineteenth-century writer explicitly made these connections: we have assembled in the foregoing paragraphs the complementary sides of English alarmism about the state of Ireland, but they do not truly make a single empirically available discourse. Generally, the anti-potato faction had little explicit interest in religion, and the debate we'll be describing was secular in tone, even downright materialist in its assumptions about human motivation and cultural practices. Nevertheless, the most horrific anti-potato rhetoric seems to borrow the extreme literalism of eucharistic doctrine when it turns to the relation between body and food. In William Cobbett's fulminations, for example, food and body are difficult to distinguish, as if, in potato eating, the Sacrament had been grotesquely inverted to produce bodies bearing an ugly resemblance to misshapen roots. Writing at the end of the potato debate in 1834 and synthesizing many of the potato opponents' images, the radical journalist portrays the Irish peasantry as people living underground, like their food, literally in the soil. The potato, he writes, "has chased bread from the cottages of this island," and with the disappearance of civilized food has come a descent into the very ground of existence. The potato eaters live, he tells his correspondent, in low mud huts full of holes:

> . . . no windows at all; but a hole or two holes in the wall; . . . the floor nothing but the bare earth; no chimney, but, a hole at

> one end of the roof a foot or two high at the end of the miserable
> shed; this hole is sometimes surrounded by a few stones . . . ; in
> cold weather the poor, ragged half-naked creatures stop up the
> hole to keep in the smoke to keep them from perishing with cold!
> The fuel is *peat,* just such as that dug out of our moors, and never
> a stick of wood.[5]

Everything about this description makes the dwelling seem subterranean: the building materials of rough stone and mud, the
fuel of peat ("as that dug out of our moors"), the strange combination of exposure and suffocation, and the repeated use of the word
"hole." As Cobbett's description goes on, the underground imagery becomes even more insistent. "Hole" comes to describe the
very dwelling just when "the root of all misery" (the potato) appears in the description:

> As to the *goods* in the hole, they are, an *iron pot,* a *rough table,* or
> board laid across two poles of stones, seats of stones. . . . The
> potatoes are taken up and turned out into a great dish, which dish
> is a shallow basket made of oziers with the bark on. The family
> squat round this basket and take out the potatoes with their hands;
> the pig stands and is helped by some one, and sometimes he eats
> out of the pot. He goes in and out and about the hole, like one
> of the family. (82–83)

Lest we think that the potato is merely incidental to this subterranean existence, Cobbett proclaims loudly and frequently that the
tuber is the channel through which Irish landlords have brought
the peasantry lower than the very ground:

> The people never could have been brought to this pass without
> the ever-damned potatoes! People CAN keep life in them by the
> means of this nasty, filthy hog-feed; and the tyrants make them
> do it, and have thus reduced them to the state of hogs, and worse
> than that of hogs. (83)

Through Cobbett's subterranean imagery, the Irish laborers have
indeed been reduced to something quite a bit lower than pigs—
something closely resembling potatoes.

As the shortest route through which the land can bear people,
the potato triggered deep fears in many and hopes in some about

the earth's fecundity. Cobbett's depictions of Irish cottiers eating the filthy root in their "holes" can be linked, for example, to persistent stories of exotic dirt-eating races; closer to home, they recall derogatory English medieval images of peasants eating dirt. The formulation is both insulting to peasants—"Peasants eat dirt, therefore peasants are dirt"—and reassuring to the landed classes—"Peasants can eat dirt, so we needn't worry about them." The complete idea has the structure of a cruel joke: the bad news is that the peasants eat dirt; the good news is that there's plenty of dirt. This absurd conflation of utter privation and abundance seems fundamental to the idea of autochthonous people, people who are part and parcel of the land, as medieval serfs were imagined to be.

A seventeenth-century mention of the Irish potato illustrates its affinity with the notion of a people who are so rooted in the soil that they cannot be eradicated even by the destruction of their grain supply. John Houghton writes of the plant's introduction to the British Isles:

> This I have been informed was brought first out of Virginia by Sir Walter Raleigh, and he stopping at Ireland, some was planted there, where it thrived well and to good purpose, for in three succeeding wars, when all the corn above ground was destroyed, this supported them; for the soldiers, unless they had dug up all the ground where they grew, and almost sifted it could not extirpate them.[6]

The rather sloppy use of pronouns in this passage underlines the main point: the "them" who cannot be extirpated short of digging up and sifting the ground could denote either the potatoes or the rebellious Irish.

As a tale of autochthonous people, though, this one is riddled with ironies. First, Irish survival is assured by a symptom of the very thing that seems to threaten it: English colonialism. Because an English colonist brought a food from an incipient colony on the other side of the Atlantic to plant in a far older colonial settlement near Cork, the Irish were later able to withstand the devastation wrought by subsequent English armies. According to the story, the colonizing drive of the seventeenth century both propelled English aggression and unexpectedly furnished provision against its deadliness. This first level of narrative irony is so satisfying that the story seems to have gone unquestioned for over a century even though some of its details are easy to refute: Raleigh was never in Virginia, and if he had been he wouldn't have found potatoes there in the late sixteenth century.[7]

A second level of irony emerges in another version of the Raleigh story, where the colonizer blunders doubly: he not only unwittingly provides the enemy with an underground food supply, but also misunderstands the sort of food he imports. Raleigh, the story goes, didn't even know what part of the potato to eat, and after tasting the bitter berries, told his gardener to destroy the plants. But, according to the operations of a peculiarly incongruous Irish providence, the roots nevertheless spread, merging, as in Houghton, with the very ground and becoming a symbol for the ineradicability of Irish Catholicism, which, despite its aboveground ruination, would maintain its subterranean vitality. The striking thing about this version of the story is that the potato is depicted as thoroughly accidental and therefore providential. Raleigh never meant to introduce a new staple food, only a variety of berry, and when the plant disappointed him, he tried to throw it away. The potato is thus the Englishman's garbage, that which has no value inside his economy, mysteriously transmogrified into salvational nutrition, manna from heaven hidden under the ground. The potato in this story is the bit of matter that not only foils the invader's intentions, but also eludes his economy of scarcity, escaping both his control and his conceptual categories and giving the Irish a foothold in what Bataille calls a general economy, where waste and wealth are indistinguishable.

These myths of the origin of the Irish potato, therefore, both use and disorganize ideas of the autochthonous relationship between ground and people. The people may be inextricable from the land, but only because the land harbors an alien stuff. Instead of being indigenous or natural, the nurturing element of this ground is foreign and accidental. Hence, instead of underlying history as the bedrock of human existence, this ground is interlaced with historical irony. The accidental potato, moreover, tosses a twist into the linear narrative of increasing English ascendancy and reminds us that what might have seemed reassuring

in the autochthonous myth when applied to English peasants—
the notion that to have the ground was to have the people—was
positively threatening to Cromwellians and Orangemen in war-
ridden seventeenth-century Ireland.

But by the late eighteenth century, when the great potato debate began, certain Englishmen had new reasons for promulgating the utopian dimension of the autochthonous myth, implying
that the potato was as plentiful as the earth itself. The potato's
English advocates started the potato debate; most of them wanted
to keep wages down by shifting the English poor off of a diet of
wheat bread and on to one of potatoes. It was in response to this
proposal that Cobbett spread his belief in the magical destructive
power of the plant, even reversing Houghton's image of the food
as the ideal provision against invasion: "It is both my pleasure
and my duty to discourage in every way that I can the cultivation
of this damned root, being convinced that it has done more harm
to mankind than the sword and pestilence united" (83). Although
passages like these, which conjure ideas of potato armies and potato locusts making their way across the Irish Sea, are unique to
Cobbett, the image on which he relied primarily, that of the
potato pulling its eaters down into an undifferentiated organic
muck, had a prior life in the utopian depictions of Ireland by
a potato enthusiast, the prolific English agricultural writer and
"improver" Arthur Young. Thirty years before Cobbett went to
Ireland, Arthur Young revived Houghton's implicit characterization of the potato as an almost preternaturally compact and un-
failing food supply. His descriptions of Irish cottiers at their meal
emphasize the benevolent fecundity of the tuber:

> . . . [M]ark the Irishman's potatoe bowl placed on the floor, the
> whole family upon their hams around it, devouring a quantity al-
> most incredible, the beggar seating himself to it with a hearty
> welcome, the pig taking his share as readily as the wife, the cocks,
> hens, turkies, geese, the cur, the cat, and perhaps the cow—and all
> partaking of the same dish. No man can often have been witness
> of it without being convinced of the plenty, and I will add the
> cheerfulness, that attends it.[8]

Where Cobbett saw human degradation, Young saw abundance,
variety, and fertility. The profuseness of this potato-eating fam-

ily is just an alternative reading of its dirt; to feed your animals
and your family out of the same dish indicated to Young a gen-
erosity that only people who have plenty can afford to indulge.
The various forms of animal life gathered round the "potatoe
bowl" have, in a sense, sprung from it. The steaming potatoes in
this passage are, to use Young's phrase, "the root of plenty," the
always-abundant fleshy plant stuff out of which the animal world
emerges. True, that world is undifferentiated—note the mixture
of pigs and persons in the description of the "family on their
hams" around the meal—but the lack of hierarchical arrangement
in this passage implies, not regression to a degraded primitivism,
but retrieval of a golden age, a peaceable kingdom, where all
God's creatures inhabit the world harmoniously.

We might see the difference between Cobbett's vision and
Young's, therefore, as the inversion of a single metamorphosis:
if in Cobbett's descriptions the Irish cottiers lived the underground life of the potatoes, in Young's the potatoes turned into
people with extraordinary ease. Cobbett expressed the dreadful
half of the dirt-eater idea, and Young expressed its hopeful half. It
would, however, be a mistake to characterize Cobbett and Young
simply as inheritors of the older images of autochthonous popula-
tions. The residues of those images persist, but they are organized
according to new ways—uniquely modern ways—of imagining
the relationship between human bodies and the earth as the
ground of material existence.

Both Young and Cobbett were concerned by what they saw
as a worsening relationship between the land and the people who
worked it in *England,* and they were interested in the role (or
potential role) of the potato either to exacerbate or to ameliorate
the new conditions. Arthur Young was an enlightened advocate
of progress through scientific agriculture. Like many "improving"
landlords of the eighteenth century, he believed that the ultimate
good of agricultural communities would be served by the most
efficient food production. Efficiency, he reasoned, was motivated
by profit seeking; profit seeking necessitated private ownership
and control of the land, which in turn required enclosures of what
had been commons. Genuinely humanitarian desires for cheap
food and a higher minimum standard of living led scientific agri-

culturalists like Young to propagandize in favor of enclosures as a step in the march of progress. Toward the end of the eighteenth century, however, this naive faith that higher profits for landlords would automatically create inexpensive and plentiful food for the working poor was somewhat shaken. Thousands of people had lost their common and forest rights, often their mainstay against starvation when the wheat crop failed, but they had not gained, it seemed, a proportional drop in the price of wheat when the harvest was good. In 1794 a disastrous harvest and widespread food rioting revealed the extent of destitution and absolute dependency among the agricultural poor. Young fastened on the potato partly as a way to compensate the poor for their loss of common rights, but mainly as a miraculous staple crop that would never fail if properly cultivated. The enclosures could continue. Progress could march on without trampling on the security or independence of the British laborer; if he were allotted three acres of subsistence tubers and a cow, he would be protected against the vicissitudes of the larger agricultural commodity market, indeed, provided against all contingencies: failed corn crops, wars, overpasturing, or protectionist legislation. Far from turning away from the enlightenment optimism of his earlier writings, his belief that the benign market and new scientific principles would bring about an era of unprecedented plenty, Young supplemented it in the 1790s with an equally fervent faith in the reliability of that thoroughly *modern* staple, the potato:

> The great object is by means of milk and potatoes to take the mass of the country's "poor" from the consumption of wheat, and to give them substitutes equally wholesome and nourishing and as independent of scarcities natural and artificial, as the providence of the Almighty will permit.[9]

Young was, consequently, very far from believing the old autochthonous myth that the poor could always somehow scratch a living out of the earth. His modified utopia required active supervision by progressive thinkers, the spread of scientific methods, and a new spirit of self-reliance, even of individualism, among laborers. Young tried to make the potato stand for all of this. It was a symbol of mankind's improvability if not his complete perfectibility. Whereas in Houghton's story the potato was an occulted form of nature's bounty brought to light by history's irony or God's providence, in Young's view the potato was pliant nature's response to human ingenuity and scientific understanding. If it wouldn't completely solve the problem of scarcity—some experience of which seemed ordained by our material nature and God's will—it was at least a significant step in that direction. Inside this meliorist vision, therefore, the potato was transformed from the Ur-food to the innovative food; Young's potato-patch utopia might even be seen as a precursor of futuristic fantasies about human societies that free themselves from "scarcities natural and artificial" by making all of their food in chemistry labs. Implicit in his potato is the dream of a humanity that has subdued its material conditions to its will not through ascetic denial, but through the discovery and propagation of unfaltering supply. The potato is the bit of matter that promises Arthur Young a new material order, a secular transubstantiation in which the human body is no longer experienced as needy and hungry, and is hence no longer riotous and unpredictable.

Like most Enlightenment panaceas, though, Young's potato had to overcome the prejudices of the benighted, some of whom, like Cobbett, objected that it violated the principles of the moral economy, and others of whom, like Thomas Malthus and David Ricardo, insisted that it violated those of political economy.

⸱⸱⸱

The phrase "the moral economy" refers to a concept developed by E. P. Thompson in his 1971 essay "The Moral Economy of the Crowd"; and, before continuing with our analysis of the early-nineteenth-century potato debates, we will take a short historiographical detour into that essay. "The moral economy of the crowd," Thompson writes, was "a consistent traditional view of social norms and obligations, of the proper economic functions of several parties within the community"[10] that, in the last half of the eighteenth century, was frequently opposed to the free-market assumptions of early political economy. Thompson uses the concept to explain the food riots of the late 1790s, the very experiences that inspired Young's potato allotments. Thompson's argument is such an important protest against historians who disregard cultural factors when analyzing economic behavior, especially behavior in response to dietary changes, that we want to spend a few pages not only reviewing what he has to tell us about the struggle over working-class food in the period, but also analyzing the terms of his own argument. His essay interests us here both because it provides the crucial concept of the moral economy and because it marks out the analytical limits that even an English *cultural* materialist historian stayed within up until the 1970s.

We must admit at the outset that Thompson never mentions Arthur Young or any other potato debater in his essay on the 1790s; indeed, he entirely overlooks the potato, and this oversight, we suggest, might indicate the limitations of the culturalist historical materialism he practices. It is, of course, easy to pick out the defects of thirty-year-old essays, and Thompson's must be acknowledged as a triumph of cultural history. First, it explodes the "abbreviated and 'economistic' picture of the food riot, as a direct, spasmodic, irrational response to hunger" (258). The historical consciousness of the rioters, Thompson insists, must be reconstructed. "How," he asks, "is their behaviour modified by custom, culture, and reason?" (187). Hunger, in other words, is a necessary but hardly a sufficient explanation of food riots. Second, the essay argues that economic historians fail to historicize their own presuppositions; relying on the idea of "economic man" to analyze earlier societies, they assume a universality of motive that is blind to cultural difference. Thompson's analysis, in contrast, insists on putting economic beliefs and behavior back into a larger cultural context. Finally, the essay subtly rejects as anachronistic a simple class-conflict model of popular uprising in the eighteenth century, substituting instead a dynamic of conflicted negotiations inside the "bread nexus" that the moral economy took for granted. Hence, the historical consciousness of the rioters was not utterly distinct from that of their governors: their "definite, and passionately held, notions of the common weal . . . found some support in the paternalist traditions of the authorities; notions which the people re-echoed so loudly in their turn that the authorities were, in some measure, the prisoners of the people" (189).

These are no mean insights. And yet, since the intervening

decades saw the development of what has come to be called the history of the body, something about Thompson's analysis seems lacking. The absence of the potato, we only half facetiously urge, marks his reluctance to submit the ideas of hunger and dearth to a more thorough cultural or historical analysis. Despite his vigilant anti-reductionism, he allows hunger and scarcity to stand as self-evident material stimuli on which a cultural analysis of response can be mounted. To be sure, he notes that the equation of provision with wheat and the equation of bread with white bread require quite a bit of cultural explanation; but he confines his discussion of the alternatives to "rougher" grain mixtures and concludes that by the 1790s millers and bakers could no longer produce, and laborers could no longer stomach, coarser household loaves. Although he draws almost exclusively on R. N. Salaman's *The History and Social Influence of the Potato* (1949)[11] for evidence that the poor would accept nothing but white bread even at the height of the scarcity, he never mentions the widespread proposals and the practical attempts to substitute potatoes for wheat. Perhaps, recognizing the availability of alternative staple foods would make the crowd actions of the 1790s seem *too* culturally determined, *too* independent of material causes, and therefore not entirely "rational." Thompson's resistance to the potato is symptomatic of cultural materialism's desire for a moral economy of explanation that assumes the reasonableness of popular action and its conformity to an implied human norm. The delicate balance between cultural variety and normative humanity in Thompson's analysis depends on an unvarying physical substratum, which the potato threatens to contaminate.

Our debt to Thompson's analysis and our distance from it on the issue of the potato mark the continuity and discontinuity between cultural materialism and the body history that followed in its wake. Viewing the moral economy, body historians would look for more than a cultural grid determining responses to the physical stimulus of hunger; they would look at hunger as part of the bodily experience of that economy. Much in Thompson's analysis already points in this direction. He demonstrates that what was at stake in the riots was the preservation of the old bread nexus (as opposed to the newer cash nexus) because it provided the flash points, the friction that enabled the rough negotiations of crowd action. That is, his analysis indicates that the laborers were struggling for the preservation of the terms of the struggle, which provided the experience of cultural inclusion. The more extended and intricate the network through which people received their staple food, the more places of potential popular intervention: "[The corn] is harvested, threshed, taken to market, ground at the mill, baked, and eaten. But at every point in this process there are radiating complexities. . . ."[12] The "radiating complexities" were the integuments of the social body itself, and it was these from which Arthur Young's potato patches would have freed the laborer: "if each had his ample potatoe ground and a cow, the price of wheat would be of little more consequence to them than it is to their brethren in Ireland," wrote Young.[13] But Thompson's description of the moral economy shows us how far such a sensation of inconsequentiality would have been from the desires of the crowd. Having a secure provision in independent isolation could not possibly have accomplished what the rioters sought, which was the experience, through friction, of their incorporation in a social body organized around bread.

The moral economy was therefore not just a cultural mediator of responses to the physical stimulus of hunger; it was itself a physiological-cultural stimulus: both the experience of inclusion inside a corporate body and a cause of the sensation of hunger. When English people refused to eat potato stews because they were "swill"—not human food—and resisted even the moderate proposal that they should add potatoes to their home-baked bread, it seems extremely likely that they were increasing their hunger. But it is also possible that they remained hungry, as they claimed they did, even when they grudgingly ate such alternatives to bread. Abundant complaints that "*squashy* stuff"[14] (eaten in no matter how large a quantity) was simply not solid enough to satisfy working people should remind us that appetite, too, has a culture and a history. Our point is not that the rejection of the potato caused the dearth of the 1790s; but the vehement refusal to accept potato substitutes for white bread when they were available points to the need for a thorough historicization of what counted as food and what felt like hunger.

Tossing the potato into Thompson's analysis of the food riots in the 1790s could, therefore, strengthen the "culturalism" of his account, but only by moving the "cultural" further into the body, by making it more than a mental structure or a set of shared understandings equivalent to "consciousness." Generally ontological agnostics, body historians do not attempt to deny the importance of matter, but they do question the proposition that physical experience is uniform and stable across time and space. Perhaps paradoxically, though, they also tend to privilege the body as a place where culture has a peculiarly tenacious hold. Because the moral economy was a mode of physical existence, and not just a way of thinking, a body historian might argue, its disruption was met with unusually violent reaction.

Cobbett's letters from Ireland[15] are the most complete, if delayed, articulation of that reaction available, and their insistence on the physical perils of noninclusion represented by the potato bears out the body historians' hunches. The letters evince a horror about the breakdown of the bread nexus that was probably shared by the English poor, who energetically repulsed the potato in the 1790s. The Irish, Cobbett reports, may be filled with potatoes, but they are nevertheless permanently deprived of the sensation of a nurturing connection to the people who own the land and ultimately control them. Since they are outside of the "radiating complexities" of the bread market, the Irish that Cobbett depicts have no points of entry into a shared community or moral economy. Indeed, in Ireland, because of the potato, there is no community. For Cobbett, potato eating marks the border, not simply between going hungry and being satisfied, but between sharing in *civilization's* nourishment and being deprived of it. The potato threatens the physical life of the poor *as humans* because it is only food, mere subsistence, unorganized into a reciprocal economy of rights and duties, expectations and negotiations. Situated at the gateway to the merely physical, the potato signifies the awful possibility that a country's staple food might not form a bond, however contested, between land and labor, countryside and city, rich and poor. Cobbett images the potato as purely exploitative bondage, which reduces people not just to animals but to harshly misused animals, when he figures it as simultaneously food and muzzle, that which stops the mouth as it fills it. God's law, he claims, forbids feeding the laborer on

> . . . infamous potatoes and salt. The law of God forbids to muzzle the ox while he is treading out the corn. . . . [I]n order that the farmers should be merciful and just, even to the animals that they employed, God commands, in the 25th chapter of DEUTERONOMY, "Thou shallt not *muzzle* the ox when he treadeth out the corn"; that is, thou shalt not pinch him, thou shalt not take from him a share of that which he has caused to come. (184)

Because potatoes are not "a share" of the master's provision, not part of what the master eats or sells, which is grain, they cannot properly recompense the laborer. Hence, no matter how plentiful the potato, it would always be nugatory nourishment and a sign of expulsion from the social body. Indeed Cobbett's image denotes an even worse state than expulsion, for the tethered oxen, although outside a proper social organism, are nevertheless slavishly bound to the masters. Similarly, the cottiers are not free from the landowners' civilization; instead, their potato muzzles place them in a uniquely modern state of pure subjugation.

If the potato threatened to break the bread nexus, violating the moral economy by forcing the laboring poor to live on a cheap subsistence crop while they continued to produce a dearer cash crop for their landlords, the political economists portrayed it as no less menacing to the cash nexus. Indeed, the political economists' unanimous condemnation of Arthur Young's potato-allotment scheme shows that, in their minds, the cash nexus and a thoroughly commodified bread nexus were inseparable. If English working people were struggling to preserve the multiple places where they could intervene to shape the social organism by insisting on eating white bread, political economists saw the wheat market as the primary means of controlling the reproduction of laborers and keeping them fit and efficient. Food rioters and political economists, therefore, were united in their opposition to the potato as a staple food. Unlike the working-class activists, however, political economists did have a use for the potato precisely as a stigmatized food.

Thomas Malthus's response to Arthur Young (in the 1806 version of *An Essay on Population*) is a convenient guide to the political economists' potato. For the sake of argument, Malthus at first brackets the possibility of potato crop failures and concentrates simply on the misery that would follow from the very plenty Young predicted:

> The specific cause of the poverty and misery of the lower classes . . . in Ireland is, that from . . . the facility of obtaining a cabin and potatoes . . . , a population is brought into existence which is not demanded by the quantity of capital and employment in the country; and the consequence of which must therefore necessarily be . . . to lower in general the price of labour by too great competition; from which must result complete indigence to those who cannot find employment, and an incomplete subsistence even to those who can.[16]

The reader might be puzzled by the word "subsistence" here. After all, Young said that the potato would insure "subsistence," making the marketplace (in grain, labor, and all other commodities) irrelevant to the issue of survival. But by "subsistence" Malthus means more than, as he puts it, "mere food" (231); he means also "decent housing and decent clothing," which can only be secured when labor itself is a relatively scarce commodity. And labor can only be scarce when food is relatively expensive. Since in a normal Malthusian world, cheap food will create an excess population, the potato is the root of misery *because* it is the root of plenty. For Malthus, the bad news was that the people were being asked to eat potatoes, and the *worse* news was that there were plenty of potatoes. Plenty of potatoes translates immediately and ineluctably into plenty of people, but into very little of anything else.

In Malthus's view, the potato was dangerous not only because it was cheap and abundant, but also because it would be grown in allotments set aside from capitalist agricultural enterprise. Hence the potato occupied a dangerously liminal place, simultaneously outside and inside the cash nexus, and the people that it nurtured were seen as similarly liminal. As a noncash crop, the potato would always be an insensitive indicator of the economy's need for bodies; if the crops are healthy, potatoes will stay cheap until a large surplus population appears. In contrast, a cash crop like wheat will quickly register the presence of too many people, for if it were very plentiful and therefore very cheap for any length of time, either rising demand would make it more expensive or some of the land on which it grew would soon be turned into pasture to increase the farmer's profit. In either case, the price of grain would go up, encouraging sexual abstinence and discouraging any further swelling of the population. Because wheat is a cash crop, in other words, its price is a sensitive mechanism that can potentially adjust the supply of people to the needs of employers in the economy at large.

The danger of potatoes thus lies in their economically extrinsic position; the extra-economic bodies that potato allotments automatically produce are not so much "redundant" in relation to the immediate food supply as in relation to the need for "productive" labor—that is, profit-making labor. Although they are sprung right from the ground and can therefore hardly be considered out of place, these potato paupers are themselves a kind of dirt because they are *not* organized into an economy. In the terms available to political economists, they could only be thought of as labor, but they have nothing to labor at besides their own reproduction. Utterly stripped-down versions of humanity, they are mere stomachs and sexual organs, multiplying to exhaustion, as in this description of a cottier's life by the radical Malthusian Francis Place:

> Once in possession of the cabin, the garden, and the girl, the Irishman sets himself and his wife to work to provide themselves with food. . . . Thus they go on, until the increase of the family makes it impossible for them to provide food enough in ordinary seasons for the healthy support of themselves and their children. . . . [W]hile a rood of land capable of producing potatoes can be had, the population may continue to increase, and must remain in its present deplorable condition . . . ill clothed, idle, dirty, ragged, and wretched in the extreme.[17]

Place's language is reminiscent of the old autochthonous myth: the Irishman and his wife set to work raising potatoes, but come up with crop after crop of children; where there is "a rood of land," there will be filthy, ragged people. And yet this is a thoroughly modern, completely Malthusian picture of humanity.

For this minimal human creature was, we might say, Malthus's invention and was fast becoming central to economic thought. According to Malthus, there are two invariant facts about human beings: they must have food, and they must have sex. A lack of either causes misery. Indeed, unless they use some vicious birth-control device, they will go on having sex until they have multiplied beyond their food supply. Only the constant threat of starvation keeps the majority of people from rampant reproduction. This rudimentary person, as critics pointed out at the time, was really just an appetite-driven body incapable of mental activity beyond the most basic Benthamite calculation: that is, the pleasure of this immediate copulation will be less than the pain of that future hunger. And yet the sheer physicality of the creature made it irresistibly attractive to political economists, for its simple pain/pleasure mechanism rendered it both predictable and organizable into a "laboring population" that would expand or contract in relation to the needs of capital. To give Malthus his due, he did not normally think that any actual persons were merely human nature in the raw; he expected people to behave according to a wide range of other cultural imperatives, all of which he classified as tending toward either vice or misery. Nevertheless, unacculturated man—we'll call him *homo appeti-tūs*—looked like a reliable part of everybody and could hence serve as the material substratum on which the economic system might rest.

It looked reliable, that is, until the potato people came into view and demonstrated how easy it might be for such a completely physical being to slip out from under the very economic structure he was supposed to ground. The potato eaters seem to have literalized *homo appetitūs* in Malthus's mind and thereby to have liberated his anarchic potential. Unlike Adam Smith's *homo economicus* (a cooler character, with more complicated calculating capacities), *homo appetitūs*, at once antisocial and practically egoless, is decidedly *non*economical. One would expect such a creature to get as far outside of restraining economic systems as possible, and the potato patch presents a likely ground for his self-exile. The very physicality that seemed to ground political economy in physiological certainty, to make its practitioners "materialists" in the nineteenth-century sense of the term, becomes a principle of disorganization when it escapes from the labor market: Malthus is "strongly disposed to believe that the indolent and turbulent habits of the lower Irish can never be corrected while the potato system enables them to increase so much beyond the regular demand for labour."[18] The bodies that can copulate and eat regardless of the demand for labor will become at once lazy and menacing. Only in the context of the economy does *homo appetitūs* turn into *homo economicus*. In short, instead of the human body providing a predictable material ground for the economy, the economy is necessary to make the body reliable.

The threat that Malthus spies in the potato, moreover, is worse than the mere irrelevance of the marketplace to *homo appetitūs,* for no bodies inside a nation can actually be completely outside of its economy. Those seemingly redundant creatures multiplying on its margins press inward as potential labor, no matter how unwilling to work, cheapening the general price of labor until the difference between the industrious and the nonindustrious has disappeared. Hence, the potato is in fact no hedge against the marketplace, but is instead that unruly thing that, itself only very indirectly controlled by the price mechanisms of the larger economy, can profoundly disequilibriate it. The economy will recover its equilibrium, adjusting itself to overpopulation, and population growth will eventually slow, but only when people become too weak even to copulate. What Malthus saw when he looked at the potato was the destructive potential of the creatures his own imagination had conjured.

And that was his optimistic vision. His pessimistic one foresaw potato crop failures, persistent infant mortality, and perhaps eventual mass starvation. Political economists certainly shared the common belief that it was difficult to stop the potato once it got going, but they also insisted that its progress was often disturbingly fitful. The population that springs out of the potato patches is, like their food, ephemeral. Note, for example, how difficult it is to tell the failing crop from the dying people in this account, which is taken from Place's *Illustrations and Proofs of the Principle of Population:*

> One great drawback on potatoes, as food for the inhabitants of a country is, that in no crop is there a greater difference in good or bad years as to the quantity produced. Two or three good years will create people, the redundancy of which population will be repressed by subsequent years of failure. . . . [Y]ears of scarcity . . . are very frequent, and these periods put an end to the false part of the population . . . raised by years of plenty. (265)

The potato garden thus produces a "false" crop of children, which seldom survives to maturity.

At first sight, it might seem that the fear of overpopulation should be mitigated by the assurance of uncertain crops and infant starvation, but the two evils could easily coexist. Place's "false part of the population" is too large for the supply of potatoes, but that might be only a small fraction of the population that is redundant in relation to the demand for labor. On closer inspection, the continuity between the ideas of constantly multiplying and constantly dying potato eaters seems more salient than their superficial discrepancy. For both ideas point to the same hyper-physical humanity. If the potato liberates the sheer physicality of *homo appetitūs* from its regulation by the marketplace, it also exposes that physicality as merely organic, corruptible, and therefore quickly perishable.

And now we have arrived at our last point about the potato in the materialist imagination: it is too biologically immanent. It was seen as both cause and symbol of the body's vulnerability. David Ricardo wrote to Maria Edgeworth in 1823 that the case for or against the potato as the people's primary food had to rest on the crop's physical security, both its evenness of yield from year to year and/or the possibility of its achieving a nonperishable, storable form. He begins with the assumption that wheat is preferable because it can be turned into the relatively durable form of flour and stored, in times of plenty, to supply the dearth of later scanty grain harvests. (It should be mentioned here that wheat flour could not be stored against potato failures because, wheat being so much more expensive, potato-dependent people would not be able to afford flour.) Lacking any such "dry" instatiation, the potato becomes an extreme instance of the problem that food in general presents to the political economist:

> We cannot, I think, doubt that the situation of mankind would be much happier if we could depend with as much certainty on a given quantity of capital and labour producing a certain quantity of food, as we can depend upon the same quantity of capital and labour producing a certain quantity of manufactured goods. It is evident that in the latter case we calculate upon results almost with absolute certainty; in the other case we must always be exposed to the uncertainty of the seasons, which will render the crop fluctuating.[19]

This intractability of nature not only throws off economic calculations about the availability of food, but also renders the cost of labor, and hence the cost of everything else, unpredictable. Unfortunately, even manufacturing, admired here for its regularity, is made vulnerable, through the workers' bodies, to an uncontrollable natural world. Under these imperfect arrangements that link us biologically to the planet, the best we can do is choose a staple food that can partially overcome its own organicism, its own tendency to decay. Ricardo is convinced that the potato is unfit for such transcendence; he meets Edgeworth's assurances that potato flour can be made and kept usable for years with undisguised skepticism and hints that the potato could wipe out the progress an advanced economy has made in liberating humankind from dependence on shifty nature. It is unredeemably organic, untransformable into a long-term storable commodity. For Ricardo, as for Malthus, the potato occupies a place that is at once extraeconomic and rudimentary in his system; he fears that the root might carry an unbearable load of biotic unpredictability into the economy's foundation, which is the worker's body.

The lumpish intransigence of Ricardo's potato, its failure to undergo preservative physical transformations, is imagistically matched by its failure to undergo metamorphoses in the marketplace. As a "short crop" (440), some potatoes will be turned into cash, but the vast majority, Ricardo notes, will be immediately consumed by their producers. You can make nothing of potatoes but more people, who (Malthus might have chimed in) will only make more potatoes. Moreover, since it is the cheapest staple, it has no *substitutes* when it disappears. People living on wheat can replace their principal food with a cheaper one, but people already living on the least expensive nourishment are left without anything affordable when their crop fails. Bread eating and smooth commodity exchanges are thus paralleled by Ricardo; in both, metamorphoses are delightfully plentiful. But the potato, in his account, stands stubbornly apart from the transformative wonders of the economy and plays the part of a memento mori.

Its liminal status inspired Malthus and other political economists to propose that the potato be institutionalized as a badge of dishonor. Far from following Cobbett's advice and discouraging the cultivation of the root of misery in England, Malthus acquiesced in Arthur Young's plan to furnish parish relief solely in the form of potatoes. The potato, Malthus hoped, would draw "a more marked line than at present between dependence and independence."[20] The tuber should remain what it already was in the eighteenth-century English imagination—a stigmatized food—but its meaning should be stabilized. It should, as it had in the minds of the bread rioters, characterize the unincorporated, but it should also define the new perimeters of the social body that mattered by equating the members of that organism with the official economy. People were no longer to think that they could casually cross over from productive laborer to part-time pauper. "Pauper" was to become a category that would stick, and the potato would help by making "an useful distinction between those who are dependent on parish relief and those who are not."[21] If you crossed the line, the parish authorities would, as it were, throw in your face the very symbol of your own indolent, turbulent, redundant, intransigent, and distressingly mortal body.

Let us conclude, then, by suggesting that imagery from the potato debate allows us to trace a shift in cultural attitudes toward the age-old concept that our bodies have their source in the soil. Both the potato's proponents and its opponents took this concept for granted. Its proponents foresaw unprecedented prosperity based on the scientifically induced new fertility of the soil. But the potato's opponents saw in it everything that is fearsome about our biological contingency. For them, the food represented a shrunken humanity, unorganized into a social totality or an economic system, mired instead in the boglike ground. The debate shows the extent to which the autochthonous body had become the locus of new, identifiably modern, hopes and fears. Above all, it had been soiled and transported to Ireland, where it could be imagined as both foreign and threateningly close. The anti-potato writers both produced and banished this ghastly nightmare of *merely* biological bodies, purposeless bodies that just multiply and die. Theirs is the bad dream of nineteenth-century materialism; it haunted the same thinkers who were making physical well-being the raison d'être of social and economic arrangements. By expatriating the autochthonous body, English materialism protected itself from its own reductio ad absurdum.

By using the potato to identify the problematic status of the body in nineteenth-century materialist thought, we hope to suggest more broadly why "materialism" has become a problematic term. We are not, to be sure, implying that our potato debaters exhaust the possible directions that the materialist imagination might take. But we do claim that they manifest a tendency typical of materialism to invoke the human body as the ground of all explanation and, therefore, to leave it unexamined as a historical phenomenon or a representational crux. In materialist history, bodies as representation cannot bear much scrutiny; indeed, they cannot actually carry much history. Hence the historians of the potato debate have tended to reproduce the blind spots of the original debaters. We hope we've turned the blind spots of those eyes into the roots of new insights.

Five

THE MOUSETRAP

For at least a thousand years the Passover Seder has included a midrash about four sons—the wise son, the wicked son, the simple son, and the son who does not know how to ask— representing four distinct attitudes toward the evening's ritual and toward the religious community it helps to define.[1] To the son who does not know how to ask, who is too young or too ignorant to seek enlightenment, the father must take the initiative and begin the story, as he is enjoined to do in the book of Exodus: "This is because of that which the Lord did for me when I came forth from Egypt." To the simple son who can at least notice that something unusual is happening but can only ask, *"Ma zot?"*— "What is this?"—the father moves from the personal to the collective and adds a crucial bit of information: "With a strong hand did God bring us out from Egypt, from the House of Bondage." But the crucial distinction is between the questions asked by the first two sons and the responses to their questions. The wise son recites a question taken from Deuteronomy (6:20): "What mean the testimonies, and the statutes / and the ordinances, which the Lord our God hath commanded you?" The wicked son recites a question taken from Exodus (12:26): "What mean you by this service?"

On the face of it, the two questions are quite similar—nothing in their original context suggests any moral difference between them—but the Haggadah treats them as diametrically opposed. To the wise son, the father patiently expounds the laws of the Passover; to the wicked son, he delivers a stinging rebuke. This is because the midrash chooses to hear in the wicked son's question a failure of identification:[2]

> The Wicked Son—what does he say? "What mean you by this service?" "You," he says, not himself. Since he has excluded himself, he has repudiated God; and you should set his teeth too on edge, replying: "This is because of that which the Lord did for me when I came forth from Egypt"; for *me,* not for him—if he had been there he would not have been saved.

You may have noticed that the reply to the wicked child is identical to that given to the child who does not know how to ask—"This is because of that which the Lord did for me when I came forth from Egypt" (Exodus 13:8); but where the words in one instance are spoken as the gentle prelude to an initiation, in the other they are recited as a denunciation, an act of exclusion that corresponds to an unacceptable self-exclusion, a refusal of communal participation. The issue here and throughout the Seder is a Jew's relation to historical memory. The Haggadah enjoins a continual renewal of the ancient experience: "In each and every generation, it is a man's duty to regard himself as though [ke-*ee*-loo] he went forth out of Egypt, as it is said, 'And thou shalt tell thy son in that day, saying, This is done because of that which the Lord did unto me when I came forth out of Egypt.'" The wicked child refuses to incorporate the memory of enslavement and the Exodus from Egypt; he refuses to swallow the story as his own.

Our words are something more than metaphorical, of course, for the Passover Seder is a meal, derived from the ancient slaughtering and eating of the paschal lamb. In the Bible certain features of the feast are carefully prescribed—for example, "They shall eat the flesh that same night; they shall eat it roasted over the fire, with unleavened bread and with bitter herbs"—as is its formal and decisive closure: "You shall not leave any of it over until morning; whatever is left of it until morning you shall burn" (Exodus 12:1–20). After the destruction of the Temple, the sacrifice of the lamb ceased to be the central ritual event of the festival, though some of its elements survived, as in the Mishnah's scrupulous attempt to reinforce the prohibition of leftovers: "After midnight the passover offering imparts uncleanness to the hands; *piggul* and *notar* impart uncleanness to the hands." *Notar*—food that is kept after its proper time—becomes *piqqul*, carrion, and hence a source of pollution. Symbolically, then, the paschal lamb begins to rot at midnight. More familiarly, of course, the Passover meal came to focus on the injunction to eat matzoth—unleavened bread—and to drink the obligatory four cups of wine. As they eat the matzoth and drink the wine, all males are required to recline on the left side—for this was the position of free men at Roman banquets—but the festive celebration of freedom is qualified by the eating of bitter herbs and, traditionally, by the injunction to show some sign of hurry or anxiety in order to re-enact the flight from the pursuing Egyptians. For the entire meal is an acting out of the Exodus story, as well as a commentary upon it, in order to fulfill the commandment that the events be experienced as though they were your own, or rather that you speak of them to your child as your own personal history. And your child in turn must make your history his own—the one who declines the memory, who does not eat the bread of affliction, who refuses to regard himself as though he personally has been brought out of the house of bondage is wicked. He has repudiated God, and his teeth must be set on edge.

Even a very small Jewish child knows perfectly well, of course, that his father has been born, say, in Boston and not in Cairo, that his uncle Abraham has played semipro baseball in Cheyenne and not slaved for the Pharaohs, and that his uncle Moses, despite his name, has not parted the Red Sea. The wicked son would seem, from this perspective, the only sane or, alternatively, the only honest person at the table. This integrity is purchased by a refusal of an ambiguous injunction: to regard yourself *as though* means in part to pretend to be something you are not—the term acknowledges some distance between your actual and your imag-ined identity—but it also means to accept something that you are, something that you may not have understood about yourself and your origin and your destiny, something that you have inher-ited from your father and he from his. To escape this inheritance the wicked son would have to refuse the supper—or so it would appear—for the ritual meal seems an irresistible realization of the

Haggadah's "as though."[3] Eating the matzoth and drinking the wine performatively make good on the claim to living memory by making that memory part of your own body even as your own body is part of the community engaged in the ritual of eating. This performance is closely related to the symbolic logic of the Eucharist, which was probably instituted, after all, at or in proximity to a Passover supper:[4]

> And as they were eating, Jesus took bread, and blessed it, and brake it, and gave it to the disciples, and said, "Take, eat; this is my body." And he took the cup, and gave thanks, and gave it to them, saying, "Drink ye all of it; For this is my blood of the new testament, which is shed for many for the remission of sins. (Matthew 26:26–28; with variations in Mark 14:22–24 and Luke 22:19–20)

In what is thought to be the oldest part of the Passover ritual, the matzoth are uncovered and held aloft, while the following words are recited in Aramaic: "This is the bread of affliction that our fathers ate in the land of Egypt."[5] How does this differ from Jesus' "This is my body," words associated with a comparable elevation of the bread in the Catholic Mass? At the moment of elevation in the Seder, historical time is drastically foreshortened; the distant past is made so intensely present that it lays claim to the material world here and now. But Jesus' words and the cultic practice that grew up around them go beyond anything intended by the rabbis who compiled the Haggadah; they pass from memory to miracle.

In the Jewish ritual, historical distance is continually reinvoked even as it is abrogated by the act of eating what is imagined as a piece of history. And the piece of history remains crucially what it always was—a piece of bread baked in a certain way. There is no transformation of its substance; on the contrary, history suffuses the object and passes into the body of the celebrant precisely to the extent that it is what it appears to be, in a plain and literal sense. Hence the claim to a direct personal experience of bondage and liberation is at once confirmed and qualified in the sentence "This is the bread of affliction that our fathers ate in the land of Egypt." The words oscillate between identification and recollection, proximity and distance, and the whole Seder similarly oscillates between a commemoration of the Exodus from Egypt and a commemoration of the rabbinical exegesis of these events. If the participants at the Seder reenact the liberation of the ancient Hebrews, they also explicitly reenact the narrative reenactment of the event by the most celebrated rabbis of late antiquity: "It once happened that Rabbi Eliezer, Rabbi Joshua, Rabbi Eleazar, the son of Azariah, Rabbi Akiba, and Rabbi Tarphon were reclining on Passover at Bene Berak, and were telling the story of the departure from Egypt all that night, until their pupils came and said to them: 'Masters! The time has come for reciting the morning *Shema.*'"[6] In the sentence "This is my body," by contrast, all traces of the rabbinical "as though" are erased, and according to Catholic doctrine, the actual substance of the bread is transmuted. Communal memory gives way to outright corporeal transformation and eating as an acknowledgment of communal membership by descent gives way to eating as the actual incorporation of the body of God.

The extreme radicalism of Jesus' speech act is underscored, of course, by the centuries of speculation, disputation, and competing institutional practice that it engendered.[7] The apparently simple sentence put enormous pressure on communal understanding of words and of matter, pressure that reached the breaking point in the sixteenth and seventeenth centuries. Are the bread and the wine the body and blood of Christ really or figuratively? Ontologically and substantially, or symbolically and in signification? How and under what conditions does something become a sign? How and at what moment does it cease to be one thing and become another? What are the entailments of the different and often incompatible terms applied to the Eucharist, terms that open an almost infinite linguistic space between God's body and a piece of common baked bread: flesh, sign, word, promise, mystery, representation, presentation, shadow, memorial, commemoration, figure, pledge, token, metaphor, metonymy, covenant, even real estate lease?[8] Should every member of the community receive the sacramental bread or only those who are worthy to receive it? If an unbeliever eats the Eucharist, has he or she actually received the body of God? Can it be efficaciously consecrated by an evil priest? Is the Lord's Supper a public, common feast or what one sixteenth-century polemicist contemptuously called "a private churlish breakfast"?[9] Can it be administered to the sick or dying in their own homes? Should observers be allowed to watch the administration of the Sacrament, as if it were a performance, or should only those who are themselves participating be present? What preparation is required before receiving Communion, and how often can or should it be received? Should it be consecrated at an altar or is a table to be preferred? Should those administering it wear special vestments? Should those receiving it kneel? Should the bread be lifted up and shown to the congregants? Should it be dipped in the wine? Should it be received in the hand or taken directly in the mouth? What happens if the sacramental bread corrupts? What is the status of the fragments that are left over and what is to be done with them?

These questions and many others like them troubled men and women in the late Middle Ages and the early modern period; they occasioned vast amounts of polemical writing, bitter denunciations, intellectual heroics, spectacular feats of the imagination, and murderous violence. As Miri Rubin's wonderfully capacious study *Corpus Christi: The Eucharist in Late Medieval Culture* argues, eucharistic interpretations are too complex, various, and unpredictable to submit to any overarching theory: "No single Eucharist is to be sought," she writes, "and no single category such as class or gender can adequately capture the variety of eucharistic meaning."[10] We have no intention of trying to do anything of the kind. But we want to make three observations: first, most of the significant and sustained thinking in the early modern period about the nature of linguistic signs centered on or was deeply influenced by eucharistic controversies; second, most of the literature that we care about from this period was written in the shadow of these controversies; and third, their significance for English literature in particular lies less in the problem of the sign than in what we will call "the problem of the leftover," that is, the status of the material remainder. This problem is never entirely absent from eucharistic theology, for, as Louis Marin observes in *La Critique du discours,* transubstantiation raises a question at the intersection of physics and linguistics. But when the Port-Royal logicians thought about the Eucharist, they focused not on matter but on words. The formula of the consecration begins with *"hoc,"* a neuter demonstrative pronoun whose function, according to the *Logic,* is to point as with a finger at the thing about which one is speaking. In the case of the matzoth, this pointing is not a problem, but how does it work in the formula of the Eucharist?[11] And what exactly is the thing at which it points? The solution for the Port-Royal logicians lies in the word *"est,"* which not only links the terms *"hoc"* and *"corpus meum,"* but also transforms the thing that *"hoc"* designates from bread into body, the body which is that of the subject who originally pronounces the words. A stable ideology of representation is challenged by a complex intuition of language as force.[12]

There is some comparable speculation in early modern England, but Reformation theology pulled in a different direction, away from the transforming power of sacramental words—words that were satirized as "hocus-pocus." English reformers focused instead upon the spiritual power of signification—*"est,"* Zwingli and others argued, here means only *"significat"*—and they focused too on the persistence and what we might call the embarrassments of matter.[13] Those embarrassments were not unfamiliar to medieval defenders of eucharistic orthodoxy, who rehearsed them as the imagined arguments of the enemies of the faith. "The beleve of thes[e] Cristen men is false, as I wene," says the rich Jewish merchant Jonathas in the late-fifteenth-century Croxton *Play of the Sacrament.* "For the[y] beleve on a cake."[14] Jonathas and his fellow Jews—who have the disquieting habit of swearing by Mohammed—purchase a consecrated Host from a corrupt Christian and put it to the test in order to mock its crudely material nature. But when they stab the Host, the Jews find to their horror that it bleeds, and their panicky reactions, which include nailing the bread to a post and casting it into an oven, only succeed in reenacting the Crucifixion and entombment for which their race was held responsible. Finally, the oven bursts asunder, and the figure of the bleeding Christ emerges. In the face of incontrovertible proof of the eucharistic miracle, the terrified Jews convert, whereupon the figure of Christ returns once again to the form of bread and is carried in solemn triumph into the church.

But the triumph was evidently less decisive than the pious authors of the miracle play hoped. For the skepticism attributed to carnal Israel continually resurfaced within the Christian community and by the early sixteenth century had flared into open and irrepressible revolt. "Is that bread," Thomas Becon asks the "mass-mongers," "which a little afore was corn in the ploughman's barn, meal in the miller's trough, flour in the baker's boulting-tub, and afterward tempered with a little water and baken of the wafer-man between a pair of hot printing-irons, come now suddenly through your charming into such dignity that it is 'the Lamb of God, that taketh away the sins of the world?'"[15] For Becon the Catholic Mass is a shameless theatrical imposture. "Like another Roscius, with his foolish, player-like, and mad gestures," the priest, decked out in "scenical and game-player's garments," puts on a performance designed to make the crowd forget that "*Hoc est corpus meum,* 'This is my body,' is a figurative speech."[16] To recite these words in an alien tongue, to pretend that they have the power to call Christ's body down from heaven, is a horrible pollution of the Sacrament, a kind of magic.[17] The gullible are induced to believe that they are actually glimpsing God: "If the priest be weak in the arms, and heave not up high enough," Becon writes, with the eye of the ethnographer and the detachment of the wicked son, "the rude people of the country in divers parts of England will cry out to the priest, 'Hold up, sir John, hold up; heave it a little higher.' And one will say to another, 'Stoop down, thou fellow afore, that I may see my Maker: for I cannot be merry except I see my Lord God once in a day.'"[18]

Becon tells a story of a Christian who took a Jew of his acquaintance, an honest and upright man whom he wished to convert, to church. The Jew enjoyed the festiveness of the service—"jolly ringing, pleasant singing, and merry organs playing"—but he declared that he was shocked to see the congregants "fall down and worship a piece of bread and a silver cup" (281–82). For Becon then, as for Luther, the Jews have refused to convert to Christianity because Christianity, in the corrupt form of Catholicism, has sunk to idolatry. Gorgeously robed magicians mumble a Latin formula and hold up a thin round cake that they claim is God: "What is idolatry, if this be not idolatry?" (274). To shock his readers into a recognition of its grotesque absurdity, Becon indulges in strange Gogol-like fantasies: Mary the Virgin gives birth to a lump of bread that sucks at her breasts; the bread walks upon the earth; the bread is stretched out and, as in the *Play of the Sacrament,* nailed to the cross. The insistent materiality pulls at the fabric of the sacred story and threatens to unravel it; such is the risk Becon must take in order to free the spiritual truth from its corrupt and idolatrous imprisonment in a piece of ordinary bread.

The threat that recalcitrant, ineradicable matter posed for eucharistic theology was not, as we have already seen, only a Reformation concern, nor was it the exclusive province of the male intellectual elite. In the heresy trials in Norwich in 1428, for example, testimony was taken against Margery Baxter, who was accused of Lollardy by her friend Johanna Clyfland in the wake of an argument in which Margery allegedly warned her (*"in lingua materna"*): "Dame, bewar of the bee, for every bee wil styngge, and therfor loke that ye swer nother be Godd ne by Our Ladi ne be non other seynt, and if ye don the contrarie the be will styngge your tunge and veneme your sowle."[19] Johanna was an orthodox believer—she told the inquisitors that she said to Margery that after the consecration the sacrament was *"verum corpus Christi in specie panis"*—but Margery had other ideas:

> You believe wrongly, since if every such sacrament were god and Christ's real body, then gods would be infinite in number, because a thousand priests and more confect a thousand such gods every day and then eat them, and once eaten emit them from their back side in filthy and stinking pieces; and you can find plenty of these gods there if you are willing to look.[20]

The scatological joke here is a vivid way of insisting on the problem of the leftover, a way of making the point that—as the Lollard John Reve put it during the same inquisition—"aftir the sacramentall wordis said of a prest at messe ther remaneth nothyng but only a cake of material bred" (111). If it is a cake of material bread, it must be chewed with teeth, swallowed, and digested. The nastiness of the natural process—that fact that the remains of the wafer must eventually pass out of the body in filthy and stinking pieces—is emphasized in order to identify matter with shameful pollution.

The only way to save Christ's Glorified Body, or rather Christian faith in that body, from material contamination is to pry it loose from the visible Church, to separate it off from the grossly physical bread and wine, by insisting that Christ—single, whole, and beyond corruption—dwells in heaven at the right hand of his Father. The Church has no power, Reformers argued, to draw Christ's body back to earth, nor could that body, if it were so drawn, violate the laws of physics. Becon told his Catholic opponents:

> It is directly against the verity and truth of Christ's natural body to be in more places at once than in one, as he must be in an hundred thousand places at once, if your doctrine be true. A stinking sodomite or a wicked whoremonger, being dressed in his fool's coat, and standing at an altar with a little thin round cake in his hand, shall with these five words, *Hoc est enim corpus meum,* and with blowing and breathing upon the bread, make Christ, the King of glory, to come from the right hand of his Father, and to touch himself in the accidents of the little cake, till ye have eaten him. . . .[21]

In the Middle Ages the Pope had extracted from the heretic Berengar a strikingly literal doctrinal confession: "The bread and wine are the true body of our Lord Jesus Christ . . . handled and broken by the hands of the priests and ground by the teeth of the faithful."[22] Even Luther, who insisted on the Real Presence, found this phraseology disturbingly crude;[23] Calvin found it monstrous.

The Reformers return again and again to the celebrated words of Augustine: "Why are you preparing your teeth and your stomach? Believe, and you have already eaten [*crede et manducasti*]."[24] It followed, according to Calvin, not that the Sacrament was pointless, but that "believers have, outside the Lord's Supper, what they receive in the Supper itself."[25] There was, as Bullinger put it, a "spiritual, divine, and life-giving presence of Christ the Lord in the Supper and outside the Lord's Supper, by which he . . . proceeds to enter our hearts, not through empty symbols, but through his Spirit."[26] Luther's theory that the body of Christ was present "in, with, and under" the bread of the Supper seemed to many Reformers to confuse the crucial distinction between spirit and matter and hence to reiterate Roman Catholic carnality. "We freely confess," Calvin wrote to the Lutheran Joachim Westphal, "that our sacred unity with Jesus Christ is beyond our corporeal understanding. . . . But must we therefore dream that his substance is transfused into us in order to be soiled with our filth?"[27] The solution is to grasp that the eucharistic formula for the bread and wine—"This is my body, this is my blood"—is a figure of speech, specifically, a metonymy in which "the sign borrows the name of the truth that it figures."[28] There are, Beza said flatly, only two possibilities: "either transubstantiation or a trope."[29]

According to the Reformers, a conspiracy of self-serving priests had contrived for centuries to transform trope into flesh, to confound what Augustine called the "visible word" with a basely "materialistic theology." The Catholic Church withholds the Host from husbands and wives who have not observed a period of sexual abstinence—as if God condemned marital love—but it is the lascivious priests themselves, the heretics argue, who have dragged the Sacrament down into the realm of the senses: you come forth to the altar with your gaudy vestments and "your shamelesse, smooth, smirking faces," Becon writes, to signify that you are ready at all times "to play *Priapus* part."[30] It is from the likes of these—from the hands and mouths and bellies of such theatrical sensualists—that the body of God must be rescued.

For the Lollards, as later for Calvinists and others, the Supper of the Lord continues to include the ritual eating of the consecrated bread—the sign must pass into and through the body—but the ritual now eschews the miraculous transformation of matter. The emphasis is on remembrance through representation: the symbol enters into the body as an exalted mnemonic device. "For Christ is not visibly present, and is not beheld with our eyes," writes Calvin, "as the symbols are which excite our remembrance by representing him. In short, in order that he may be present to us, he does not change his place, but communicates to us from heaven the virtue of his flesh as though it were present."[31] "As though it were present"—we are brought close once again to the

Passover Seder and its injunction to eat and remember under the sign of "as though." But for Calvin, and for Protestants more generally, the Supper of the Lord does not finally center on the carnal rite of remembrance. The crucial agent is not historical memory, written on the flesh, but feeling faith, a faith that soars away altogether from the limitations of matter. "The sacrament is corruptible," writes the Anglican John Jewel in his controversy with the Catholic John Harding; "Christ's body is glorious, and void of all corruption. The sacrament is in the earth: Christ's body is in heaven. The sacrament is received by our bodily mouth: Christ's body is received only by faith, which is the mouth of our soul."[32]

Committed as they were to the Aristotelian distinction between substance and accidents, Catholic theologians had always recognized that there was in the Sacrament of the Mass a material residue, and committed as they were to a principle of exhaustiveness, they had vigorously debated its status. The issue of digestion was officially resolved by the argument that after the consecration, the bread was miraculously changed in substance into Christ's body, but the appearance of bread, the accidents or species, was unchanged.[33] The substance, Albertus Magnus declared, remained only as long as the form of the Eucharist continued intact; once the wafer was dissolved in the mouth (or, in Gratian's formulation, once it was touched by the teeth) it was no longer Christ's body.[34] But this sophisticated doctrine did not entirely resolve the problem of the leftover, even for church intellectuals, and heresy trials throughout the late Middle Ages, along with conflicting practices within the Church itself, suggest that it continued to be a vexing problem for a wide spectrum of people. The consecrated bread had been transformed by the touch of the transcendent, but its material accidents stubbornly persisted and were unnervingly subject to the disgraces to which all matter is vulnerable.

In the poisoned atmosphere of the sixteenth century, this vulnerability became a particularly charged point of contention between Catholics and Protestants. This accounts for several strange moments in the first examination of the Protestant Anne Askew in 1545: in the notes that she is said to have smuggled out of the Tower of London to John Bale, she relates that a priest, sent to question her on her beliefs, asked her, "If the host shuld fall, and a beast ded eate it, whether the beast ded receyve God or no: I answered, Seynge ye have taken the paynes to aske thys questyon, I desyre yow also to take so moche payne more, as to assoyle it your selfe. For I wyll not do it, bycause I perceyve ye come to tempte me. And he sayd, it was agaynst the ordre of scoles, that he whych asked the questyon, shuld answere it. I tolde hym, I was but a woman, & knewe not the course of scoles."[35] The question was not random: it was also asked by the chief secular interrogator: "My Lord Mayor laid one thing unto my charge which was never spoken of me, but of them: and that was, whether a mouse eating the Host received God, or no? This question did I never ask; but, indeed, they asked it of me, whereunto I made them no answer, but smiled."[36] By the middle of the sixteenth century, Catholics expected Protestants to try to mock them with the Host-eating mouse; thus, for example, Becon taunts the mass-mongers for believing that "not only the godly and faithful eat the body of christ in the supper, but also the ungodly and misbelieving; yea, the cats, rats, mice, dogs, owls, flittermouses."[37] The taunts must have stung, for the lord mayor tries to turn the tables and lure the heretic into the mousetrap. Anne Askew's smile is a wonderfully poised response, for it gives away nothing and implies that the problem is after all the Catholic Church's and not hers.

"We suffer anxiety if anything of the cup, or even of our bread fall to the ground," Tertullian wrote, and the anxiety was reiterated through the ensuing centuries.[38] Elaborate measures were taken during the Middle Ages to protect the Host from contamination or pollution. The Mass table was situated in an elevated and enclosed place and covered by a ciborium to prevent dust from falling upon the cloth or the wafers. Though they had the right to make ornaments for the priest's apparel and napkins for the holy table, women were forbidden to approach the altar or touch the chalice, the paten, and the corporale. Before celebrating Mass, the officiating priest was combed by church servers with ivory combs so that nothing unclean might fall from his hair onto the holy things. During Mass a servant raised and lowered a *fla-*

bellum (fan) at the side of the priest to keep flies from alighting on the bread or cup.[39] Priests wore maniples or *"sudaria,"* small pieces of cloth embroidered with gold, over their wrists at Mass, so that they could wipe away any drops of perspiration that might otherwise fall upon the bread and wine. After breaking the Host, the priest was supposed to keep his thumb and forefinger closed, so that no crumbs could fall from his hand; later he was supposed to rub these fingers together over the chalice, so that the small particles might drop into the holy vessel.[40] According to Durandus, "After the celebrant has taken in the sacrifice, he must not allow himself to cough or spit. Neither must he eat the Host as men do other food, but he should hold it in his mouth with discretion, modesty, and caution, using his front teeth and moistening it with his tongue, so that no crumb can fix itself in the cavities of his teeth."[41] After Mass, priests would use a separate basin to wash their hands, along with the paten and chalice, in order to collect any particles of the Host. In the later Middle Ages, pipes were laid from the washstand, carrying the water either directly to the earth or by means of a spout into the churchyard outside— in either case, only onto consecrated ground. Alternatively, ordained as early as 1212, priests were supposed to drink up the rinse water.

But as churchmen recognized, these extraordinary measures would never be perfect, and there would inevitably be accidents, thefts, and disasters, including the mouse about which Anne Askew was interrogated. Aquinas reports that "some have said that, as soon as the sacrament is touched of a mouse or a dog, the body and blood of Christ straightway departeth from it," but he regards this reassuring view as a derogation of the truth of the Sacrament. John of Burgos declares flatly that a mouse, eating the Host, receives the body of Christ— *"Mus . . . comedens hostiam suscipit corpus Christi"*—and, though there is considerable disagreement and uncertainty, other theologians concur.[42] If the bread has been miraculously transformed, then all of it—not only the leftover wafers but the crumbs on the altar cloth—must be protected from defilement. Protestant polemicists seized on these opinions and maliciously rehearsed the more extreme moments of Catholic eucharistic fervor. Hence Jewel quotes Peter of Palus:

"The mouse's entrails must be drawn, and the portion of the sacrament that there remaineth, if the priest be squeamish to receive it, must reverently be laid up in the tabernacle, until it may naturally be consumed." "If the priest be squeamish to receive it"— ideally, that is, the priest should eat the bits of wafer recovered from the mouse's entrails, just as "St Hugh of Clunice much commendeth Goderanus, a priest, for receiving the like portions" vomited up by a leper. "St Laurence's gridiron was nothing so bad," Goderanus is said to have reported afterward.[43] "I protest," writes Jewel after dwelling for pages on this subject, that its "blasphemy and loathsomeness" is intolerable; "neither would I have used this unpleasant rehearsal, were it not that it behoveth each man to know how deeply the people hath been deceived, and to what villany they have been brought" (784).

These are the vicious little amusements of sixteenth-century intellectuals. But, as Anne Askew and her inquisitor both understood, the stakes for all the faithful were high. Along with questions about the materiality of the supreme signifier, they involved the nature and limits of the religious community: Who has legitimate access to the holy? What do you need to believe in order to become part of Christ's body and to make Christ's body part of yours? Where do you locate and how do you ward off threats of pollution? What is the proper relation between the Eucharist— "a most Maiesticall & diuine obiect," in the words of a late-sixteenth-century English Catholic priest—and the "exorbitant desyres" of the human body, "this sacke of durte? this meate for wormes, this gate of sinne? this bodye of myne?"[44] The skirmishing about the mouse is for Protestants a way of exposing the Catholic Church's alleged idolatry, materialism, and indifference to the faith of its members, while for the Church it is a necessary if awkward corollary to its central dogma and to its assertions of institutional power. A priest—any priest, regardless of his personal failings or the failings of his parishioners—had the power, through his performance of the ritual of consecration, to initiate and preside over the miraculous transformation of matter. And if matter was actually transformed, how could the faithful be indifferent to the disposition of even the tiniest fragments? The concern was not merely decorum, though decorum was important enough, but rather the fate of the precious body of God.

⟋

We claimed earlier that the literature of the period was written in the shadow of these controversies, and we want at least to gesture toward making good on this claim. The point is not only that explicitly religious works are affected—as they manifestly are—but also that apparently secular works are charged with the language of eucharistic anxiety. "Now, Hamlet, where's Polonius?" Claudius asks. "At supper." "At supper? Where?" "Not where he eats," Hamlet replies, "but where a is eaten."[45] The significance of these words extends beyond the cruel and callous joke about Polonius; *the* supper where the host does not eat but is eaten is the Supper of the Lord. A theological resonance here may seem implausible, and not only because Polonius is an extremely unlikely candidate for the role of sacrificial offering: after all, though Protestants actively promoted substituting the phrase "the Supper of the Lord" for the Catholic "Mass," the word "supper" retained its principal meaning of the last meal in the day: "About the sixth hour," as one character puts it in *Love's Labour's Lost*, "when beasts most graze, birds best peck, and men sit down to that nourishment which is called supper" (1.1.227–29). Hamlet, to be sure, makes the grim point that Polonius will himself be the nourishment served up at this supper, but there scarcely seems to be any sacrificial meaning attached to his body. When at the scene's end Hamlet declares, with appalling coldness, that he'll "lug the guts into the neighbour room," we are far from an allegory of the most sacred mystery of the faith.

Yet just as we dismiss the strange resonance in the phrase "Not where he eats but where a is eaten," the next lines make it sound again: "A certain convocation of politic worms are e'en at him. Your worm is your only emperor for diet" (4.3.20–22). Scholars duly note the allusion to the Diet of Worms, where Luther's doctrines were officially condemned by the Holy Roman Emperor, but the question is what work the allusion is doing. Two answers have been proposed—showing that Hamlet was a student at Wittenberg and marking the earliest date for the play's events—but its principal function, we think, is to echo and reinforce the theological and, specifically, the eucharistic subtext, not only in the bitter jest that was just spoken but in the reverse riddle that follows: "A man may fish with the worm that hath eat of a king, and eat of the fish that hath fed of that worm." "What dost thou mean by this?" Claudius asks, and Hamlet replies, "Nothing but to show you how a king may go a progress through the guts of a beggar."

Somewhere half buried here is a death threat against the usurper-king—and Claudius understands perfectly well that the rapier thrust at the rat behind the arras had been aimed at him rather than Polonius—but Hamlet's words, with their strange blend of rage, disgust, and curiosity, reach beyond his immediate enemy, as they have already reached beyond Polonius, to touch another king, the royal father whose body is rotting in the sepulcher. And as if Hamlet's imagination knew no bounds, as if it were compelled to thrust further and still further, until it reached the ultimate point, it seems to touch another king as well, the king of kings whose transubstantiated flesh could go a progress through the guts of a beggar.

But why should the prince's imagination be seized by images of royal or even divine decomposition? After all, Hamlet has just seen the ghost of his father in Gertrude's closet—"My father, in his habit as he lived" (4.4.126), he tells his mother—and he had earlier seen him looking exactly as he had looked on the battlefield, in "that fair and warlike form," as Horatio puts it, "In which the majesty of buried Denmark / Did sometimes march" (1.1.45–47). The two apparitions are strikingly different, the one in full armor ("so majestical," says Marcellus [1.2.124]) and the other in a nightgown, but in each case the father's body is intact and his face is evidently visible.[46] Hamlet is confronted in effect with animated versions of the effigies sculpted on sixteenth-century tombs: *representacions au vif,* in the language of contracts from the period, "lifelike" figures arrayed in costumes befitting their worldly dignity and comfort.[47] But tombs in this period often had another effigy carved just below the *representacion au vif:* a *representacion de la mort.* This horrible image in the shadows of the lower register—a depiction of the decaying corpse eaten by mice and worms—is what Hamlet's imagination seems continually to force into his consciousness, compelling him, as his mother complains, to "seek for thy noble father in the dust" (1.2.71). From this perspective, the apparition of his father in the intact, uncorrupted forms found on the upper register of the period's tomb sculpture only pulls Hamlet's attention down to the still more dreadful image that lurks below, the image of the decaying corpse.

"Thou know'st 'tis common—all that lives must die," Gertrude tells her son, "Passing through nature to eternity" (1.2.72–73). It was this "passing through nature" that the *representacion de la mort* was presumably meant to underscore, by insisting upon the transience of the flesh: "Let the soul depart but one half hour from the body," the Catholic Robert Persons wrote in his *Christian Directory* (1582), "and this loving face is ugly to look on: let it ly but two days in the grave, or above ground dead, and those who were so earnestly in love with it before, will scarce abide to behold or to come near it."[48] Consolation lies elsewhere; to dwell obsessively upon the flesh, to persevere in mourning the fate of the body, is to pursue what Claudius calls "a course / of impious stubbornness" (1.2.93–94). Hamlet, in the usurper's devious but deeply perceptive view, is anything but a model of filial piety; rather his "obstinate condolement" is a form of aggression not only against the natural and supernatural order of things, but also against the very father he professes to mourn: "Fie, 'tis a fault to heaven, / A fault against the dead, a fault to nature" (1.2.101–2). Claudius is in effect accusing Hamlet of being the wicked son, behaving not as if his father's spirit had passed through nature to eternity, but as if instead it had been transformed into the most degraded form of matter.

This transformation played, as we have seen, a crucial role in the polemic that raged around the Mass, a polemic that lies just below the surface of Hamlet's caustic, riddling words about the Diet of Worms, the fat king and the lean beggar, the royal progress through the intestines. If these words allude to a grotesquely materialist reimagining of the Eucharist, if they conjoin "a fault to heaven" and "a fault against the dead," if they complete a circuit that links Hamlet's prospective father-in-law Polonius and his "uncle-father" Claudius to his earthly and heavenly fathers, they would seem to bear out the charge that Hamlet is the wicked son. By insisting upon the vulnerability of matter and its grotesque metamorphoses, by dwelling upon the transformation of the dead into endlessly recycled food, by dragging a king through the guts of a beggar, Hamlet bitterly protests against the ghostly transmission of patriarchal memory and against the whole sacrificial plot in which the son is fatally appointed to do his father's bidding. But how is it possible to reconcile this apparently skeptical, secular protest with Hamlet's obsessive quest to fulfill precisely the task that the ghost has set him?

The answer is that a skeptical, secular insistence on irreducible corporeality paradoxically originates in an attempt to save the Eucharist from the taint of the body. It is only by ritually defiling the Host, by imagining the Sacrament passing through the belly of the beast, by dwelling on the corruptibility of matter and its humiliating susceptibility to chain-eating that the spirit can be liberated. "But now what do thei with him, hauing thus transformed him," the preacher John Bridges asked about the Host in the Catholic Mass, in a sermon he preached at Paul's Cross in 1571,

> forsoth euen as the cat doth with the mouse, play with it, dandle it vp & downe, hoise it ouer her head, tosse it hither & thyther, & then eate it cleane vp: euen so for al the world, did they order Christ. Marke a Priest at Masse, and marke a Cat with a mouse, & tel me then what difference. Nor if Christ were not eaten vp of the Priest, did he so escape the Priests handes: Nay, euen as a mouse kept in a trap till she pine to death, as a birde in a pitfal til she be starued, as a caytif in a dungeon til he be famished, so was Christ thrust vp into a copper pixe, and there hanged vp tyll euen the wormes did eate hym, and scraule [*sic*] all ouer hym, and the very hoarie moulde dydd rotte him, and then was he taken down and burned, bycause he could keepe himselfe no better. O cruell *Canibali*, O barbarous Priests.[49]

"Behold the masse-Priest with his baked god," writes Thomas Adams in 1615, in a similar vein, "towzing tossing, and dandling it, to and fro, vpward and downward, forward and backward, till at last, the iest turning into earnest, he choppes it into his mouth at one bitte; whiles all stand gaping with admiration."[50] Since neither Bridges nor Adams was by any means proposing to do away with the wafer, their ridicule had its obvious dangers, but the risk of mocking the most sacred thing had to be taken in order to secure the integrity of belief and the purity of the sacrifice. This is the logic of Protestant polemics against the Mass, and this too is the logic of Shakespeare's tragedy.

Even before he learned of his mother's adultery and his father's murder, Hamlet had been sickened by the "too too solid" (or "sallied" or "sullied") flesh. Later in the play, after he has encountered the ghost, he will use many images that link this materiality with corruptibility, but here the dominant associations are not with the vulnerability of nature but rather with what for Hamlet is its nauseating vigor, its uncontrollable, metastatic power to renew itself: " 'Tis an unweeded garden / That grows to seed; things rank and gross in nature / Possess it merely" (1.2.135–37). Why unchecked fecundity should be the focus is explained by his obsession in the rest of the speech with his mother's remarriage: it is as if the death of his father should properly have brought about the death of desire, the end of renewal and increase, the disappearance of matter.

Hamlet's longing is for a melting or thawing of the flesh, a turning of solid into liquid and then the "resolution" of liquid into dew.[51] But the flesh does not simply vanish; instead, it is caught up in unending cycles of renewal, strikingly figured by the recycling of leftovers: "Thrift, thrift, Horatio. The funeral bak'd meats / Did coldly furnish forth the marriage tables" (1.2.180–81). In Hamlet's bitter jest, food prepared for his father's funeral has been used for his mother's marriage, a confounding of categories that has stained both social rituals in the service of thrift. At issue is not only, as G. R. Hibbard suggests,[52] an aristocratic disdain for a bourgeois prudential virtue, but a conception of the sacred as incompatible with a restricted economy, an economy of calculation and equivalence. Such calculation has led Gertrude to marry Claudius, as if he were his brother's equal: "My father's brother," Hamlet protests, "but no more like my father / Than I to Hercules" (1.2.152–53). Her remarriage, like the reuse of the funeral baked meats, is a double defilement: it has sullied Gertrude's flesh, which becomes a leftover to be gobbled up by the loathsome Claudius, and, since "Father and mother is man and wife; man and wife is one flesh" (4.3.53–4), it has retroactively stained old Hamlet by identifying his noble spirit with the grossness of the "bloat King" (3.4.171).

The source of the pollution, according to the ghost, is unbridled sexual appetite:

> lust, though to a radiant angel linked,
> Will sate itself in a celestial bed
> And prey on garbage. (1.5.55–57)

The disgust provoked by the leftover is here intensified by the image of the person who, though sated, continues to eat and to eat garbage—not simply refuse, but, literally, "entrails."[53] The ghost breaks off his meditation on lust in order to recount the scene of his murder, but Hamlet becomes obsessed with his mother's sexual appetite, which seems to loom larger in his consciousness than the killing of his father. His charge that Gertrude has murdered her husband—"A bloody deed—almost as bad, good-mother, / As kill a king and marry with his brother" (3.4.27–28)[54]—gives way to a desperate, nauseated indictment of her filthy desires:

> Nay, but to live
> In the rank sweat of an enseamèd bed
> Stewed in corruption, honeying and making love
> Over the nasty sty. (3.4.81–84)

The lines are the culmination of a powerful current of imagery in the play, not all of it in Hamlet's own speeches, related to something sticky, greasy, cancerous, or mildewed in, around, or of the body, something that leaves a horrible stain or that swells and bursts inwardly or that is detected by a rank taste or a lingering smell.

Claudius, who intuitively shares many of Hamlet's deepest perceptions, reproaches himself for not dealing sooner with his nephew's dangerous madness:

> We would not understand what was most fit,
> But, like the owner of a foul disease,
> To keep it from divulging, let it feed
> Even on the pith of life. (4.1.19–23)

Hamlet is, by implication, a disease within Claudius's own body, a body that is coextensive with the state. If, as Marcellus suspected, "something is rotten in the state of Denmark," this "something" is Hamlet. "Do it, England," Claudius declares, ordering his tributary state to put Hamlet to death, "For like the hectic in my blood he rages, / And thou must cure me" (4.3.66–68). And when this cure fails, Claudius, turning to Laertes, imagines himself as the physician who must break through the skin to lance the dangerous infection: "But to the quick of th'ulcer" (4.7.95.10). The metaphor had already been used by Hamlet, devising the "Mousetrap" as a means to expose what lay hidden within his uncle: "I'll tent him to the quick. If a but blench, / I know my course" (3.1.573–74). And Hamlet returns to it again when he is pleading with his mother not to dismiss his words by attributing them to madness:

> It will but skin and film the ulcerous place
> Whilst rank corruption, mining all within,
> Infects unseen. (3.4.138–40)[55]

The image repeatedly is of some horrible substance, itself a life-form but one inimical to any life one actually holds dear, growing in the darkness, feeding and spreading and ultimately killing.

Even before he had encountered the ghost and learned its secret, Hamlet had had intimations of this ghastly living thing hidden within an apparently healthy living body: "some vicious mole of nature" (1.4.18.8), he termed it. "Mole" is usually glossed as an external blemish, and the subsequent phrase "the stamp of one defect" would seem to support such a meaning, but there is a latent sense as well of something deep inside a person, burrowing in the darkness like a blind mole, or growing within like the tumors or the false conceptions that were also in this period called moles, or restlessly gaping and feeding like the female genitals that were by Galen compared to moles.[56] With that sublime, half-mad verbal lightning that flashes blindingly throughout the play, confounding the vicious and the innocent, the excremental and the divine, Hamlet in the next scene returns to the image, hysterically addressing his father's ghost, whom he hears moving beneath the ground: "Well said, old mole. Canst work i'th' earth so fast?" (1.5.164).

Hamlet does not speak again of the blind mole, but the image lingers perhaps in the digging of Goodman Delver the gravemaker or in Hamlet's contriving against the treachery of Rosencrantz and Guildenstern to "delve one yard below their mines" (3.4.185.7). Above all, the horror, disgust, and weird humor that it evokes in Hamlet are powerfully reiterated in his response to his mother's desires. His mother's failure to see—her inability to distinguish between her first husband and the loathsome Claudius—comes to stand in Hamlet's mind for the sexual viciousness of her nature. "Have you eyes?" he asks. "Could you on this fair mountain leave to feed, / And batten of this moor? Ha, have you eyes?" (3.4.65–66). "Eyes without feeling," he continues in a second quarto passage, "feeling without sight" (3.4.70.8). Hamlet's identification of this corrupt and corrupting and blind infection, this horrible life-within-life, with his mother's sexuality leads him to forget the vengeance to which he has dedicated himself, or so the ghost charges, interrupting Hamlet's tirade about the "enseamèd bed" to remind him of his purpose: "Do not forget. This visitation / Is but to whet thy almost blunted purpose" (3.4.100–1).

The time is out of joint, and the spirit of the father has charged his son with setting it right. But the task becomes mired in the flesh that will not melt away, that cannot free itself from its deep bonds with mother and lover, that stubbornly persists and resists and blocks the realization of the father's wishes. Generativity— the capacity for bodies, and specifically for women's bodies, to engender more and more flesh—comes to obsess Hamlet, as if it were the source of contamination that he must somehow get free of before he can serve his father's spirit:

> Get thee to a nunnery. Why wouldst thou be a breeder of sinners?
> I am myself indifferent honest, but yet I could accuse me of such

things that it were better my mother had not borne me. . . . Go
thy ways to a nunnery. Where's your father? . . . Let the doors
be shut upon him, that he may play the fool nowhere but in's own
house. . . . I have heard of your paintings, too, well enough. God
hath given you one face, and you make yourselves another. You
jig, you amble, and you lisp, and nickname God's creatures, and
make your wantonness your ignorance. Go to, I'll no more on't.
It hath made me mad. I say we will have no more marriages. . . .
To a nunnery, go. (3.1.122–49).

The object of the loathing here appears to be breeding itself, or
rather the sexual desire that women, by the way they look and
move and speak ("You jig, you amble, and you lisp"), arouse in
men, leading them to play the fool.

Somewhere behind Hamlet's words is Erasmus's genial perception, in the *Praise of Folly,* that without the folly of sexual
desire the world would not long continue, but the humanist's vision, here as elsewhere in the play, has been turned into disgust
and a longing to free the spirit, Hamlet's father's spirit and his
own, from the corrupting taint of the flesh. Sexual desire has led
Hamlet's father to make his mother a breeder of such worthless
sinners as Hamlet himself is: "it were better my mother had not
borne me." In this self-annihilating wish, Hamlet's father is un-
coupled from his mother, and all future coupling will cease: "I
say we will have no more marriages."

"I hoped thou shouldst have been my Hamlet's wife," Gertrude
says sadly over Ophelia's corpse. "I thought thy bride-bed to have
decked, sweet maid / And not t'have strewed thy grave" (5.1.227–
29). But long before Ophelia's death, the bride-bed and its pleasures have been poisoned by Hamlet's anxiety about desire, his
disgust at generation, and his rejection of marriage. "For if the
sun breed maggots in a dead dog, being a good kissing carrion—
have you a daughter?" Hamlet asks Polonius, who replies that he
has. "Let her not walk in the sun" (2.2.182–85). The association
of ideas here links Ophelia to the carcass of a dog, lovemaking
to the kissing of rotting flesh, and conception to the breeding of
maggots. Hamlet's words also contain a famous textual crux that
leads back to the theological issues with which we have been concerned. Warburton in the eighteenth century proposed that the

true reading was "a God, kissing carrion." If the emendation, which Samuel Johnson thought so "noble" that it "almost sets the critic on a level with the author," is correct, it would express in the most direct way possible the deep anxiety about the yoking of the divine spirit to corrupting and corruptible matter that haunted eucharistic controversies for centuries. That anxiety, the play seems to suggest, is not only eucharistic but also incarnational: it is enfleshment that corrupts. Disgust at the idea of the Incarnation is an ancient theme, associated with many Christian heresies and, not without justification, with Jews. The twelfth-century Hebrew chronicle of Rabbi Eliezer bar Nathan, recounting the persecution of Jews during the First Crusade, tells of a Jew named Shemariah in the Rhineland who killed his wife and children, to save them from defilement, and then unsuccessfully tried to kill himself. The chronicler reports that the Christians said to him (implausibly enough), "Although you have acted in a defiant manner, your life shall be spared if you adopt our erroneous belief. Otherwise, we will inflict a violent death upon you, burying you alive with those you have slain." Shemariah answered, "Heaven forfend that I should deny the Living God for a dead, decaying carcass."[57]

At the very least, Hamlet's task, imposed upon him by the ghost, is complicated by his own and his father's entanglements in the flesh. When alive, old Hamlet was not exempt from the thousand natural shocks that flesh is heir to, and even after death he carries about him a strange quasi-carnality, for he was taken "grossly, full of bread, / With all his crimes broad blown, as flush as May" (3.3.80–81). "Full of bread"—the words distinguish between someone living in the midst of his ordinary life and someone who, anticipating death, puts his spiritual house in order through fasting.[58]

Hamlet is disgusted by the grossness whose emblem here is the bread in his father's stomach, a grossness figured as well by drinking, sleeping, sexual intercourse, and above all perhaps by woman's flesh. The play enacts and reenacts queasy rituals of defilement and revulsion, an obsession with a corporeality that reduces everything to appetite and excretion. "We fat all creatures else to fat us, and we fat ourselves for maggots. Your fat king and your lean beggar is but variable service—two dishes, but to one table. That's the end" (4.3.22–25). Here, as in the lines about the king's progress through the guts of a beggar, the revulsion is mingled with a sense of drastic leveling, the collapse of order and distinction into polymorphous, endlessly recycled materiality. Claudius with his reechy kisses and paddling fingers, is a paddock, a bat, a gib, and this unclean beast, like Becon's priapic priest, has poisoned the entire social and symbolic system. Hamlet's response is not to attempt to shore it up but to drag it altogether into the writhing of maggots. Matter corrupts: "If you find him not within this month," Hamlet says, finally telling Claudius where to look for Polonius's corpse, "you shall nose him as you go up the stairs into the lobby" (4.3.35–36).

The spirit can only be healed by refusing all compromise and by plunging the imagination unflinchingly into the rank corruption of the ulcerous place. Such a conviction led the Reformers to dwell on the progress of the Host through the guts of a mouse, and a comparable conviction, born of intertwining theological and psychological obsessions, leads Hamlet to the clay pit and the decayed leftovers that the grave diggers bring to light. "How abhorred in my imagination it is," Hamlet says, staring at the skull of Yorick. "My gorge rises at it" (5.1.178–79). This is the primary and elemental nausea provoked by the vulnerability of matter, a nausea that reduces language to a gagging sound that the Folio registers as "Pah." Revulsion is not an end in itself; it is the precondition of a liberated spirit that finds a special providence in the fall of a sparrow, sacrificially fulfills the father's design, and declares that the readiness is all.[59]

But this is not quite all. We remarked earlier that there was some risk in the strategic insistence on the problem of the leftover, and we think we can glimpse it again at the close of *Hamlet.* For if there is a detachment from the body that culminates in Hamlet's impossible words, "I am dead, Horatio," there is at least the shadow of a different kind of detachment, a detachment from the spirit. "Remember me," the spirit of Hamlet's murdered father solemnly commands, and his son swears to erase all "baser matter" from the book and volume of his brain. But the communion of ghostly father and carnal son is more complex, troubled not only by the son's madness and suicidal despair but by the persistent, ineradicable materialism figured in the progress of a king through the guts of a beggar. The mind that dwells upon that progress has not succeeded in erasing all but the father's commandment; rather it manifests something of the restless curiosity of Montaigne, who muses that "the heart and life of a triumphant emperor is the breakfast of a little worm."[60] Montaigne's reflection comes in the course of the "Apology for Raymond Sebond," that is, in the great essay whose skeptical materialism radically undermined his own father's spiritual guide. "There is nothing so horrible to imagine," Montaigne writes in a haunting passage of this essay, "as eating one's father."[61] But there are, he observes, nations that regard this act as testimony of filial piety, "trying thereby to give their progenitors the most worthy and honorable sepulture, lodging in themselves and as it were in their marrow the bodies of their fathers and their remains, bringing them to life in a way and regenerating them by transmutation into their living flesh by means of digestion and nourishment" (438). There are echoes here of eucharistic piety and a sense of the vulnerability of the flesh, but the thoughts slip away from Catholic and Protestant orthodoxy alike, toward a tolerant acceptance of the dizzying variety of customs and the natural processes of the body.

Similarly, when Hamlet follows the noble dust of Alexander until he finds it stopping a bung-hole, he does not go on to meditate on the immortality of Alexander's incorporeal name or spirit.[62] The progress he sketches is the progress of a world that is all matter. "'Twere to consider too curiously to consider so," warns Horatio; he has heard, however fleetingly, the voice of the wicked son.

Six

THE NOVEL AND
OTHER DISCOURSES OF
SUSPENDED DISBELIEF

B ut the wicked son speaks in the familiar tongue of the
Enlightenment, so that a listener might hear in Hamlet's
words just the beginning of a new phase of thought that resonates
through both ideology and its critique in the modern period.
Hamlet's reluctance to accept the destiny marked out for him by
his father's spirit touches a doubt, first about the mingling of spirit
and flesh, and then about the very existence of spirit, which per-
vades modernity. The wicked son's combination of genealogical
inconsequentialism ("What has your past to do with me?") and
ontological materialism becomes commonplace then, and both
are underwritten by a new positive valuation of doubt.

The World Without Faith and the Wicked Son's Ideology

The wicked son's keynote, in this Enlightenment phase of his
existence, is doubt of all revealed doctrine, and his cadence is
common sense. If truth is available, he says, our senses and intellect will find it; truths are reasonable, discoverable. We do not
need revelation; above all, we can do without belief. Defining
himself primarily against belief, the wicked son may be taken as
a prototype of the most successful modern ideologists. He does
not enter into doctrinal dispute, but instead seeks to do away with
doctrine altogether. Often he demystifies in the name of the
seemingly natural, the manifest, the given, the evident. Sometimes his ideology can hardly be distinguished from everyday
practices and understandings, with their high tolerance for contra-   *163*

diction and cognitive dissonance. At other times, when he turns his doubting eye on common sense itself, he exerts new pressure on our understanding; but the wicked son's first task is to disable faith, to declare it obsolete, unnecessary, a thing of the past.

And what a bloated, ripe target the doctrine of the Real Presence afforded him, with its minutely detailed and ostentatiously counterintuitive claims! Unavailable to the natural intellect, the Real Presence sat for Catholics at the very apogee of discursive awareness as a veritable test of faith; it did not nestle down into the fabric of common sense, like ideology. If it had been made to seem commonsensical, it would have lost its point, for it was designed to strain believers and put them through a trial of fidelity. That's why the accents of English Protestantism modulated so subtly into those of the wicked son. For Protestants opposed to the doctrine of the Real Presence, the bread at the Supper of the Lord is merely what it seems—bread. They continually invoked truths reasonable, natural, and discoverable. Of course, at some point, they needed to speak of the Blood of the Lamb, and then they ceased to sound like Hume or Voltaire. But the cleverest Protestant polemicists against the Real Presence are able to defer this invocation for a considerable length of time and in the meanwhile to indulge themselves in a great deal of wit at the expense of credulous Catholics, who ignore the evidence of their senses and believe in palpable absurdities.

Not that Protestantism served historically simply as a way station on the road to skepticism. Against determined agnostics, Protestants (like Catholics) pointed out that even the most thoroughgoing skeptic must ultimately take something—perhaps what he calls "common sense"—on faith. And if one is bound, willy-nilly, to believe something, the argument continues, then skepticism has limits. Indeed, some fideistic thinkers used skepticism as a fundamental component of their arguments for faith. Moreover, if one must believe something, then the fact that a proposition—for example, "The Bible is the Word of God"—rests on faith cannot, in itself, discredit it. Skepticism, in short, has often been pressed into the service of religious faith.

Nevertheless, their compatibility should not be overemphasized. When the Enlightenment thinker takes, say, the reliability of his senses "on faith," he is not making an *act* of faith resembling that of the religious believer. It is, in fact, odd to confuse these two notions of "faith," for the holder of the first regrets it as merely a lamentable operational necessity, whereas the holder of the second cultivates it as an active theological virtue, the exercise of which is a gift of God's grace. Involuntarily taking something "on faith" because it cannot be otherwise established is the outcome of exhaustion, finitude, or laziness, whereas believing in something is the result of vigilance. In the sixteenth century, Enlightenment determination might be represented by Bacon's struggle against exhaustion and his ambition to test most rigorously precisely those things that were most widely held true. In the seventeenth century, this disposition becomes even more opposed to that of religious faith, as it admits and welcomes the constant presence of *uncertainty* in the quest for knowledge. That one learns to rely on propositions in the register of the merely probable is hardly proof that *faith* is always with one. When an enlightened thinker discovers some unexamined assumption, he brings it to consciousness and acknowledges it as an operational premise, which can then be tested and, if necessary, discarded, or held with some degree of certainty. But neither when he holds an assumption unconsciously nor when he holds one hypothetically is his belief comparable to an item of religious faith, which cannot be unconscious, subjected to empirical verification, or maintained in a provisional status. The dialectic of faith and doubt belonged to the old regime; Enlightenment man comes to know only the play of certainty and uncertainty, twin progeny of doubt, on the field of probability.

Often, though, he uses the vernacular analogy between unexamined assumptions and religious beliefs for his own polemical purposes, especially when he engages in ideology critique. When Karl Marx set out to discredit the ideology of commodities, for example, he unmasked it as a kind of religion, a modern version of the Real Presence. To understand the mystifications of the marketplace, "we must have recourse to the mist-enveloped regions of the religious world," where "the productions of the human brain appear as independent beings endowed with life."[1] Imagining themselves to be hard-headed realists, he claims, par-

ticipants in the market economy are actually deluded into believing that an intangible "spirit," exchange value, is an intrinsic
quality of the commodity itself. Marx's trope implies that "this
bread is the body and blood of Jesus Christ" has as its secular
version "this bread is five pence." The copulative "is" certainly
means vastly different things in these two propositions, as the
two massive discourses explicating the verb in these contexts (the
doctrine of the Real Presence and the discipline of political economy, respectively) attest, but Marx wishes to demonstrate that,
despite its considerable discoveries, the disciplinary discourse
cannot dispel the "fetishism of commodities," for it, too, is captivated by "the whole mystery of commodities, all the magic and
necromancy" (87). Marx, playing the wicked son to his political-
economist forefathers, thus relies on the already firmly established presumption that an idea requiring faith is ipso facto untenable. The wicked son's creation, modernity under capitalism,
had only partially completed its historic task of ridding itself
of the need for credulity.[2] Reaching all the way back to anti-
eucharistic polemics for its legitimacy, Marx's critique of ideology
redeploys the wicked son's tropes and carries on his project of
doubt and demystification.

Doubt, endless doubt, has been the motor of modern thought,
and Marx was not the only thinker to direct it at "bourgeois"
ideology itself, to take as a special object of skepticism "mere productions" of the human brain and hand that "appear as independent things endowed with life." Marx's description of religion as
a misrecognition of mankind's own inventions comes, of course,
from Ludwig Feuerbach. When Marx extended Feuerbach's insight through his own analysis of the fetishism of commodities,
his ideas converged with a vigorous line of skeptical conservative
thought. Sainte-Beuve, for example, reflecting on the Revolution
of 1848, also stressed that seemingly natural and autonomous life-
forms are really fabrications.

> La civilisation, la *vie*, sachons-le bien, est une chose apprise et
> inventée. . . . Les hommes, après quelques années de paix, oublient
> trop cette vérité: ils arrivent à croire que la culture est une chose
> innée, qu'elle est pour l'homme la même chose que la nature.[3]

Sainte-Beuve's purpose is, to be sure, the opposite of Marx's: the French critic wished to protect an established social order by designating it a fragile achievement, while the German revolutionary wished to discredit it. They nevertheless share the underlying claim that people must be reminded of the constructed nature of "civilization," that they must be taught to doubt the naturalness and inevitability of their social world, or they will soon be unable to tell the difference between illusion and reality, between essential, beneficial creations and mere sham. For Sainte-Beuve, revolution rather than capitalism is the venue where art and life find their final absurd inversion: "Dans les scènes scandaleuses ou grotesques qui ont suivi la Révolution de février, qu'a-t-on vu le plus souvent? Le répétition dans la rue de ce qui s'était joué sur les théâtres" (38).

In all stripes of nineteenth-century social thought, doubt is what can be counted on, and it therefore cannot be used to separate ideology critique from ideology.[4] Whatever the criteria by which one might distinguish them—whether it be falsehood as opposed to truth, complicity with class oppression as opposed to its subversion, or common sense as opposed to science—the mere deployment of doubt will not suffice. "Ideology" and "critique" tend to indicate contextual judgments about the possible political ramifications of ideas, especially their potential for encouraging or discouraging the acceptance of the relations of power that are in place. Much of what is judged "ideology" on the basis of this criterion presents itself as the unmasking of some other ideology, and a corrosive skepticism is perhaps just as likely to go hand-in-glove with a defense of the social status quo as to propel a revolutionary impulse.

In Sainte-Beuve's outlook, though, we can recognize one trait, usually ignored by analysts, that might help differentiate the discourses promoting the acceptance of the new social and economic dispensations from those retarding their acceptance: modern ideologies often replaced faith with credit. Leaving behind the religious dialectic of doubt and faith, they entered the realms of provisional truths, propositions and arrangements to which we extend temporary contingent assent, without having to believe them true or right under all conditions. This is the territory of speculation, with its infinitely calibrated degrees of acquiescence, that allows one to calculate risk. Sainte-Beuve turns this speculative frame of mind to what are usually called ideological uses when he implies that the social order should be credited, not because it's natural or divinely ordained, but because the forces of chaos will overtake any civilization that seems to falter: "La sauvagerie est toujours là à deux pas; et, dès qu'on lâche pied, elle recommence" (38). In the same spirit of wary assent, people learned to accept paper money and invested in the national debt, not because they were so credulous as to believe that the treasury held enough specie to redeem all of their paper at once, but because they understood that any such demand would lead to anarchy and that the credit they advanced collectively obviated their need to hoard precious metals privately. Doubt is crucial to the workings of capitalism, for profits are supposedly earned in direct proportion to risks. Those who are willing to extend credit on little surety stand to reap the greatest benefits. The speculative mentality so basic to capitalism thus resembles Freud's version of fetishism—in which, although the fetishist does not forget that he gives the object (the bond, the promissory note, the shoe, and so on) its phantasmatic power, this consciousness does not make the object less powerful—more closely than Marx's.[5]

The literary is also born under the rising star of dubiety, for in literature we self-consciously savor the fact that "the productions of the human brain appear as independent beings endowed with life." Our awareness that a literary work is entirely invented only enhances our wonder at its vitality. Affirming nothing, denying nothing (to paraphrase Sidney), the literary is the perfect consort of doubt. It indulges feigned acts of faith but requires only that we suspend our *dis*belief, as an element is suspended in a solution that it thoroughly permeates. Our pleasure in Hamlet's vividness, for example, comes from knowing—and marveling—that he is an invention.[6] An invention, moreover, with a strangely diffuse source, for the relative obscurity of Shakespeare's life, the scantiness of his biography, even the tenacity of crackpot theories about his real identity have made him a figure for both the ineffability of individual genius and the creativity of the species as a whole. To relish the illusion of Hamlet's vivacity is, thus, not to forget that he's a human invention, but to delight in what seems *our* originary power. Literature, we might say, is not a relief from disbelief (as Coleridge's use of the word "suspension" has led some erroneously to think), but rather a particular way of enjoying it.

By the mid-nineteenth century, the great age of the novel, the progress of "demystification" could be taken for granted. Doubt was self-assured; indeed, it was so well established that writers had begun to stress the fabricated nature of the whole social world, not just of money or credit. The novel corresponds to this phase of self-confident doubt, a doubt that can almost go without saying, for nineteenth-century fiction is the most highly developed genre of the probable, an explicitly fictional form that does not ask its readers to believe its characters actually existed or the events really took place, but instead invites us to appreciate the *believable* as such. Reading them, we extend credit to representations of the social without becoming credulous about their specifics. Seemingly of our own accord, moreover, we repeatedly qualify and compromise our demands on the strict typicality of the novel's general social representations in order to encounter the unexpected. We respond to the implicit promise of the figure's alluring fictionality, which stimulates our desire to witness palpable human fabrications that "appear as independent beings endowed with life." To achieve the illusion of vivacity, to seem like "independent" individual beings, the characters that make up the social milieu must continually exceed their exemplary functions and depart from social types. And hence the reality effect of the novel *opposes* its representational role, and readers collude in the pragmatic adjustments between these two functions. The truism that the social is not "natural," but is instead made according to particular desires and interests, is rehearsed in reading novels, an activity requiring that we help fabricate a "world" (which we know is not The World) for the purpose of achieving specific narrative pleasures.

Novels may therefore be said to activate a fundamental practice of modern ideology—acquiescence without belief, crediting without credulousness—while significantly altering its disposition, transforming the usually guarded wariness into pleasurable expectations. Whether this transformation strengthens one's attachment to dynamics of domination or, obversely, establishes expectations of pleasure unrealizable in the social world; whether, in the latter case, those expectations prove in themselves engrossing enough to compensate for the experience of social powerlessness or, instead, inspire resistance; whether fictional realism makes the ideological subject by providing those very experiences of resistance, or simply has no social or political effects whatsoever: these controversial issues are unresolvable by either literary theory or critical analysis. For an "ideological effect" is not something a text contains in the same way that a well contains water or a battery energy, to be drawn or tapped by any user. It is, rather, something that might occur in reading under certain conditions; when literary critics undertake ideology critique, they judge how texts might have affected hypothetical readers at different times and places, sometimes supplementing their accounts with other kinds of historical evidence. And their speculations have the same status, and are subject to the same rules of evidence, as any other historical speculation.

We might, however, venture the generalization that novels do limber us up to cross ontological levels with ease, to poise ourselves on provisional ground, to assent for the moment while keeping our readiness to depart from the fictional world. Indeed, departing is the lure, for in addition to wanting to satisfy narrative desire, one also longs to be finished with it, to have done with all the making and unmaking, to feel a sense of superiority to the social process. One may never expect to leave behind the social web, which has reciprocally made its makers, but the nineteenth-century novel at least promises the satisfaction of concluding. We know this promise will be disappointed, that closure won't quite give us the lofty and disengaged serenity we seek, that expectation is all, but that does not stop us from looking forward, through our demystified eyes, to a conclusion that will always just be an ending. There is pleasure, it turns out, even in the lack of closure, which prompts us to open another novel, to subscribe to a new set of explicitly hypothetical expectations. We might say that the round of novel reading acts as a ritual renewal of our unspoken consent to work on the social.

This chapter will suggest that because the wicked son's ideology and his ideology critique are equally concerned with the status of imaginary entities, one might profitably look to the nineteenth-century novel for an elaboration of their mutual interdependence and their mutual elusiveness. The provisionality that neither ideology nor its critique can completely acknowledge in the categories they share—such as "imagination," "society," "consciousness," and "individual"—is taken for granted in the novel, and yet it operates all the more powerfully. Dickens's *Great Expectations* will be the text, for its narrator is himself a wicked son who buries, resurrects, and reanimates *Hamlet*'s leftovers in a world ostensibly free from both fathers and spirits.

The World Without Fathers and the Wicked Son's Imagination

Pip's expectations have nothing to do with his father, for no one could seem more completely defunct in body, spirit, and fortune than the "Philip Pirrip, late of this parish" who is declared "dead and buried" (along with "Georgiana wife of the above" and "Alexander, Bartholomew, Abraham, Tobias, and Roger, infant children of the aforesaid") in the opening pages of *Great Expectations* and *never* mentioned again.[7] The wicked son's nefarious suggestion that the past is past, over and done with, and that none of it has anything to do with *him* is at once common sense and painful reality to little Pip as he scans his surroundings and sees only a landscape like a blank sheet, ruled but not lettered: "The marshes were just a long black line . . . ; and the river was just another horizontal line, not nearly so broad nor yet so black; and the sky was just a row of long angry red lines and dense black lines intermixed" (1). As a figure for the as yet unwritten social world of this (or perhaps any) orphan, the blankness of the initial setting makes Pip's wicked-son mentality seem like an opening gambit: tell me the story, it seems to say, that will people this desolation and end my isolation. But the letters in the churchyard promise no stories; they are comically complete, words and icons combined, and seem to leave no room for curiosity about their overly represented and therefore everlastingly finished referents: "The shape of the letters on my father's [tombstone], gave me an odd idea that he was a square, stout, dark man, with curly black hair. From the character and turn of the inscription, '*Also Georgiana Wife of the Above*,' I drew a childish conclusion that my mother was freckled and sickly" (1). Moreover, the dinner-table stories Pip is told raise the theme of familial identification and gratitude only to render it hilariously absurd:

> "Besides," said Mr. Pumblechook, turning sharp on me, "think what you've got to be grateful for. If you'd been born a Squeaker—"
>
> "He *was*, if ever a child was," said my sister, most emphatically. . . .
>
> "Well, but I mean a four-footed Squeaker," said Mr. Pumblechook. "If you had been born such, would you have been here now? Not you—"
>
> "Unless in that form," said Mr. Wopsle, nodding towards the dish [of pork]. (24)

Pip could have been the eaten, not the eater; Dunstable the butcher might have "come up to you as you lay in your straw, and he would have tucked up his frock to get a penknife from out of his waistcoat-pocket, and he would have shed your blood and had your life. No bringing up by hand then. Not a bit of it!" To sit at a meal in thankful consciousness that one is not the food—that's about all it means to be born into a human family in *Great Expectations*.[8]

This minimal sense of social engagement, in which the child obeys under threat of cannibalism while inwardly dissenting, is established early ("You do it . . . and you shall be allowed to live," the convict tells Pip in the first scene. "You fail . . . and your heart and your liver shall be tore out, roasted and ate.") as both the excuse and the precondition for Pip's expectations. In the next stage of his career, his imaginary social relationships (his belief that he is Miss Havisham's heir and Estella's intended) replace both the convict's raw threat and Mrs. Joe's and Mr. Pumblechook's ludicrously coerced claims on his indebtedness, but this seeming increase in civility is merely a delusion, shared by other characters, but not by the reader, who hears the evidence that Pip is offered to Estella as a sacrificial boy on which to practice her man-slaying skills: "Break their hearts my pride and hope, break their hearts and have no mercy!" (89). And we also witness his stubborn refusal to recognize his sacrificial status despite its reiteration: "[Give] up your whole heart and soul to the destroyer!" Miss Havisham somewhat incautiously advises him.

In this world where no memory of the father intrudes, the son can hardly be said to be free. His debts are not canceled by his father's absence, but are instead rendered nightmarishly absurd because unredeemable. The "open secret" of the plot is that the socially acknowledged debts are figments of the collective imagination, ruses of revenge and resentment, which Pip willfully helps create despite all evidence of their dangers and illusions. The plot's famous symmetry consists in the recognition that behind Pip's imaginary debt, the savage compact of the opening scenes reappears. And the moral would seem to be that the wicked son, who pretends to owe his ancestors nothing, will ultimately capitulate, will finally take responsibility, not because he has come to see the rightness of the social order or the naturalness of his obligations, but because he sees that his very survival was always already a capitulation, a sacrifice of some sort.

To be sure, by the time Pip's debt to the criminal Magwitch comes fully due in the third volume of the novel, it has been considerably softened and sentimentalized. A nascent bond of sympathy with the convict, in fact, already differentiates between Pip's first, wholly involuntary, communion in the churchyard[9] ("The man . . . turned me upside down and emptied my pockets. There was nothing in them but a piece of bread. . . . I was seated on a high tombstone, trembling, while he ate the bread ravenously" [2]) and the second, coerced but guilty, feeding, in which Pip imagines Provis to be "like a large dog of ours" (16). Pip's domesticating imagination chimes with the convict's own self-pity ("You'd be but a fierce young hound indeed, if at your time of life you could help to hunt a wretched warmit, hunted as near death and dunghill as this poor wretched warmit is!") as they work out, through their canine metaphors, a rudimentary fellow-feeling in some realm seemingly more primitive and also more innocent than modern society. And by the time of the second meal, the implied sentimental alternative to the sacrificial plot has already been established in "the freemasonry of fellow-sufferers" (8) shared by Pip and Joe, which is explicitly extended to the contrite convict when he is caught on the marshes Christmas night:

> ". . . I'm sorry to say, I've eat your pie."
> "God knows you're welcome to it—so far as it was ever mine," returned Joe with a saving remembrance of Mrs. Joe. "We don't know what you have done, but we wouldn't have you starved to death for it, poor miserable fellow-creatur.—Would us, Pip?" (36)

However, this confraternity of the oppressed is never an independent alternative to the sacrificial dynamic, of which it is finally only another permutation. Formed in defiance of Mrs. Joe the shrew, a traditional figure of misrule, it tames the lawless compact between Pip and "his convict" only to allow the boy's "guilty secret" to shade into his later, apparently justifiable guilt about abandoning Joe in favor of his expectations. Because Joe is supposed to serve as the counterweight to all those who claim Pip's gratitude, because he modestly deserves what the others noisomely try to exact, Pip can endlessly play out the motifs of the Christmas dinner table, can consciously berate himself with ingratitude throughout the period of his expectations, can even provoke a chorus of harassing boys and girls (Trabb's Boy, the Avenger, Biddy, Bentley Drummle) to signify the state of his conscience. Where his childish, primal, irrational shame leaves off, his reflective adolescent guilt takes over, giving him that inward sensation of resistance to paying a debt while he is actually meeting every stipulated social obligation. Joe is both the reminder of the falseness of those obligations and the proof that Pip really is wicked after all, incapable of filial gratitude.

When Pip becomes unable to bear his debt to Joe, their fellowship is thus reabsorbed into the sacrificial plot to which it had once seemed an alternative, but where it had also, in fact, begun. For Joe's kindly protection of Pip and docile sufferance of Mrs. Joe's persecutions are understood by the blacksmith as expiations of his own brutal father's sins. Joe's whole life is a sacrifice to the destroyer:

"My father, Pip, he were given to drink, and when he were over-took with drink, he hammered away at my mother, most onmerci-ful. It were a'most the only hammering he did, indeed, 'xcepting at myself. And he hammered at me with a wigour only to be equalled by the wigour with which he didn't hammer at his anvil. . . . In time I were able to keep him, and I kep him till he went off in a purple leptic fit. And it were my intentions to have had put upon his tombstone that Whatsome'er the failings on his part, Remember reader he were that good in his hart." (42)

The tribute Joe plans for his father takes us back again to the novel's opening encounter with the parental tombstones. It recalls the odd literalism of Pip's encounter, its comic confusion of its material and semantic properties. But these seem inappropriate to Joe's language. Just as the syntax of the last sentence of his speech does nothing to prepare us for the direct address of the epitaph ("Remember reader") or the capitalization of the first words of the planned couplet's lines ("Whatsome'er," "Remem-ber"), the very story he is telling, which is about the reasons for his illiteracy, should preclude his ability to visualize his composi-tion or misspell "heart" as "hart." Indeed, illiteracy is the price Joe has paid for being the good son, since his father beat him when he tried to go to school, "which, you see, . . . were a draw-back to my learning" (42), and forced him to work. The tribute Joe actually paid—leaving school and supporting his father—therefore should prevent him from visualizing the tribute of an epitaph. Ascribing such textual features as capitalization and odd orthography to Joe's imaginary consciousness would seem, there-fore, to be something of a lapse. We might excuse it, though, by reading the textual features of Joe's intended tribute, not as expressions of his probable individual imagination, but as part of the novel's pattern of representing the dead as creatures replaced by stony letters, characters so hard ("hart") that you must give them your heart and must redeem them with your imagination. The demands of the dead render both good and bad sons child-like, putting them on the narrow threshold between things and signs, forcing them, it seems, to the origins and limits of the symbolic.

Nevertheless, the behavior of Pip and Joe at the tombs of their parents is strikingly different. Pip, as we've seen, seems uninterested in them; he lets the letters comprehend them entirely. Joe, on the other hand, wants to remember and honor his father, although he is comically incoherent about the nature of his father's merits and can express only a generalized filial piety. Joe is not sure just what his father's story means, but he knows it means something *for him.* Whereas Pip, the narrator, never comes near the topic of his own father; whatever his story was, it has no relevance for Pip's own story. Joe is a large child who has given his whole heart and soul to the destroyer without a murmur, and he therefore abides in a liminal place, always blundering and stumbling at the threshold of symbolic and social orders. Resolute in his atonement, he figures the dutiful son as a lovable dupe, relatively static and disempowered. Pip, on the other hand, reaps the retribution of disillusionment and heartbreak, the standard punishment meted out in the nineteenth century to novel heroes, most of them wicked sons, who leave their fathers' tombs behind unregarded and expect to encounter great things in the larger world.[10] The sacrifice is made, one way or the other.

Indeed, no child seems safe in *Great Expectations;* Pip and Joe are only the most obvious sacrifices. But Estella—who is apparently martyred to her mother's jealous rage, then deprived of a heart by Miss Havisham's revenge, and finally beaten out of her one protection, her stony indifference, by her husband—is even more completely wasted by visitations of the unknown parents' sins than any of the male children. Mrs. Pocket—another mistress of misrule, whose delusions of aristocratic grandeur and constant misremembering of her deceased grandpapa's "position" occasion the near-infanticidal neglect of her own children—repeats the slaughter of the innocents in the mode of social satire. In the Pocket household, the maternal grandfather is a ridiculous stand-in for patriarchal authority. Imperiled children are, indeed, so common in this novel, and their families so routinely bloodthirsty or uncaring, that its whole social world appears to be one large Moloch's feast. Mr. Pocket, a father forgotten and ignored in his own household, hysterically voices what might be the whole novel's motto: "'Hear this!' he helplessly exclaimed to the elements. 'Babies are to be nutcrackered dead, for people's . . . grandpapa's positions!'" (183).

And yet, one must admit, there is something quaintly anti-quated about Mr. Pocket's formulation, implying as it does that children are sacrificed, as in *Hamlet,* to the patriarchal representative of the family. More in keeping with the general dynamic of death-dealing in *Great Expectations* is this speech of the lawyer Jaggers, describing the point of view of a suppositional lawyer, who is obviously himself:

> Put the case that he lived in an atmosphere of evil, and that all he saw of children, was their being generated in great numbers for certain destruction. Put the case that he often saw children solemnly tried at a criminal bar, where they were held up to be seen, put the case that he habitually knew of their being imprisoned, whipped, transported, neglected, cast out, qualified in all ways for the hangman, and growing up to be hanged. (391)

This impersonal damage, judicially administered in the interests not of a family, but of that higher-order abstraction called "society," appropriately seems to have no individual human representatives. The children in Jaggers's description are acted upon by unseen forces: they are "held up to be seen," "imprisoned," "whipped," and "transported," but the holders, imprisoners, whippers, and transporters, everywhere, are specifically invisible. Jaggers's speech reveals the triumph and the terror of the wicked son's imagination: having freed himself from particular figures authorized and empowered to exact his sacrifice, he replaces the father's ghost with a whole demoniacal society, any member of which might suddenly rouse himself to deliver the hapless child over for judgment. For in the wicked son's world, all parents are effectively dead, all children therefore truant, and the social world confronting them necessarily vengeful and resentful. Jaggers's speech resonates in the silence surrounding "Philip Pirrip, late of this parish."

The World Without Fathers and the Social Imaginary

The sacrifice of the children is, to be sure, most thoroughly accomplished at the lower end of the novel's social spectrum. The children depicted in Jaggers's speech are, after all, the "spawn" of the criminal underclass, the vagrant lumpen proletariat, who are presented here as a *social problem.* Our placement of the speech inside the pervasive pattern of child sacrifice in the novel is not intended to deflect attention from its social specificity, but instead to suggest that pauper children come into view as, specifically, a *social* problem inside the skeptical, individualist mentality we've ascribed to the "wicked son," for it is there that the very concept of "society," with its lateral class divisions, takes shape. As an abstraction denoting the totality of relations among more limited forms of human sociation (such as families, polities, guilds, ranks, industries, dynasties, states, and so on), "society" is first conceived in the eighteenth century and becomes an identifiable object of inquiry in the nineteenth.[11] Its conceptualization, moreover, is generally recognized to coincide with the appearance of the isolated "individual" as the primary human subject, and the pairing of these two abstractions, often locked in conflicted interdependence, has been found to dominate bourgeois ideology even as it laid the groundwork for ideology critique itself, which, after all, depends on the assumption that there is such a thing as society.

When we notice that the attempts of the wicked son to free himself from the determinations of the family merge into a nightmarish vision of isolated, endangered children, who can then be perceived as a *social problem,* we are rehearsing some of the principal motifs of what is often called "bourgeois thought." It might be said that *Great Expectations* allows us to see those grand categories in the making, for it reminds us frequently, if anachronistically, of rudimentary stages in the very idea of the social, which often seems to be struggling into existence against the powerful resistance of the narrator's consciousness. *Great Expectations* does not present "society" as a static abstraction, but instead gradually configures its outlines through a series of imaginary projections and counterprojections.[12]

Both the rudimentariness of the social in this novel and its overtly imaginary nature can be traced back to that silence surrounding "Philip Pirrip, late of this parish," a silence signaling not only the wicked son's victory, but also the death of the plot of genealogical identity and rightful inheritance. Before *Great Expectations,* that plot had been drawing its last gasps for decades in Dickens's novels, like a patient kept alive on a respirator. Most

nineteenth-century novelists had long before left familial determinations behind and launched their heroines and heroes into
the wider waters of social destinies. In England, stories like Tom
Jones's and Evelina's, which climax with the discovery of *who* one
is, had much earlier been replaced by those of Anne Elliott or
Becky Sharp, who make their own destinies independently of
their origins. Dickens's novels were an exception to this pattern.
Right up until *Little Dorrit* and *A Tale of Two Cities,* the family
secret dominated his plotting; heroes and heroines alike learned
their rights, their duties, and their destinies when they found out
what the previous generations had done. Dickens even seemed
intermittently aware that his plots were old-fashioned and sometimes drew attention to their archaism; through its "Remember
Me" motif, for example, *Little Dorrit* reaches all the way back to
Hamlet for a reference point.

Then, quite suddenly, Dickens creates a hero, Pip, whose destiny and family identity are completely separate, so disjoined that
the undutiful son's implicit query—"But what has *my father's* past
to do with *me?*"—goes entirely unanswered because it is unasked,
for the first time in this author's career. Pip is not a foundling or
a bastard, like Oliver Twist or Esther Summerson, so no mystery
attaches to his birth; neither has he inherited through his family
a problematic legacy, like Charles Darnay, Arthur Clennam, or
John Harmon; and his story is not propelled, like Nicholas Nick-
leby's or David Copperfield's, by some traumatic disinheritance.
As points of origin, or as figures to escape, avenge, outdo, or even
remember, Pip's parents play no role. When Magwitch, in another of Dickens's Shakespearean moments, reappears as the terrifying paternal "ghost" ("Look'ee here, Pip. I'm your second father. You're my son" [320]), Pip's life, like Hamlet's, is no longer
his own—but not because his identity dictates his fate, for Pip
inhabits the world of lone individuals, in which the question
"Why me?" has a remarkably uninformative but always apt rejoin-
der: "Why not?"

In *Great Expectations,* Dickens veered away from his usual
plotting so abruptly that all of the coordinates of his fiction seem
to have been thrown out of alignment. We unexpectedly find ourselves inside a consciousness that has so thoroughly extinguished

all curiosity about its kin, that has emerged so insouciantly as the family's sole male survivor, that "society" itself seems to have been put on the edge of extinction. Instead of generating a more differentiated and fully-formed social world than those usually encountered in Dickens's work, the sudden death of the genealogical identity plot produces a more rudimentary and phantasmal milieu, one that barely rises to the appellation of "social." The hero *ex nihilo*, whose grand ambition is to get as far as possible from everything associated with his "common" home, finds nothing like the complex web of human interactions normally encountered by novelistic innocents who make their way from the provinces to the city. Pip's metropolitan environment not only fails to resemble the realized societies of Balzac's Paris or Eliot's Middlemarch, but also bears little likeness to Dickens's normal London. Sparsely populated, with a higher-than-usual proportion of eccentrics, this is a milieu of the margins and the brinks, where thresholds are jealously guarded and people's behavior is rigidly determined by the few environments they repetitively visit: Jaggers's office, Pip's and Herbert's rooms, Wemmick's fortified house (satiric symbol of the individual in a hostile society), the courtroom, the prison. Having gone to London to raise himself in society and learn its ways, Pip keeps finding himself on its edge, in the precincts of criminal law, where society constitutes itself primarily and primally through the expulsion of its transgressors.[13] In the relative absence of the social building blocks of family histories, occupations, economic enterprises, and so on, Pip's "society" seems to be stuck in the rut of this primitive act of self-formation through the extrusion of the criminal.

But that act can never really be definitive in this basically punitive version of the social, where cohesion depends on exclusion and society's sole function is only to police its margins. For under these conditions, the gratifications of social life, its very raison d'être, disappear. The point is made obsessively in the repetitious comic business of the first volume, where each of Pip's "socializing" episodes—the Christmas dinner, the apprenticeship to Joe, the attendance at Mr. Wopsle's dramatic reading of "George Barnwell"—comes to resemble a criminal proceeding. And we may take Pip's experience as typical, for, as we've seen, the children are almost all on probation and are therefore identified with the discarded convicts. Pip's panic-stricken imaginary fluctuations back and forth across the line separating "society" from its outside are only a hyperbolic recognition of the general threat, and therefore the general instability, produced by this crude social state.

The overtly *imaginary*[14] nature of those fluctuations, however, points to the other side of this novel's genealogical lack. When the plot of identity and rightful inheritance suddenly disappears and society is reduced to its mechanisms of exclusion, a novelistic space becomes available for seemingly random imaginary bonds. Hamlet may doubt the provenance of his father's ghost, but he knows his duty to his father's memory derives from genealogical necessity, whereas Pip's duty to Magwitch results from an accidental identification, which, to use Marx's phrase, "achieves an independent life." Like Old Hamlet, Magwitch has a species of revenge in mind when he adopts the blacksmith's apprentice: in his greater wealth and gentility, Pip is to triumph over the colonists who spurned the convict. But Pip is only the instrument of Magwitch's revenge by a combination of chance encounter and imaginative force: "When I was a hired-out shepherd in a solitary hut, not seeing no faces but faces of sheep till I half forgot wot men's and women's faces was like, I see yourn" (304). Just as Pip had once looked at Magwitch sympathetically, associating him with a pet dog, Magwitch looks at a wilderness of sheep and sees the sympathetic child's face in his mind's eye. On the social margins where this novel lingers, the rudimentary form of social constitution may be criminal exclusion, but human bonds are made explicitly through imaginary identification. Joe imagines Pip to be the little boy he once was and resolves to reverse the dynamic of his own childhood by being the hardworking but gentle blacksmith his own father was not. Miss Havisham imagines Estella to be the instrument of her revenge, the one who will reverse the genders of love and betrayal in her own story. And Magwitch makes a third in this pattern of explicitly nonbiological, phantasmatic self-reproduction.

Hence, out of a complex desire for fellowship in the wilderness, a desire to replace the child he lost, and resentment against other

colonists, Magwitch creates not just a bond with Pip and a right
to his allegiance, but Pip himself: "It was a recompense to me,
look'ee here, to know in secret that I was making a gentleman.
The blood horses of them colonists might fling up the dust over
me as I was walking; what do I say? I says to myself, 'I'm making
a better gentleman nor ever *you*'ll be!' " (306). Nor is it only the
older generation of characters that makes the younger out of hap-
hazard materials. Pip, as we saw earlier, made a feeling creature
out of Magwitch in his own imagination, who in turn "makes"
Pip's life as a "recompense" to both Pip and himself, simultaneously fueling and assuaging his project of social revenge. No
wonder Pip compares himself to both Frankenstein and Frankenstein's monster when Magwitch returns to claim his creation:
"The imaginary student pursued by the misshapen creature he
had impiously made, was not more wretched than I, pursued by
the creature who had made me" (320). The circuit of vivification
and indebtedness is only completed when Pip becomes hostage
to Magwitch once again by receiving the power of life and death
over him: "Nothing was needed but this; the wretched man, after
loading wretched me with his gold and silver chains for years,
had risked his life to come to me, and I held it there in my keeping" (320).

   This is the moment at which the characters' imaginative power
(to create or vivify each other) and the law's power (to exclude
or obliterate people) intersect in the plot, and Pip finds himself
again at the margin, where he started out. Pip must now renew
the project of keeping Magwitch alive by taking on the function
of the excluder; that is, he can only save Magwitch's life by getting
him out of the country, since the convict's banishment is for a
life term and returning is a capital crime. The expulsive "society"
has been neatly spatialized by this sentence, so that it literally
includes only those who are suffered to remain on the British
Isles, and much of the action of the novel's third volume is de-
voted to getting Magwitch as close to the literal edge of the kingdom as possible. The opening chapters' marshes (a word in which
we can hear both "marges" and "mare" or "sea") are recalled in
the riverside setting of the chapters describing the attempted escape, and Pip must also repeat the initial communion as at once

a voluntary act of salvation and an enforcement of the sentence of banishment. Pip, indeed, intends to share the exile; hence, were the entire circuit of projective identification to complete itself, Pip would be at once the elective excluded and the agent of exclusion.

But he fails in this ambition, for the orphaned mind that has conjured the compulsively expelling society seems driven to imagine its utmost penalty, its power to impose the final exclusion—death. The novel seems unable to conclude without first stopping at the scene of the death sentence:

> . . . I saw two-and-thirty men and women put before the Judge to receive that sentence together. . . .
>
> . . . Penned in the dock, as I again stood outside it at the corner with [Magwitch's] hand in mine, were the two-and-thirty men and women, some defiant, some stricken with terror, some sobbing and weeping, some covering their faces, some staring gloomily about. There had been shrieks from among the women convicts, but they had been stilled, and a hush had succeeded. The sheriffs with their great chains and nosegays, other civic gewgaws and monsters, criers, ushers, a great gallery full of people—a large theatrical audience—looked on, as the two-and-thirty and the Judge were solemnly confronted. (433)

In this, one of the most crowded locations of the novel, the gap between those who will be inside and those who will be cast out seems widest. Its juxtapositions—the chains and nosegays; the ludic "theatrical audience" and the deadly serious prisoners; the stark, still demeanor of the convicts and the judge, on the one hand, and the grotesque civic sideshow surrounding them, on the other—stress that this routine ceremony is designed to create the greatest possible mental distance between those who have been "a scourge to society" (433) and those who constitute its members. Other details—the solemn repetition of the archaic-sounding number "two-and-thirty," the convicts being "penned" promiscuously in the dock, like animals—are obviously intended to evoke the idea of ancient sacrifice, and the scene also harks back to Jaggers's description of the numerous child criminals "held up to be seen" at the bar. This scene fleshes out the spectral agents of his speech and populates the courtroom with more fully-imagined bodies, so that the convicts seem the children of his vision grown up: "he had reason to look upon [children] as so much spawn, to develop into the fish that were to come to [the law's] net" (391).

But if this scene dramatizes the final sacrificial separation, it is also a scene of the return of the sacrificed through the aperture of Pip's imagination. When we fill in the ellipses in the above quotation, the narrator's wonder at the vivacity of these figures in his mind rivals his retrospective astonishment at the scene itself:

> But for the indelible picture that my remembrance now holds be-
> fore me, I could scarcely believe, even as I write these words, that
> I saw two-and-thirty . . .
>
> The whole scene starts out again in the vivid colours of the
> moment, down to the drops of April rain on the windows of the
> court, glittering in the rays of April sun. Penned in the dock . . .

This novel contains few such references to the moment of writing, and here they push into the foreground Pip's almost involuntary role as medium. The images press on the narrator: he seems barely to summon them; they "start out again," like dormant things suddenly come to life. Animation seizes the building itself, which weeps uncannily in the sunshine. And a reminder of Pip's mediating retrieval lingers in that word "penned"; he has "penned" them to save them. The scene becomes a self-conscious triumph of immortality through the word, a celebration of description as resurrection. The more detailed their depiction, the more completely these dead revive: ". . . and some of them were supported out, and some of them sauntered out with a haggard look of bravery, and a few nodded to the gallery, and two or three shook hands, and others went out chewing the fragments of herb they had taken from the sweet herbs lying about" (434). The detail about the herbs—for example, stressed by the repetition of the word, which both connotes springtime and reminds us of the filth and stink of prisoners, which carries the minuscule suggestion that some were distracted by a tiny, commonplace enjoyment at the moment of their doom—bespeaks a refusal on the part of these dead to disappear utterly. In short, the evocation of Magwitch's condemnation "for his return to the land that had cast him out" itself becomes a mode of return, even from the last exclusion.

The dreadfully reduced social world and the imagination it stimulates are thus locked in a paradoxical struggle to the very end, a struggle precluding finality. The same orphaned mind that conjures a society maintaining itself by setting rafts of helpless people adrift on the seas of oblivion brings them back by the very intensity with which it imagines their loss.

The World Without Spirits and Discourses of Suspension

It brings them back, but it does not bring back Philip Pirrip Late of this Parish or Georgiana Wife of the Above, who remain dead letters, mere inscriptions. Their continuous absence, we've claimed, signals the demise of the genealogical plot; but, we've further argued, far from saving the son from his obligations to the past, the genealogical lack only exposes him to sacrifices randomly exacted. The smooth grooves of familial identification are missing, and affiliation follows accidental, impromptu paths in an excess of explicitly imaginative activity. Finally, we've noted that the narrator's imagination, goaded on by the very lack from which it springs, appears as the hyperexcited medium through which the lost objects of identification return. In the wicked son's novel, the activity of endowing "the productions of the human brain" with life is not hidden to maintain an ideological illusion, but is instead promoted as the salvific counterpart to society's expulsions.

We are now in a position to notice and explore one of the oddities of these objects of identification, these productions of the human brain: they are often not only dead people remembered, but also people remembered as the already reanimated dead. Even in the earliest stillness surrounding Philip Pirrip Sr. and Georgiana, the restless undead are stirring. Pip first imagines their behavior as he watches Magwitch,

> picking his way among the nettles, and among the brambles that
> bound the green mounds, he looked in my young eyes as if he were
> eluding the hands of the dead people, stretching up cautiously out
> of their graves, to get a twist upon his ankle and pull him in. (4)

And a few paragraphs later, observing the convict's limping progress toward "a gibbet with some chains hanging to it which had once held a pirate," Pip imagines him to be "the pirate come to life, and come down, and going back to hook himself up again" (5). In the midst of his "first most vivid and broad impression of the identity of things," Pip knows for sure that "the small bundle of shivers growing afraid of it all and beginning to cry was Pip," and the only other human being in this wilderness is immediately consigned to the ranks of the undead.

The convict's appearance as a threatening revenant should no doubt be linked to the wicked son's guilty consciousness, which produces a figure for the paternal repressed at the very moment of the boy's first awareness of separate existence, and, by implication, of his own escape from the calamity that has overtaken his parents.[15] One could even say that the comic flippancy of the preceding paragraph describing the parental tombstones, its insouciant refusal to separate letters from persons and hence to register loss or absence, provokes the parents' angry retaliation. Ancestral return seems implicit as well in Pip's first perception of Miss Havisham, which obviously recalls the sickly "Also Georgiana, Wife of the Above":

> I saw that the dress had been put upon the rounded figure of a young woman, and that the figure upon which it now hung loose, had shrunk to skin and bone. Once I had been taken to see some ghastly waxwork at the Fair, representing I know not what impossible personage lying in state. Once, I had been taken to one of our old marsh churches to see a skeleton in the ashes of a rich dress, that had been dug out of a vault under the church pavement. Now, waxwork and skeleton seemed to have dark eyes that moved and looked at me. (53)

But the novel's undead are not simply the jealous parents returned, for there are, to begin with, too many of them straddling the zones of life and death. Mrs. Joe, after being felled by Orlick and "left for dead . . . , come[s] to life again" (404) and lingers on the threshold for several years. Compeyson, the novel's most ontologically problematic character, when observed by Mr. Wopsle from the stage, looks as though he is haunting rather than spying on Pip: "I saw that you were quite unconscious of him, sitting behind you there, like a ghost" (365). And Estella, entombed in Miss Havisham's house, turns out to be the missing corpus delicti revived, the presumed slaughtered child of Magwitch and Molly, whose absent body allows her mother to be acquitted on a charge of murdering another woman. Molly herself, always held "in suspense," is a theatrical dumb show of arrested animation, at once overwrought and phantasmal:

> . . . extremely pale, with large faded eyes, and a quantity of streaming hair. I cannot say whether any diseased affection of the heart caused her lips to be parted as if she were panting, and her face to bear a curious expression of suddenness and flutter; but I know that I had been to see Macbeth at the theatre, a night or two before and that her face looked to me as if it were all disturbed by fiery air, like the faces I had seen rise out of the Witches' caldron. (201)

As an auto-icon of a captive murderer, Molly further brings to mind the "two dreadful casts on a shelf, of [executed criminals'] faces peculiarly swollen, and twitchy about the nose," also displayed by Jaggers. Contemplating one of these, Pip asks, "Is it like him?" "Like him?" replies Wemmick. "It's himself, you know" (189). Then turning to the cast, Wemmick apostrophizes, "Why you must have come down in the night and been peeping into the inkstand, to get this blot upon your eyebrow, you old rascal."

One could go on multiplying such instances, but the point has probably been amply made by now: as Magwitch puts it, "There's o'er much coming back" in this novel. And many of the undead inhabit states of suspended animation like the one implied in Joe's description of Miss Havisham's final condition:

> "Is she dead, Joe?"
> "Why you see, old chap," said Joe, in a tone of remonstrance, and by way of getting at it by degrees, "I wouldn't go so far as to say that, for that's a deal to say; but she ain't—"
> "Living, Joe?"
> "That's nigher where it is," said Joe; "she ain't living." (441)

The manifestations of the undead in *Great Expectations* seem too numerous and various to fit into the trope of the parents' return.

Moreover, their insistent association with imaginative activity makes them look more like figures in a fantasy of mastery than monsters returning from the repressed. Their presentation underscores that certain modes of perception and certain figures of speech allow an incessant play of the imagination across the life-death divide: characters come to death, and to life, "by degrees." Part of the explanation for the replacement of the dead by the undead, therefore, is that the novel can thus rehearse, in its fable, its imagery, and its rhetoric, a general function of novels: animating and suspending animation. The pleasures of pretending to flesh out a moribund structure, to put blood and muscle on a conceptual abstraction, to lay it by for future use, then to resuscitate it are the pleasures of the fictional mode. These pleasures are all the more apparent in serial publications like *Great Expectations*, which require that the reader's interest be suspended from one installment to the next, often through the technique of a suspenseful plot. And, since we know that the periodically reappearing simulacra, indicating absence as they do, will necessarily have a whiff of death about them, it only seems appropriate that *Great Expectations* should linger in the graveyard to bare its rites of fiction.

We've mentioned before that the novel's generic readiness to disclose the open secret of its fictionality would seem to fit a dominant nineteenth-century "ideological" tendency toward epistemological flexibility. Complicating Marx's formulation that ideology entails a "fetishistic" belief in the independent life of mere human inventions, we've argued that instead ideology has required a mode of supplementing disbelief with a willingness to enter into known illusions, a disposition to take obvious inventions of the human hand and brain for independently living entities under certain conditions and for certain purposes. The continuity of skepticism underlying both fiction and the ideology of the modern period would, then, seem an obvious nexus in which to place *Great Expectations'* revenants, since they, too, invite us to play with the difference between animate and inanimate beings. Explicitly, in this case, we are invited to pretend that bodies can be held at the brink of life or moved gradually in and out of a vital state through the operations of the mind. Pip becomes an allegory for the reader, both frightening himself with the ghastly figures and indulging the wish that he had the power to think the dead back to life.

There is, however, more to the subject of suspended animation than these generalizations can compass, for the life-death boundary was remarkably controversial in the nineteenth century. It was haunted not only by epistemological doubt, but also by ontological uncertainty. If Pip (or the reader of fiction) was gratifying a human wish to reconceive the mortal passage, he had plenty of company in several disciplines. Indeed, the lifting of the life-death distinction out of commonsense daily understandings (which had little to say about it) and into disciplinary *discourses* (where it was endlessly worried) is one of modernity's characteristic promotions. In general, what Foucault called the modern *episteme* aimed to take nothing for granted and relentlessly converted much of what we've been calling the bedrock of ideology (all that goes without saying) into the stuff of its investigations. "Let there be discourse" was its implicit slogan,[16] and many questions that had previously seemed relatively easy to answer—such as, "Is this body alive?"—became problematic. Moreover, they tended to stay problematic, for unlike religious doctrine, modern discourse was designed to expand the horizon of the unknown in its quest for scientific understanding. Hence, as we trace the discursive affiliations of *Great Expectations* in the following pages, we should note at the outset that we are not seeking a context of "beliefs" about life and death, but are, rather, outlining devices of doubt.

Although the literature of the early nineteenth century is replete with complaints against materialism for having rendered the universe mechanically nonvital, the opposite might just as well have been asserted: that materialism dramatically expanded the zones of the organic, vastly multiplied the entities that could be described as alive or dead, and reduced the sphere of things to which those categories would simply not apply. Materialist explanations of the nature of vitality, for example, are noticeably flexible about its location; "life" can lurk in numerous, previously unexpected places: in electricity, in magnetic "force," in a subtly all-pervading liquid; indeed it can be latent in the whole of inorganic, or inanimate, matter, which, with the development of organic chemistry, could be conceived as a vast storehouse for the building blocks of the organic. If not itself actually and actively alive, inorganic matter seemed pregnant with life potential, and redescribing "life" *as this potential* immanent in matter was a crucial late-eighteenth- and nineteenth-century development.

The vitalization of matter was crucial because it marked so many disciplines and fields of endeavor. Classical political economy, for example, spread the medium of "life" throughout the marketplace by conceiving of value as stored-up labor and commodities as expended vigor. While this abstracted value manifests itself in objects primarily at the moment of their exchange (that is, as commodity value), it nevertheless remains latent in manufactured objects. The labor theory of value thus converted the entire built human environment into a depository where the energy of millions of lives has been amassed.[17] Marx's reasoning followed that of the political economists when he also described capital as "dead labor," and his repeated Gothic images of capitalism as a vampire are merely unusually lurid instances of the pervasive uncanniness in materialist economics.

Even the soi-disant anti-materialists of the period repeat these imaginative patterns. The social theorists who were steeped in German romanticism, such as Coleridge and Carlyle, promoted a vitalist organicism supposedly at odds with "scientific" materialism, but the very language of their protests against Enlightenment thought reverberates with its dominant note, carrying and expanding the theme of the implicit liveliness of matter. "The universe," announces Carlyle's Teufelsdröckh, "is not dead and demoniacal, but living and my home." "Living" and "dead" come increasingly to exhaust the possibilities; those entities that are demonstrably neither, such as the merely inanimate, are integrated into the spectrum, often as mixed or marginal instances; and this trick of thought rebounds on the way people are imagined, insinuating that we may ourselves be borderline cases. Ruskin, for example, describes people, buildings, and architectural traditions as composed of both living and dead elements in *The Seven Lamps of Architecture*. Indeed, he goes so far as to describe even life itself as both living and dead: ". . . false life is, indeed, but one of the conditions of death or stupor, but it acts even when it cannot be said to animate, and is not always easily known from the true."[18] He emphasizes that great buildings are alive not only metaphorically, but also literally, for their very forms are full of "sympathy," which is communicated to the observer (72). Although Saint Mark's may not be able to move and breath, it nevertheless possesses a quickening potential, which is the essence of art. The life-death spectrum dominated Ruskin's aesthetics ever more completely as his influence grew; in footnotes added to *Seven Lamps* in 1880, he proclaimed, "The real question is only—are we dead or alive?" (149–50).

"Are we dead or alive?" may seem a very fanciful question, but it echoed the same uncertainty that preoccupied the no-nonsense medical profession: "When a medical man is sent for on a sudden to a person who has fallen into a state of insensibility, and finds him lying motionless, the first question which would arise in his mind is, whether the person is really dead; and although the question seems easy of solution, it is really not. . . ."[19] Medicine is the most obvious discipline charged with exploring the life-death threshold, and it was the doctors who claimed, in the late eighteenth century, to have discovered that humans might linger there for much longer periods of time than had previously been thought. The discovery of "suspended animation," or "apparent death," cast doubt on what had for centuries seemed the certain signs of death. Dr. James Curry wrote at the end of the eighteenth century, "The time is still within the recollection of many now living, when it was almost universally believed, that life quitted the body in a very few minutes after the person had ceased to breath," a mistaken belief that led to premature burial or to the conclusion, in cases of recovery, of "Divine Interposition."[20] But, Curry assures his readers, medical science has now made the "happy discovery of an essential difference between *Absolute* and *Apparent Death.*"

There was, in fact, very little consensus about the exact nature of the "essential difference." For Curry himself and the vast majority of doctors interested in "morbid states," it consisted simply in recoverability, and further metaphysical implications were irrelevant. Although progress in medical knowledge certainly both stimulated and was driven by an interest in suspended animation, that interest produced no single, positive set of new beliefs, but instead merely strengthened the skeptical disposition. Bodies that looked quite lifeless might instead be dormant, and doctors were repeatedly cautioned not to trust too readily to appearances. Curry's ringing announcement of the discovery of "apparent death" was mainly a way of introducing a lengthy description of how physicians should go about testing for death, a procedure that was fast becoming one of the most important parts of forensic medicine. Even for the run-of-the-mill doctors, the average practitioners who simply wanted to avoid burying anybody alive, physical death had become not only something to lament, avoid, certify, or wonder at, but also something to disbelieve, and the place that seemingly moribund bodies occupied on the life-death continuum had become uncertain.

The tests for death, moreover, themselves uncovered so many baffling phenomena that speculation about what we might call the ontology of life and death arose in certain quarters of the mainstream medical profession and on its unorthodox fringes. During the nineteenth century, "suspended animation" was used as evidence in several competing theories of life. At one extreme we find the mechanical materialism deriving from the eighteenth-century clinician John Fothergill, who thought apparent death proved that the body was like a clock, which could be stopped and started again.[21] Although this was not a typical nineteenth-century view, it survived in some quarters throughout the century and even found its way into both communist and fascist medicine in the twentieth century.[22] On the other extreme, the late-nineteenth-century—putatively anti-materialist, and certainly anti-scientific—founders of the Society for the Prevention of Premature Burial had what might be called "occult" interests in the subject and a determined purpose of discrediting the authority of the medical profession. Between these extremes, most early- and mid-nineteenth-century doctors who cared to think about the subject at all seem to have subscribed to a form of "soft" vitalism, positing the existence of a "vital principle," a kind of "energy" given to the organism in a fixed amount at the outset of its life. Early vitalists had thought the vital principle and the vital functions inseparable, but the phenomenon of suspended animation seemed to contradict that position. It suggested, instead, that the functions of life could temporarily cease, while the vital principle somehow persisted. This perceived split proved momentous, for it seemed to require the redefinition of life as *potential* life and of death, not as the mere observable cessation of functions, but as the loss of the *capacity* for life. As the medical historian Martin Pernick explains, "The absence of vital potential could never be directly demonstrated save by physical destruction of the body; diagnostic tests could confirm life, but could only infer death."[23] In short, the discovery of "apparent death" not only perforated the boundary between life and death, making death in the extant body an uncertain inference, but also created a new unlocated life in abeyance. The disappearance of the difference between life and its potential augmented the general tendency to conceive all matter as in some state of relative vitality. In short, "suspended animation" could be thought of as an apt metaphor for the new uncanniness of matter itself.

Most physicians were no doubt uninterested in such metaphors, but some were willing to speculate about the relation between the vital power and seemingly inanimate objects. Others were interested in the partial vitality of bodies or in the conveyance of vitality from one to another. "Suspended animation," that is, allowed vitality to leak out of its usual vessels and thereby encouraged speculation about the nature of life. Mesmerism, known in the early Victorian period as "animal magnetism," interested an impressive array of British scientists in the 1830s and continued to attract proselytes (although against increasing opposition) throughout the century.[24] Dickens was one of many perfectly sane Victorians who seriously entertained its notion "of an universal magnetic power, distinct from that of the common magnet, depending upon a fluid pervading all living and inanimate matter, and the source of all in art and nature."[25] His close friend Chauncy Hare Townshend defended the hypotheses that the fluid pervading all matter was itself both vital and the medium of all vitality. The existence of such a medium, too "subtle" to be detected by our normal senses, was conjectured to transfer the body's life to some other location during episodes of apparent death, allowing a vital spark to travel while the body itself was dormant. Moreover,

Townshend sometimes suggested that people might send "emanations" of themselves across distances through that medium, so that their bodies might be located in one place and their selves, viewable in a subtle form, in another. Significantly, Dickens dedicated *Great Expectations* to Townshend.

The relation between Townshend's book *Facts in Mesmerism* and Dickens's novel might, indeed, serve as a model for the way his novels incorporate neighboring discourses. *Great Expectations* makes several friendly gestures toward Townshend's book. For example, the original undead couple, Magwitch and Miss Havisham, are implicated in the perpetration of spectral projections. Pip has a vision of Miss Havisham hanging from the ceiling of the old brewery the first time he visits Satis House, and her delirious brother claims that she is haunting his deathbed, prompting Compeyson's objection, "Why, you fool, don't you know she's got a living body?" (330). Magwitch, too, is suspected of projecting his image to Pip across great distances. Miss Havisham's and Magwitch's elopements out of their bodies certainly confirm their suspension on the threshold between life and death; the passage describing Magwitch's emanations, moreover, shows us just how capacious that space had become:

> I began either to imagine or recal that I had had mysterious warnings of this man's approach. That for weeks gone by, I had passed faces in the streets which I thought like his. That, these likenesses had grown more numerous, as he, coming over the sea, had drawn near. That, his wicked spirit had somehow sent these messengers to mine, and that now on this stormy night he was as good as his word, and with me. (308)

Because Magwitch's appearances come in the form of likenesses in other faces, because his so-called "spirit" travels through others, he reduces their faces to demonic semblances of himself. Hence, the pervasiveness of a subtle living fluid, through which some intelligences can travel outside of their bodies to inhabit others, seems to diminish the independent significance of the bodies one encounters, to immerse and thereby dilute their being. The newly conceived liveliness of the universe tends to dislodge the particular lives of the channelers, the media, who lend themselves to the traveling force and become its mannequin-like messengers. Dickens's comradely allusion to Townshend's book might be said, therefore, to draw a paradox out of it: the spread of Life, in the abstract, increases the population of the zombies.

The passage not only incorporates Townshend's speculations into a darker and more self-contradictory dynamic—where animating the universe suspends the lives of its inhabitants—but also obliquely comments on the event's ontological status. It indicates a distinction between imagining and recalling only to render the difference irrelevant, hinting that the imagination might be as trustworthy an organ of perception for such phenomena as any other, and that its employment might not necessarily affect the veracity of the experience. Each report of an "apparition" in *Great Expectations* contains reservations about its "objective" reality, for the novel, as we've said repeatedly, is generically a skeptical discourse. But those very reservations are used, in this passage and elsewhere, to create the understanding that it doesn't matter whether or not events are imagined or recalled, whether one sees or merely thinks one sees. Partly it doesn't matter because one is, after all, reading a novel, so the truth value of any statement is suspended. But here one detects a further use of the toleration that always, to some extent, attends fictionality: skepticism in these passages modulates into a *positive indifference* to ontological levels, signaling the special susceptibility of the novelistic sensibility. The above passage, for example, seems to want us to notice that an everyday narrative technique—foreshadowing—is being morphed into a mystical accomplishment, as if to hint that novels generally are open to profound and hidden layers of reality.

The novel, however, has no interest in promulgating such an openness as a new belief system, and its absence of truth claims mirrors the skeptical rhetoric of the British mesmerists themselves. Townshend's *Facts in Mesmerism*, as the title implies, asserts only that certain phenomena had been witnessed by himself and others for whom he could vouch, but it avoids urging its readers to adopt on faith the explanations put forward by Mesmer himself. Indeed, it blames enthusiastic mesmerists for asserting the existence of unseen forces before having soberly documented the phenomenal effects: "Do we not, in conducting an important analysis, first ascertain the phenomena, their characteristics, and the circumstances under which they appear; and then, after long and careful induction, name, but with caution, some pervading principle into which they may all be harmoniously resolved?"[26] Townshend wishes, for the moment, to suspend metaphysical speculation in scientific procedure, and hence he adopts an empiricist's posture of doubt: "Credulity has done [mesmerism] worse service than incredulity" (12). Dickens wishes to do something similar—to suspend mesmerism's hypotheses in the formal operations of the novel: Is the appearance of Miss Havisham at the deathbed of her brother a hallucination produced by his bad conscience, in time-honored novelistic fashion, or is it literally a spectral emanation? For Townshend, the reality of spectral emanation might ultimately be proven, but in the novel, the difference between Pip's imagining the phenomenon and its independent reality is immaterial. Outside, in other discourses, Townshend vied for credibility with his detractors; both groups cited the evidence of controlled experiments and clinical observations, attempting to meet the criteria for scientific certitude. But in the novel, competing truth claims cease to compete; one entertains the possibilities both that Pip's imagination is overwrought and that it is accurately receiving a message projected from afar, for either is compatible with the foreshadowing technique, without trying to decide between them. Briefly put, in passages like these, the novel's usual encouragement of fluid movement among ontological levels becomes momentary permission to ignore them.

Dickens's novel, then, does not exactly conform itself to mesmerism or any of the various discourses that were redrawing the life-death boundaries; instead it uses their rhetoric of uncertainty to enhance its own range of suspended possibilities.[27] On the life-death boundary, the "maybes" were multiplying, and the novel, attracted by the resemblance to its own conditional mood, was drawn in that direction. The attraction, moreover, was mutual, for the status of the imaginary was a popular theme among those studying states of suspended animation and out-of-body vitality. Indeed, of all the possibilities abroad there, perhaps the most relevant to *Great Expectations* was the implication that *maybe* the products of the imagination are, in some sense, alive.

The work of yet another of Dickens's friends, Dr. John Elliotson, explicitly addresses the connection between suspended bodily processes and vigorous imaginings. Like Townshend, Elliotson was interested in states of "mesmeric" trance; but unlike Townshend, he dismissed all talk of migrating souls as so much claptrap. Elliotson's pristine materialism and empiricist integrity won him Dickens's deep respect; here was a professional scientist bravely confronting the brink of consciousness, even persecuted for his inquiries by his own profession, but who nevertheless maintained an adamant disbelief in all putatively supernatural phenomena. It was Elliotson who showed Dickens plaster casts of executed criminals, like those in Mr. Jaggers's office, and who assured him that the mesmeric trance was a workaday tool for learning about the nervous system. He doubted the existence of a vital fluid, insisting that it should be materially discoverable, for "is not fluid still matter?"[28] He rightly perceived that what passed for "supernaturalism" or even "spiritualism" was the spawn of materialism itself, and he maintained that mesmerism's limited results should be examined for their physiological significance.

Indeed, Elliotson managed to assimilate everything, even Christianity, into his materialist worldview. He went so far as to claim that the Bible, rightly read, holds that human immortality is not that of an immaterial soul, but the revived life of the resurrected body: "It is the peculiar doctrine of scripture, in distinction to that of most heathen philosophers and people, that the resurrection will be positively of *body*,—that in our *flesh* we shall see God" (47). In his standard textbook *Human Physiology*, he urges this form of materialism as orthodox Anglican doctrine, and cites Bishop Summer, Bishop Law, and William Paley in support of his contention that belief in an immortal soul is mere superstition, either pagan or Roman Catholic: "The heathen doctrine was grounded on the supposed inherent immortality of a supposed substance distinct from the body. The Christian doctrine teaches the resurrection of what we obviously are—*bodies*" (48). Modern enlightened Protestant Christians should accept Law's proof from Scripture that, "by the words *soul* and *spirit*, no immaterial, immortal principle in man is meant, but merely person, the superior and inferior mental faculties, living creature, &c.; by *death*, a total cessation of existence; by *the life hereafter,* a second *bodily* existence" (47). Although Elliotson seems to deprive the dead of that weird semilife with which materialism frequently invested them, his view nevertheless renders their state merely temporary, conceiving it as a gap, a syncope or pause in existence, a suspension of the being that was and will be a second time.

But Elliotson was certainly also fascinated by "apparent death," and his skeptical engagements with mesmerism convinced him that there were states of trance so deep that their subjects were entirely insensible. He relates several instances of self-induced suspension:

> My readers will remember the extraordinary, but unquestionable, case of colonel Townshend [no relation to Chauncy Hare Townshend], who some time before his death possessed the power of gradually reducing the action of his heart till it became imperceptible and for half an hour he appeared really dead. Bernier informs us that Indian Brahmins and Fakirs can throw themselves into somnambulism, and even teach the art. Cardanus professed to be able to place himself in ecstatic insensibility. St. Austin tells of a priest, named Restitutus, who could become insensible and lie like a dead man whenever he pleased, insensible of blows, punctures, burning. . . . (691–94)

His list ends with the case of a man in India who had himself buried alive for a month and when disinterred, "gradually recovered his senses and the use of the limbs." Always worried about seeming too credulous, Elliotson adds, "There may be after all some trick: but Cornet Macnaghten once suspended him for thirteen days in a close wooden box." He attributes mesmeric trance to "a *power* acting, I have no doubt, constantly in all living things, vegetable and animal" (685; emphasis added). Even for the hardnosed Elliotson, therefore, the concept of life as a generalized "power," as a pervasive potential, seems to depend on, as well as to imply, correlative states in which life processes are partially in abeyance.

And in these states, the imagination quickens; for when the "vital force" is not occupied in the animation of the body, it may all the more fully spend itself on mental activity divorced from the subject's immediate sensible surroundings. Suspension and trance, Elliotson thought, are on a continuum with normal sleep, and in describing the relation of bodily torpor to mental vividness that obtains in dreaming, he unfolds a general energetics of body and mind, which will help us understand how an imaginary being might be said to live.

Much of what Elliotson has to say about trance states comes in lengthy quotations from the phrenologist Francis Gall (who had divided the brain into various organs) describing the redirection of "life" in dreaming: "All the vital energy is concentrated on one organ, or upon a small number of organs, while others are in repose; so that the energy of the former becomes necessarily more energetic."[29] Elliotson frames his discussion as a rebuke to the purveyors of mesmeric "marvels"; recounting many of their stories simply to discredit them and many others to explore their probability in terms of his own understanding of the energetics of the body, he insists that the legitimate phenomena known as *sommeil lucid* can all be ascribed to the redistribution of the life force among the plurality of organs. To read him is to encounter the extensive calibrations of disbelief inspired by the phenomena of *sommeil lucid,* some of which are registered only in the subtlest ironic inflections:

> Dr. Haycock, Professor of Medicine at Oxford, would deliver a good sermon in his sleep; nor could all the pinching and pulling of his friends prevent him. (632)

Or,

> An American lady . . . preached during her sleep, performing regularly every part of the Presbyterian service, from the psalm to the blessing. . . . We know individuals who have heard her preach during the night in steam boats; and it was customary, at tea parties in New York . . . , to put the lady into bed in a room adjacent to the drawing-room, in order that the dilettanti might witness so extraordinary a phenomenon. (634)

But when it comes to stories of composing literary works in one's sleep, Elliotson believes them readily and recounts them soberly; he considers it completely plausible that the powers of literary creativity might "occasionally display more energy [in the sleeping] than in the waking state."[30] For if the brain is really a "plurality of organs," the inactivity of most of its functions in sleep would allow a surfeit of energy to those that do not require sensory input, such as fantasy and imagination: "We therefore cannot be astonished if some, like Augustus La Fontaine, make admirable verses in their sleep. . . ; if on waking in the morning some, like Franklin, find a work completed which had been projected on going to bed." Vividness of images and rapidity of conception, we are told, characterize mental activity in the dreaming state, but volition is usually dormant. Hence, writers themselves have had "superstitious notions" about the source of their increased creativity, attributing it to visitations of spirit, or "inspiration," instead of to the concentration of their own "animal life" in the appropriate organs. A properly skeptical, materialist, and (in Elliotson's version) Protestant investigator would explain that during the torpid state of most of the body's organs, the productions of the imagination become the peculiar repositories of an influx of actual organic life.

Such imaginary entities thus seem possessed of an independent life because their creators did not experience their creation; but there is another sense in which one might argue that they actually are alive, if life and the potential for life are one. They contain "life" not because, as superstitious people once believed, they are engendered by a deathless spirit or "soul," but rather because they are the results and receptacles of concentrated and rapidly expended animal energy, which remains accessible in them. For the more intense the energy invested in the imaginary product, the more automatically it will become an "exciting cause" of further organic activity. Of course, the same could be said, and was said, of any human creation; it "contains" the energy expended in its production. That insight underlay the nineteenth century's theory of value and stimulated a materialist, animistic vision of manufactured objects, known to Karl Marx as "commodity fetishism." But *imaginary* creations seemed particularly full of suspended vitality because their consumption duplicates their production. Reading or listening, once again the seemingly unwilled conceptions arise and our consciousness of our surroundings grows hazy. In contrast, although a horseshoe may get its value from the labor embodied in it, it doesn't stimulate a repetition of its making in its consumer. Because a similar state of passive activity seems attained in both the composition and the consumption of, for example, "Kubla Khan," the poem might be said to suspend, to hold *in potential,* the same string of involuntary images and the very state of mental excitation that obtained in the dreaming brain of Coleridge. Of all the bits of officially inanimate yet vital matter afloat in the materialist universe, the imaginative text, especially the text composed in a dormant state, was perhaps the liveliest.

Elliotson's physiological treatment of the imagination in the context of sleep, trance, and other states of bodily suspension attributed to imaginary things a literal life, and hence his relentless skepticism yielded similar results to Townshend's flightier speculations: both stretched the concept of life and temporarily overrode ontological barriers. They shared a common nineteenth-century energetics that sometimes made it difficult to distinguish, malgré Marx, between the products of the human mind and hand and independently living things. We can find episodes in *Great Expectations* that echo Elliotson's *Human Physiology.* For example, Elliotson discusses the activity of the imagination under the threat of death as a kind of waking dream in which

> we always conceive with an intensity equal to sensation,—an impossibility in the waking state, unless under extraordinary excitement. . . . Another instance of increased excitement . . . is the extreme rapidity of conception, so that a succession of events may be crowded into a dream which we are certain cannot have lasted more than a few moments—a rapidity which takes place in the waking state only under the strongest excitement, as in the fear of instant death.[31]

Compare Pip's description of his thoughts when he thinks himself about to die:

> It was not only that I could have summed up years and years and years while he said a dozen words, but that what [Orlick] did say presented pictures to me, and not mere words. In the excited and exalted state of my brain, I could not think of a place without seeing it, or of a person without seeing them. (405)

But specific instances of *Human Physiology*'s incorporation as a resource for describing Pip's mental processes seem less important than its more general scientific authorization to view the imagination as a life-giving organ and the imaginary work as the suspended vivacity of its author.

Although Dickens seems not to have written anything in his sleep, it is remarkable how often he himself and his contemporaries linked his writing to dreams, visions, states of delirium, even hallucination. In his last illness, he described himself writing through his prostration, "I don't invent it—really I do not—*but see it*, and write it down."[32] And two years after his death, George Henry Lewes explained that Dickens "was a seer of visions": "When he imagined a street, a house, a room, a figure, he saw it not in the vague schematic way of ordinary imagination, but in the sharp definition of actual perception, all the salient details obtruding themselves on his attention. He, seeing it thus vividly, made us also see it."[33]

And in this seeing, there is no need for believing. As Coleridge, *the* nineteenth-century expert on the imagination (Elliotson quotes him copiously), had long before explained, the involuntary nature of imagining makes belief unnecessary:

> It is laxly said that during sleep we take our dreams for realities, but this is irreconcilable with the nature of sleep, which consists in a suspension of the voluntary and, therefore, of the comparative power. The fact is that we pass no judgement either way: we simply do not judge them to be unreal, in consequence of which the images act on our minds, as far as they act at all, by their own force as images. Our state while we are dreaming differs from that in which we are in the perusal of a deeply interesting novel in the degree rather than in the kind.[34]

Because the images have "their own force," they do not require belief; they "act" without its permission. No amount of knowing that these creatures are imaginary can lessen their vivacity. Or, to put it another way, because they're virtually alive, you don't care whether or not they're real.

Lewes was among those who found the combined vitality and unreality of Dickens's works distressing. Like Elliotson, he was an empirical psychologist who assigned each mental function to a separate organ of the brain and seems to have thought that Dickens's imaginative organ was nothing short of pathological: "Dickens once declared to me that every word said by his characters was distinctly *heard* by him; I was at first not a little puzzled to account for the fact that he could hear language so utterly unlike the language of real feeling, and not be aware of its preposterousness; but the surprise vanished when I thought of the phenomena of hallucination."[35] The vivacity of Dickens's exaggerations created corresponding "hallucinations" in readers, Lewes maintained, finally displacing the actual experience of embodied people: "His types established themselves in the public mind like personal experiences. Their falsity was unnoticed in the blaze of their illumination. Every humbug seemed a Pecksniff, every jovial improvident a Micawber, every stinted serving-wench a Marchioness."[36] For Lewes, who favored more scientific modes of social categorization as well as more realistic modes of fiction, the automatic transfer of impressions from Dickens's inflamed imagination to the reader's blocks the normal perception of reality.

Lewes's complaint recalls Marx's assertion that we are victims of an imposture, that a secondary order of beings, mere fabrications, has passed itself off as the category of primary actors in the social world. Marx and Lewes articulate the sinister implications of the materialist invigoration of the universe: the more the inanimate comes alive, the more the living themselves seem subordinated to their own products. The hallucinations of the undead author, now permanently suspended and all too retrievable in his novels, displace the reader's "personal experience" and install themselves as organizing social categories, just as, Marx tells us, commodities supersede their makers in the marketplace. Both these visions arise inside the nineteenth-century discourse of social and biological energetics, which we've been exploring through the topic of suspended animation, and express the fear that society only comes alive as a distorted simulacrum, in a blaze of hallucinatory energy that casts its true outlines into the shadows. Lewes, however, seems more cognizant than Marx that inside the terms of this discourse, no amount of demystification can deprive these beings of their power, which derives not from their successful impersonation of reality, but from the energy invested in them. Requiring no belief, they are invulnerable to doubt and demystification.

The Undeath of the Wicked Son

And yet one might claim that Hamlet, that powerful imaginary being, is subjected to an extended farcical demystification in *Great Expectations*. One might even say that the grotesque performance of the play that Pip and Herbert attend tries to render *Hamlet* unreal compared to the novel. The represented performance could be seen as a foil designed to confer the illusion of reality on the novel's own preposterous (to use Lewes's word) representations. As such the play-within-the-novel could be said to function like Hamlet's own advice to the player, which is alluded to when Wopsle, the miscast Hamlet, recites the well-known recommendation that the player not saw the air, and a sulky man in the gallery shouts, "And don't you do it, neither; you're a deal worse than him!" The fact that Wopsle's elocution is "unlike any way in which any man in any natural circumstances of life or death ever expressed himself about anything" may make Dickens's expression ("so unlike the language of real feeling," according to Lewes) sound normal. Wopsle's stagy oddity might even lead a reader to pass over the narrator's own odd suggestion that someone in a "natural circumstance . . . of *death*" could express himself at all.

And yet the play-within-the-novel is more than a foil; it is also a measure of the distance between Hamlet's plot and Pip's, and as such it concedes the earlier work's priority and superior gravitas. We've pointed out that Pip, like Hamlet, is assigned the task of avenging a father—not, to be sure, his biological father, nor the blacksmith who has taken on the nurturing of Pip, but his social father, the man who has secretly made his social identity. This "filial" obligation, as we've also seen, is not at all like that imposed on Hamlet by his father. Hamlet has to murder his uncle; Pip ostensibly has only to assume a new class identity, for it is in making a gentleman that the despised outcast Magwitch seeks redress for his exclusion. There is, then, no tragic destiny for the hero of *Great Expectations,* and Dickens seems highly aware of the falseness—melodramatic exaggeration, sentimentality, sensationalism—that the note of Shakespearean tragedy would strike in this composition, so he explicitly repeats it here only as farcical satire, in which the audience refuses to observe the decorum of separation from the events on stage. Its constant interventions— advice tossed down from the gallery, along with nuts—destroy the possibility of elevation upon which tragedy depends. And the poverty of the illusion-making—the doubling (and tripling and quadrupling) of roles, the tawdriness of the actors, the inadequacy of the costumes and sets—emphasizes the incongruity between the tragic drama and this debased locale. "On our arrival in Denmark, we found the king and queen of that country elevated in two arm-chairs on a kitchen-table, holding a Court" (239), the episode begins, and the whole production seems continuous with the precinct of the kitchen, the scene of Pip's early tortures, the place from which he tried to escape and to which he will aspire when he asks Biddy to marry him in the extremity of his chastening.

As this description suggests, Shakespeare's play is not itself the object of the satire in this travesty; Pip's pretensions are certainly implicated, but those of the little theater company, especially those of its leading man, Mr. Wopsle, are the audience's, and the narrator's, main targets. Indeed, the Shakespearean text's utterly secure stature underwrites the comedy of incongruities. A settled familiarity with Shakespeare's tragic *Hamlet,* played straight or read seriously, is assumed for the purposes of farcical juxtaposition against this outlandish manifestation. Hence, the opening description of the king and queen in their kitchen-table elevation contains a delicious refusal either to stand within the well-known represented world of Shakespeare's play or to stand altogether outside it in the farcical ineptitude of the performance, a refusal also demonstrated by the audience's waggish charade of accepting the illusory premises: "On the question whether 'twas nobler in the mind to suffer, some roared yes, and some no, and some inclining to both opinions said 'toss up for it;' and quite a Debating Society arose. . . ." And again, "When [Wopsle] appeared with his stocking disordered . . . a conversation took place in the gallery respecting the paleness of his leg, and whether it was occasioned by the turn the ghost had given him" (240). Less knowingly, Joe finds himself caught between the play and the performance as he decries the audience's tendency "to be continiwally cutting in betwixt [Wopsle/Hamlet] and the Ghost with 'Amen!' . . . Which I meantersay, if the ghost of a man's own father cannot be allowed to claim his attention, what can, Sir?" (208–9). Wopsle, the former clerk in Pip's village church, who thought that his sonorous voice should entitle him to the ministry, does not make Hamlet seem ridiculous. His confusion of theatrical and liturgical performance ("Did you observe . . . that there was a man in the gallery who endeavoured to cast derision on the service—I mean, the representation?" [243]) leads him to intone both Shakespeare and the Psalms in a nonsensical singsong, but the joke is on Wopsle. Mouthing the words of Shakespeare, in however deep and loud a voice, does not result in an incarnation of the character, who remains an elusive referent, a contrasting memory.

The satire, therefore, strikes most obviously at upstart players, and perhaps by implication at the perils of dramatic representation in general:

> The late king of the country not only appeared to have been troubled with a cough at the time of his decease, but to have taken it with him to the tomb, and to have brought it back. . . . It was likewise to be noted of this majestic spirit that whereas it always appeared with an air of having been out a long time and walked an immense distance, it perceptibly came from a closely-contiguous wall. This occasioned its terrors to be received derisively. (239)

A long anti-theatrical tradition had instanced the difficulty of presenting Old Hamlet's ghost ("this fellow in the cellarage," as Hamlet himself quips) to prove the superiority of closet drama, which dispensed with the inconvenient foibles of representative bodies. The travesty hints that performances in general might be impediments, rather than aids, to illusion-making. To stay safely ensconced in the play, it implies, one might have to forego its embodiment. Hamlet lives vividly in the imagination despite

Wopsle, and many influential nineteenth-century writers argued that even the most competent thespian incarnation would be a pale reproduction of the images the text can present more directly to the mind's eye.

Is it stretching the point to discern in this failed attempt to incarnate the National Bard's vision, this boisterous incantation that reanimates nothing, yet more Victorian mockery of fetishism? The episode certainly combines some playful, competitive jostling of the ancestor, some acknowledgment of the tragic drama's greater profundity compared to the novel, some assurance that the ancestor survives even his most debased representations, and a suggestion that all performances are debasements. But the narrative concentration on physical trifles that are absurdly invested with deep significance also invokes the larger issue of how to activate the latent beings suspended in the culture. Mr. Wopsle's dresser, "a Jewish man with an unnatural smear of eyebrow," is a most determined fetishist, insisting that Hamlet comes alive mainly through the advantageous display of expensive stockings, and he is only one step further along in absurdity from Wopsle, who imagines that the depth of his voice insures the profundity of his Hamlet. Indeed, the collapse in Wopsle's mind of the church and the stage makes a kind of hocus-pocus out of his performance, especially when combined with the dresser's advice that he rehearse with wafers on his ankles to remind him to keep his stockings in full view: "The last Hamlet as I dressed, made the same mistakes in his reading at rehearsal, till I got him to put a large red wafer on each of his shins, and then at that rehearsal . . . I went in front, sir, to the back of the pit, and whenever his reading brought him into profile, I called out, 'I don't see no wafers!' And at night his reading was lovely" (243).

If this is partly a satire on fetishism, however, it would come very close to implicating Dickens's own artistic practice, for he had long been accused of a preposterous reliance on material trifles to trigger or express the most significant mental states. For example, in a passage that shares Karl Marx's disgust with the attribution of life and independent power to the inanimate, Hippolyte Taine repeats what was already a common complaint about Dickens's novels in 1856: "Living thoughts are controlled by inanimate things; . . . clouds, flowers, leaves, play their several parts; hardly a form of matter without a living quality; no silent thing without its voice."[37] Does the Hamlet farce point back to Dickens as a fetishist; does it give us Wopsle and his dresser as ridiculous versions of the novelist? Or does it instead attempt to distinguish between the novelist's method, which, we've claimed, invokes the vitality of matter and finds material locations for the imaginary, and some more archaic, prematerialist form of fetishization?

Of course it can be said to do both. The idiotic randomness of the things to which Wopsle and his dresser assign importance assures us by contrast that the novelist's associations are just; in the words of John Forster, defending Dickens against Taine's attack, Dickens's trifles evince a "feeling of the subtlest and most effective analogies, . . . from which is drawn the rare insight into the sympathies between the nature of things and their attributes."[38] The mistake of Wopsle and his dresser is not that they try to conjure with trivialities, but that they use the wrong ones; it is simply laughable to imagine a "true sympathy" between the nature of Hamlet and his socks (although, of course, that's just what the characters in *Hamlet* do). The Hamlet farce represents the failure to find the appropriate signs for the conveyance of an imaginary being; the fetishes are powerless to engage the vital impulse that might have been passed from mind to mind through other means. And yet the energy of Shakespeare's Hamlet seems to survive; apparently he remains untouched, neither entangled, enervated, nor degraded by matter that contains no "subtle analogy" to him.[39]

There can be, in other words, no *mousetrap* for Hamlet in this materialist universe. Since the creatures of the human mind are not spirits but degrees of mental energy with psychological and analogical, not metaphysical, relations to the sensory world, they cannot be captured and sidetracked into the "wrong" matter. If Hamlet is distantly referenced in this farce, the effect is one of comic incongruity, not sacrilegious distress. In this flattened ontological space, where everything is equally real and potentially alive, the energetic principle cannot be trapped and debased; ideational beings live in and through the physical, where they are utterly at home. In this sense, the Victorian's Hamlet is more independent and incorruptible than the Roman Catholic's Christ. Hamlet cannot get stuck in the wrong places; incarnation holds no terrors for him.

Hence, when Pip dreams that he must perform Hamlet, he imagines further that he plays opposite "Miss Havisham's Ghost"; the ambiguity of phrasing allows both the sense that the vengeful father has been replaced by the vengeful mother (that Pip encounters not the paternal injunction but some far more incoherent female plot) and the sense that the father's part is taken by the female actress ("Miss Havisham's Ghost" is like "Wopsle's Hamlet"). Although this incorporation of the father's idea by the woman's body seems connected to Pip's inability to play the part as written by Shakespeare (he dreams that they perform "before twenty-thousand people, without knowing twenty words of it"), assigning the part to Miss Havisham does not in itself seem any more absurd than assigning Hamlet to Pip (Miss Havisham's ghost is not like Wopsle's Hamlet). The casting is right for this phase of Pip's expectations and has even been anticipated on one of Pip's earliest visits to Miss Havisham's house, where he hears the mice "rattling behind the panels," as the wasted woman bitterly announces "sharper teeth than teeth of mice have gnawed at me" (82).[40] Even when a suitably masculine father enters the drama, the intermediacy of the feminine remains necessary to their relationship: Estella's paternity, not Pip's, becomes the mystery to be uncovered, and Pip learns, when he takes Magwitch for his foster father, that he had all along been a substitute for the convict's missing daughter. Pip's assignment is to find, not to obscure, the feminine connection.[41] The ease with which the father-son plot wends its way through various female figures demonstrates that there may still be something the matter with mothers in 1860, but that something is no longer matter itself.

But if materialism rendered *Hamlet*'s ontological issues obsolete, why do nineteenth-century materialists—from Auguste Comte to Karl Marx, from Hippolyte Taine to George Henry Lewes, from Charles Dickens to George Eliot—still harp on fetishism? One answer lies in the already-remarked resemblance between materialism and fetishism. When there are no ontological distinctions to insure a hierarchy of importance, one might fear slipping into a preoccupation with mere trivialities, be nervous about investing trinkets with significance, be alarmed at the difficulty of articulating the criteria of significance. Under these conditions, "fetishism" becomes a convenient scapegoat. Further, when life becomes potential life and is diffused throughout the physical universe, anti-fetishism blames the inability to tell the difference between living and inert objects on a primitive naïveté. By making fun of the fetishist's collapse of the very metaphysical differences they themselves had rendered untenable, the materialists reestablished ontological levels without taking responsibility for them. No wonder the discourse of fetishism appears alongside materialism. Fetishism, we might say, is materialism's leftover; the fetish haunts the materialist as the holy mouse turd haunts the Catholic. And just as in Protestantism where the attack on the Real Presence both saved and threatened the doctrine of the Incarnation, in materialism the denigration of fetishism both protects and imperils the ideology's central insights.

Does our generation's greater tolerance for fetishism signal the end of the wicked son's ascendancy? Probably not. Indeed, it would seem rather to indicate the thorough success of his logic, for the current widespread disenchantment with the project of ultimate demystification must be yet another manifestation of the skeptical impulse. His questioning may now sound more modest, less arrogantly self-assertive in some quarters. In others, though, he seems to have developed a cynical edge, as if proud that his questions are unanswerable. The fact that disbelief no longer needs a scapegoat like fetishism might, therefore, indicate a more comfortable self-sufficiency. The wicked son declares his independence from all ontologies, including materialism. Apparently unfazed by burgeoning religious revivals, and relieved of his earnest nineteenth-century "scientism" and his previous reliance on theoretical "foundations," the wicked son rolls complacently into the next millennium.

Introduction

1. The first editorial board was chaired by Svetlana Alpers and Stephen Greenblatt; it included Paul Alpers, R. Howard Bloch, Frances Ferguson, Joel Fineman, Catherine Gallagher, Denis Hollier, Lynn Hunt, Steven Knapp, Thomas Laqueur, Walter Michaels, Michael Rogin, and Randolph Starn. Two members of the preceding discussion group, Leo Bersani and D. A. Miller, declined to join the editorial board in the first years of the journal.

2. Johann Gottfried von Herder, *Reflections on the Philosophy of the History of Mankind*, ed. Frank E. Manuel, trans. T. O. Churchill (Chicago: University of Chicago Press, 1968), p. 58.

3. Herder's historicism abjures the attempt to find the optimal climate for civilization, but it by no means eschews the strong environmentalism characteristic of social theorists who regarded the organic structure of a society as intimately bound up with adaptation to a particular place. Hence, he argues, the warmer regions of the East stimulate early and extremely intense sexual desire, leading to early marriages and hence to the subjugation of women, which in turn leads to licentiousness and hence to the warped fertility that creates a disproportionate number of female babies, and hence to polygamy, and so on. Herder, *Reflections on the Philosophy of the History of Mankind*, pp. 62ff.

4. Johann Gottfried von Herder, *Against Pure Reason: Writings on Religion, Language, and History*, trans. and ed. Marcia Bunge (Minneapolis: Fortress Press, 1993), p. 50.

5. Herder, *Reflections on the Philosophy of the History of Mankind*, p. 91.

6. Herder, *Against Pure Reason*, p. 51.

7. Herder, *Reflections on the Philosophy of the History of Mankind*, p. 59.

8. Herder, *Against Pure Reason*, p. 43.

9. Herder, *Against Pure Reason*, p. 143.

10. Herder, *Against Pure Reason*, p. 151.

11. Herder, *Against Pure Reason,* p. 151.

12. Ezra Pound, "I Gather the Limbs of Osiris," *New Age* (1911–12); we owe this reference to Andrew Lawson. William Carlos Williams, *In the American Grain* (New York: New Directions, 1956), p. v.

Chapter One

1. Clifford Geertz, "Thick Description: Toward an Interpretive Theory of Culture," in *The Interpretation of Cultures* (New York: Basic Books, 1973), p. 9.

2. The promise is conveyed, among other means, by such features as the changed typeface (used, in the case of such a long excerpt, instead of quotation marks) and the brackets that denote the writer's scrupulosity in signaling any additions or alterations to what he had originally written in his journal: "The French [the informant said] had only just arrived." Such printing conventions do a considerable amount of work in establishing the particular nature of the piece of writing.

3. Gilbert Ryle, "Thinking and Reflecting" and "The Thinking of Thoughts: What Is 'Le Penseur' Doing?" in *Collected Papers,* vol. 2 of *Collected Essays, 1929–1968* (London: Hutchinson, 1971), pp. 465–96.

4. For a critique, from the standpoint of social science, of Geertz's way of suggesting the vital presence in the cultural texts themselves of their range of meanings, see Mark A. Schneider, *Culture and Enchantment* (Chicago: University of Chicago Press, 1993), pp. 55–82.

5. "Ideology as a Cultural System," in Geertz, *The Interpretation of Cultures,* p. 208.

6. *1 Henry IV,* 3.1.51–53. All citations to Shakespeare are from *The Norton Shakespeare,* ed. Stephen Greenblatt et al. (New York: W. W. Norton & Company, 1997).

7. It is not the case that Flaubert's novel lacks ethnographic interest, but the level of self-conscious mediation is completely different from what we hope to find in a native informant's narrative.

8. Erich Auerbach, *Mimesis: The Representation of Reality in Western Literature,* trans. Willard R. Trask (Princeton: Princeton University Press, 1953), p. 3.

9. The first German edition had one less chapter, but in the English edition Auerbach added a chapter on *Don Quixote.*

10. *Mimesis* puts in the largest possible frame perceptions that had obsessed Auerbach for his entire career and had been articulated both in his 1929 study of Dante, *Dante als Dichter der irdischen Welt,* and his crucially important 1944 essay "Figura."

11. Auerbach does, however, imply at times that European techniques of representation did in fact "advance" toward an ever greater power: "The inner history of the last thousand years is the history of mankind achieving self-expression: this is what philology, a historicist discipline, treats.

This history contains the records of man's mighty, adventurous advance to a consciousness of his human condition and to the realization of his given potential: and this advance, whose final goal (even in its wholly fragmentary present form) was barely imaginable for a long time, still seems to have proceeded as if according to a plan, in spite of its twisted course." In "Philology and *Weltliteratur*," trans. Marie and Edward Said, *Centennial Review* (1969): 5.

12. See discussion of this point in Luiz Costa Lima, *The Dark Side of Reason: Fictionality and Power*, trans. Paulo Henriques Britto (Stanford: Stanford University Press, 1992), pp. 483–84.

13. Karlheinz Barck, "Walter Benjamin and Erich Auerbach: Fragments of a Correspondence," *Diacritics* 22 (1992): 82.

Chapter Two

1. In *The Postmodern Condition: A Report on Knowledge* (trans. Geoff Bennington and Brian Massumi [Minneapolis: University of Minnesota Press, 1988]), Jean-François Lyotard counterpoised the *petits récits* of postmodernism to the historical *grands récits* of modernity. David Simpson, in *The Academic Postmodern and the Rule of Literature: A Report on Half-Knowledge* (Chicago: University of Chicago Press, 1995), demonstrates that the desire to forestall totalizing historical systems by telling anecdotes lies at the root of the discourse that differentiates itself as the "literary" in the eighteenth century (41–71).

2. Joel Fineman, "The History of the Anecdote," in *The New Historicism*, ed. H. Aram Veeser (New York: Routledge, 1989), p. 61.

3. Roland Barthes, "The Discourse of History," trans. and intro. Stephen Bann, *Comparative Criticism: A Yearbook* 3 (1981): 3–20. The essay was first published in *Social Science Information* in 1967.

4. Amos Funkenstein gives a concise history of counterhistory as "the systematic exploitation of the adversary's most trusted sources against their grain" in his essay "History, Counterhistory, and Narrative" in *Probing the Limits of Representation: Nazism and the "Final Solution,"* ed. Saul Friedlander (Cambridge: Harvard University Press, 1992), pp. 66–81. He gives a fuller account in chapter 4 of *Theology and the Scientific Imagination from the Middle Ages to the Seventeenth Century* (Princeton: Princeton University Press, 1986), where he cites Walter Benjamin's use of the phrase "to brush history against the grain." Benjamin is discussing the task of the "historical materialist," but many of his "Theses on the Philosophy of History" would fit our conception of counterhistory. See Walter Benjamin, *Illuminations*, ed. and intro. Hannah Arendt, trans. Harry Zohn (London: Jonathan Cape, 1970), pp. 255–66. We are indebted to these essays, which make a connection between Marxism and counterhistory. We are expanding the term even further here to include anti-narrative historical studies, skeptical metahistorical work (such as that of Paul Veyne, Michel de

Certeau, and Hayden White), radical "history from below," and counter-factual history.

5. See especially Funkenstein's *Theology and the Scientific Imagination*, pp. 273–89. For an alternative account of the professionalization of history, see Anthony Grafton's *The Footnote: A Curious History* (Cambridge: Harvard University Press, 1997).

6. See, for example, Robert W. Fogel's *Railroads and American Economic Growth: Essays in Econometric History* (Baltimore: Johns Hopkins, 1964).

7. While continuing to consider himself a Marxist, Thompson left the British Communist Party in 1956, after complaining that it encouraged foregone conclusions in historical analysis: historians were being asked "to make 'correct formulations' within a schematized system of doctrine, rather than to return again and again to social realities." Quoted in Dennis Dworkin, *Cultural Marxism in Postwar Britain: History, the New Left, and the Origins of Cultural Studies* (Durham, N.C.: Duke University Press, 1997), p. 49. Dworkin's book gives an overview of Thompson's dissatisfaction with British determinist Marxist orthodoxy and his later more public battle against Althusserianism.

8. E. P. Thompson, *The Making of the English Working Class* (London: V. Gollancz, 1963), pp. 12–13.

9. From "Interview with Edward Thompson," *RHR* (1976): 15.

10. Quoted in E. P. Thompson, "The Crime of Anonymity," *Albion's Fatal Tree: Crime and Society in Eighteenth-Century England* (New York: Pantheon Books, 1975), p. 256.

11. Thompson, *The Making of the English Working Class*, p. 13.

12. The two essays in question are "The Moral Economy of the English Crowd in the Eighteenth Century" and "The Moral Economy Reviewed," in *Customs in Common: Studies in Traditional Popular Culture* (New York: New Press, 1993), pp. 185–351. The first of these essays was originally published in 1971.

13. Isaac D'Israeli is usually credited with inventing the genre of alternate history in his essay "The History of Events that Never Happened," *Curiosities of Literature* (1791–93; reprint, New York: Garland, 1971).

14. Sally Alexander, "Women, Class and Sexual Differences in the 1830s and 1840s: Some Reflections on the Writing of a Feminist History," *History Workshop* 17 (spring 1984): 127.

15. Paul Hirst, *Economy and Society*, I, 1972, quoted in "Editorial," *History Workshop* (no. 6, 1978): 3.

16. Raymond Williams, *Politics and Letters* (New York: Schocken Books, 1979), p. 168.

17. Ibid., p. 142.

18. Raymond Williams, "Lucien Goldmann and Marxism's Alternative Tradition," *The Listener* 89 (23 March 1972): 375–76. For an overview of Williams's relation to Marxism, see John Higgins, *Raymond Williams:*

Literature, Marxism, and Cultural Materialism (New York: Routledge, 1999).

19. Joan W. Scott took both E. P. Thompson and Raymond Williams to task for grounding their histories in reports of prereflective experience and recommended that historians should instead focus "on processes of identity construction." "The Evidence of Experience," *Critical Inquiry* 17 (no. 4, summer 1985): 797. Williams, however, conceived of "experience" as a fugitive and problematic phenomenon, rather than as a bedrock of identity. For an account of nonfoundationalist concepts of "experience," see Martin Jay's "The Limits of Limit Experience: Bataille and Foucault," *Cultural Semantics: Keywords of Our Time* (University of Massachusetts Press, 1998), pp. 62–78.

20. Williams, *Politics and Letters*, p. 168.

21. Raymond Williams, *The Long Revolution* (New York: Columbia University Press, 1961), p. 73.

22. Raymond Williams, *Writing in Society* (London: Verso, 1984), pp. 162–63.

23. English translation published in *Michel Foucault: Power, Truth, Strategy*, eds. Meaghan Morris and Paul Patton (Sydney: Feral Publications, 1979), pp. 76–91. The piece was originally published in *Les Cahiers du chemin* 29 (15 January 1977): 12–29. We are grateful to Christopher Nealon for bringing this essay to our attention.

24. Michel Foucault, *The Order of Things; an Archaeology of the Human Sciences* (translation of *Les Mots et les choses*) (New York: Random House, 1973), p. xv.

25. James Miller, in *The Passion of Michel Foucault* (New York: Simon & Schuster, 1993), makes "limit-experience" the key to understanding Foucault's life and work. For a discussion of "experience" and French poststructuralists, see Martin Jay, "The Limits of Limit-Experience: Bataille and Foucault."

Chapter Three

1. In a response to this paper (Center for Hermeneutical Studies, May 1995), Harry Berger Jr. notes that, perhaps in response to Uccello, Joos "restores the standard tipped-up Flemish ground plan that implies a high viewing point bird's-eye view, and that also resists the drive into deep space by bringing—bending—the higher, putatively more distant objects toward the picture plane, as if for better viewing." The effect, Berger suggests, is at once to allow the viewer extraordinary access and to maintain a certain distance: "opening, showing all, inviting the eye in to travel around only loosely constrained by perspective effects—but making it hard for you to imagine yourself walking in—or able to walk in and stand." Not all the figures in the painting, however, submit to the same scheme and hence are seen from above. As Berger notes, the witnesses, the patron and his group, are "foreshortened a little so as to imply a lower viewing point—i.e., you

see them from below." This shift perhaps implies a slight invitation to the viewer to imagine himself or herself in this group, though not one of the apostles who are taking Communion directly from Christ.

2. John E. Booty, *John Jewel as Apologist of the Church of England* (London: SPCK, 1963), p. 152.

3. Marilyn Aronberg Lavin, "The Altar of Corpus Domini in Urbino: Paolo Uccello, Joos Van Gent, Piero della Francesa," *Art Bulletin* 49 (1967): 1–24.

4. For the relation in altarpieces between historical time and eternal truths of Christian doctrine, see Lotte Brand Philip, *The Ghent Altarpiece and the Art of Jan van Eyck* (Princeton: Princeton University Press, 1971), pp. 167–68. In an altarpiece, Philip observes, Christ had to be present both as sacrificing priest and as sacrifice (cf. the discussion of the representation of the lamb in the upper and lower panels in Gent, 62ff.). Philip (62n.) cites Aquinas: "Sacerdos gerit imaginem Christi, in cuius persona et virtute verba pronuntiat ad consecrandum. . . . Et ita quodammodo idem est sacerdos et hostia" (*Summa* III, 83, 1–3).

5. Thomas Cranmer, *A Defence of the True and Catholick Doctrine of the Sacrament* (London, 1550) in *The Work of Thomas Cranmer*, ed. G. E. Duffield (Philadelphia: Fortress Press, 1965), p. 145.

6. Anna Padoa Rizzo observes that the duchess (Battista Sforza) was herself involved in the creation at Urbino of a Monte di Pietà, which was in turn linked to the anti-Semitic rhetoric of Uccello's predella and possibly of Joos van Gent's main panel. *Paolo Uccello* (Firenze: Cantini, 1991), pp. 111–17.

7. The itinerant friars encouraged the Holy Week *sassaiola*, the traditional stoning of Jewish houses at the close of the Easter procession. See Ariel Toaff, *Love, Work, and Death: Jewish Life in Medieval Umbria*, trans. Judith Landry (London: Vallentine Mitchell & Co., 1996), pp. 179–86. They also generally called for enforcement of the so-called "badge for Jews"—a circle of yellow cloth for men, to be attached to the left-hand side of the garment, above the belt, and circular earrings for women. See Diane Owen Hughes, "Distinguishing Signs: Ear-Rings, Jews, and Franciscan Rhetoric in the Italian Renaissance City," *Past and Present* 112 (1986): 3–59. In the Uccello predella, discussed below, the Jewish man is not wearing the badge, but his wife's headscarf may have signaled Jewishness, since a yellow veil was introduced at approximately this time as a substitute for the distinctive earrings. See Jeremy Cohen, *The Friars and the Jews: The Evolution of Medieval Anti-Judaism* (Ithaca: Cornell University Press, 1982). For papal policy, see Shlomo Simonsohn, *The Apostolic See and the Jews*, 3 vols. (Toronto: Pontifical Institute of Mediaeval Studies, 1988–1990).

8. In the ewer and basin on the floor there is, it seems, a further narrative allusion, to the washing of the disciples' feet.

9. Lavin, "The Altar of Corpus Domini in Urbino," p. 13.

10. Lavin, "The Altar of Corpus Domini in Urbino," p. 16.

11. Part of the pleasure and interest of the invitation is that there can be competing or overlapping meanings: in England, according to Eamon Duffy, the High Mass began with "an elaborate procession round the church, at the commencement of which salt and water were solemnly exorcised, blessed, and mixed," while at its end a loaf of bread presented by one of the parishioners was blessed, cut up, and distributed to the congregation. Eamon Duffy, *The Stripping of the Altars: Traditional Religion in England, 1400–1580* (New Haven: Yale University Press, 1992), pp. 124–25. It is at least possible that these ceremonies had their equivalents in Italy and were reflected in the salt, water, and bread on the left-hand side of the table. Such meanings would not be incompatible with an allusion to the Jewish sacrificial meal, but would pull in a different direction, away from Isaac, as it were, and toward Sixtus.

12. Baldesar Castiglione, *The Book of the Courtier*, trans. Charles Singleton (New York: Doubleday, 1959), p. 357.

13. Anna Padoa Rizzo rejects Pope-Hennessy's hypothesis that Uccello lost the commission for the main panel after his work was criticized; rather, she suggests, he was recalled to Florence, necessitating that the painting of the main panel be done by Joos van Gent (and, she argues, by Piero della Francesca [111–17]). The influence, if not the direct involvement, of Piero is suggested by Mario Salmi, *Paolo Uccello, Andrea del Castagno, Domenico Veneziano*, trans. Jean Chuzeville (Paris: Weber, 1937), p. 38.

14. Lavin, "The Altar of Corpus Domini in Urbino," p. 3.

15. In *Outcasts: Signs of Otherness in Northern European Art of the Late Middle Ages*, 2 vols. (Berkeley: University of California Press, 1994), Ruth Melinkoff gives several images of the Last Supper that show Christ feeding the wafers to his disciples: a Passion Altar by Master Bertram (late fourteenth century), Hanover, Niedersächsisches Landesmuseum Landesgalerie; Kings College Chapel; Jörg Ratgeb (c. 1500–1510), Rotterdam Museum, Boymans-van Beuningen.

16. John Frith, *A Christen Sentence*, appendix C in Thomas More, *Letter to Bugenhagen; Supplication of Souls; Letter Against Frith*, in *The Complete Works of St. Thomas More*, ed. Frank Manley et al. (New Haven: Yale University Press, 1990), 7:429.

17. For an example of the complexity of the doctrinal response to the objection that an incarnate body could not violate the laws of physics, see Thomas More's *Letter Against Frith*, in *The Complete Works*, 7:249ff.

18. See Charles Ziha, "Hosts, Processions and Pilgrimages in Fifteenth-Century Germany," *Past and Present* 118 (1988): 48ff. Cf. Peter Browe, *Die eucharistichen Wunder des Mittelalters* (Breslau, 1938), esp. p. 56 n. 53 and p. 157.

19. In a critique of this paper at the Center for Hermeneutical Studies, Deborah Shuger argues that this distinction is the whole point of Uccello's panel, which she associates with the humanist attack on medieval credulity.

20. For an account challenging the popular origins of anti-Semitism in the earlier Middle Ages, see R. I. Moore, *The Formation of a Persecuting Society: Power and Deviance in Western Europe, 950–1250* (Oxford: Basil Blackwell, 1987).

21. The positions could be in tension even in the rhetoric of an individual preacher. Hence, for example, Bernardino of Siena begins by speaking against usurers in general, not against Jews in particular, but as he warms to his subject, the condemnation becomes more pointed and more extreme: "Il denaro è il calore vitale di una città. Gli usurai sono sanguisughe che si applicano con delizia a divorare un membro malato, dal quale succhiano il sangue con insaziabile ardore. Quando il sangue e il calore abbandonano la estremità del corpo per fluire al cuore, è il segno della prossima morte. Ma il pericolo è piu incalzante quando le ricchezze di una città sono nelle mani degli ebrei. Allora il calore non ha più il suo normale corso verso il cuore. Come nella peste, si dirige verso il membro malato del corpo; poiché ogni ebro, sopprattutto quanto è prestatore, e nemico capitale cristiano." ("Money is a city's vital heat. Usurers are leeches that apply themselves with delight to devour a sick limb from which with insatiable ardor they suck the blood. When blood and heat abandon the extremities of the body in order to flow toward the heart, it is a sign that death is near. But the danger is greater when a city's riches are in the hands of the Jews. For then the vital heat no longer has its normal course toward the heart. As in cases of plague, it flows toward the sick limbs of the body. Therefore every Jew, above all the Jewish moneylender, is a Christian's mortal enemy.") Quoted in Robert Bonfil, *Gli ebrei in Italia nell'epoca del Rinascimento* (Firenze; Sansoni, 1991), p. 27.

22. The soldiers wear contemporary costumes but have "S.P.Q.R." on their shields and standards. Lavin suggests that the insignia gives them an air of "antiquity" (the miracle had, after all, taken place more than a century before), while another interpreter proposes that it gives them an "Italian" rather than "French" identity (Pierre Francastel, in Lavin, "The Altar of Corpus Domini in Urbino," p. 7).

23. As Berger has pointed out to us, the light that floods into the room seems to come—can only come—from the opening made by removing the wall.

24. Caroline Walker Bynum, *Holy Feast and Holy Fast* (Berkeley: University of California Press, 1987), p. 67.

25. The story is attributed to "I. Markes Iesuite, in a book of his written of late, and intituled, The Examination of the new Religion, page 128" and is cited in John Gee, *The Foot out of the Snare: with a Detection of Svndry Late Practices and Impostures of the Priests and Iesuits in England* . . . (London: Printed by H. L. for Robert Milbourne, 1624), pp. 28–29.

26. In *Les Intellectuels chrétiens et les juifs au Moyen Âge* (Paris: Cerf, 1990), Gilbert Dahan observes that Host desecration is strictly parallel to

charges of ritual murder and was regarded as a greater crime: "la répétition de la Passion se faisant alors non par l'intermédiaire d'un homme,
c'est-à-dire l'image de Dieu, mais pour ainsi dire directement dans la chair
même de Dieu, matérialisée sous les espèces de l'hostie" (27). (In the context of our analysis, it is particularly worth noting the complex play here
on representation or image and 'direct' reality—namely, the bread!)
Dahan cites as prehistory the ruling at the Fourth Lateran Council by
Innocent III against the "abominable acts" committed by Jews with their
Christian wet nurses: when the latter have had Communion, the Jews
make them throw away their milk for three days: "Henri de Suse nous
explique qu'ainsi les juifs comprennent que le Corps du Christ s'est diffusé
dans les organes des nourrices. Ils croient donc eux aussi en la trans-
substantiation et cela à la fois explique leur comportement, quand ils se
vengent sur les hosties consacrées, et souligne la gravité de leurs actes,
puisque c'est véritablement Dieu qu'ils attaquent" (28).

27. Protestants cited instances when such bleeding was not accidental:
"Anno 36 of Henry the Eighth, a Priest did pronounce at Pauls Crosse,
and there confessed in publick, that hee himselfe saying Masse, pricked
his finger, and bebloudied the Corporas with the Altar-clothes, purposing
to make the people beleeue, that the Host had bled miraculously." Gee,
The Foot out of the Snare, p. 42.

28. For the relation between Jewish unbelief and Jewish doubt, see the
problem addressed in a quodlibet by Henri de Gand: "Utrum Iudaeus
pungens hostiam consecratam, qui videns sanguine emergente ex puncturis
ipsam rubescere et viso miraculo conuertitur et baptizatur, debeat pro isto
delicto puniri a iustitia publica." ("If a Jew stabs a consecrated host and,
seeing that it reddens with blood flowing from its wounds, converts and is
baptized in response to the miracle, should he be punished by public justice for his crime?") Henri's second argument in favor of punishment
hinges on whether Jews could be expected to punish such a person: "Nisi
Iudaeus iste super dicto facto punietur a public iustitia secundum legem
Christianam, tunc maleficium illud maneret impunitum, quia Iudaei non
punient illud secundum legem suam." Henri de Gand, *Quodl* XIV, q. 15,
ed. de Paris 1518, ff. 470v–472v, quoted in Dahan, *Les Intellectuels chrétiens*, p. 105.

29. In the most careful account of the painting, Lavin (7) refers to the
passage as a hole, though the term does not seem entirely accurate.

30. In *Pictures and Punishment: Art and Criminal Prosecution during the
Florentine Renaissance* (Ithaca: Cornell University Press, 1985), Samuel Y.
Edgerton Jr. remarks of this scene: "In spite of the painter's almost whim-
sical style, we detect in this and his other scenes of the story a peculiar
sympathy for the unfortunate Jews, an attitude perhaps stirred in him by
firsthand confrontation with the actual horror of the similar event in Florence" (148). Not all observers detect this peculiar sympathy. Mary Pitta-
luga, for example, suggests that Uccello's exquisite use of color—his

"pure, fantastic effervescence"—in these scenes effaces any anxiety that the scene might otherwise arouse (*Paolo Uccello* [Roma: Tumminelli, 1946], p. 19); and the claim that the violence is entirely aestheticized is seconded by Franco and Stefano Borsi: "Even in the scenes showing the hanging and burning at the stake, the composition's balance and the elegance of the knights and their standards create an atmosphere more akin to a tournament" (*Paolo Uccello*, trans. Elfreda Powell [New York: Harry Abrams, 1994], p. 260).

31. On the worsening situation of Jews in northern Italy in the late fifteenth century, see Attilio Milano, *Storia degli ebrei in Italia* (Torino: Einaudi, 1963), esp. pp. 197ff. On Jewish banking in Urbino, see Gino Luzzatto, *I Banchieri ebrei in Urbino nell'età ducale* (Padova: Arnaldo Forni, 1902). Particular attention should be paid to the repercussions for Jews of the charges of ritual murder made in the city of Trent in 1475 by Bernardino of Feltre. See R. Po-Chai Hsia, *Trent 1475: Stories of a Ritual Murder Trial* (New Haven: Yale University Press, 1992).

32. For an illuminating formal and doctrinal analysis of a eucharistic altarpiece, see Aloys Butzkamm, *Bild und Frömmigkeit im 15. Jahrhundert: Der Sakramentsaltar von Dieric Bouts in der St.-Peters-Kirche zu Löwen* (Paderborn: Bonifatius, 1990). Margaret D. Carroll has a suggestive analysis of the relation between a painting's formal design and anti-Semitic ideology in "Dürer's *Christ among the Doctors* Re-examined," in *Shop Talk: Studies in Honor of Seymour Slive* (Cambridge: Harvard University Press, 1995), pp. 49–54.

33. See, for example, Hasdai Crescas, *The Refutation of the Christian Principles* (c. 1398), trans. Daniel Lasker (Albany: State University of New York Press, 1992): "Jeremiah has already said: 'Can a man make gods for himself? No gods are they!' And they make him every day. There is no difference between making him by hand or by word, since their priests believe that they make God by word when they say, 'This is my body; this is my blood'" (61). See also Daham, *Les Intellectuel chrétiens;* and D. Berger, *The Jewish-Christian Debate in the High Middle Ages: A Critical Edition of the Nizzahon Vetus* (Philadelphia: Jewish Publication Society of America, 1979), p. 225.

Chapter Four

1. This debate is discussed at length in Redcliffe N. Salaman's *The History and Social Influence of the Potato* (Cambridge: Cambridge University Press, 1949). Salaman's book is an unsurpassed achievement, and much of the evidence for our own, much quirkier, analysis comes from its pages.

2. The kind of body history referred to here began appearing in Europe and the United States in the 1960s. Drawing on medical and scientific history, the histories of sex, gender, and corporeal political discourse; of disciplinary institutions; of the family, food, exercise, sport, and work,

these histories demonstrate that the body has not only been perceived, interpreted, and represented differently in different times, but also that it has been lived differently. Examples include Michel Foucault's *The History of Sexuality*, trans. Robert Hurley (New York: Pantheon Books, 1978–1986); Barbara Duden's *The Woman Beneath the Skin: A Doctor's Patients in Eighteenth-Century Germany*, trans. Thomas Dunlap (Cambridge: Harvard University Press, 1991); and Thomas Laqueur's *Making Sex: Body and Gender from the Greeks to Freud* (Cambridge: Harvard University Press, 1990). See also these collections: Catherine Gallagher and Thomas Laqueur, eds., *The Making of the Modern Body: Sexuality and Society in the Nineteenth Century* (Berkeley: University of California Press, 1987); Michel Feher, Ramona Naddaff, and Nadia Tazi, eds., *Fragments for a History of the Human Body*, 3 vols. (New York: Zone Books, 1989).

3. Raymond Williams, *The Sociology of Culture* (New York: Schocken, 1982), pp. 209–10.

4. Biologists, by the way, no longer categorize the part of the potato plant we eat as a "root," but rather as a fleshy underground stem.

5. *Cobbett in Ireland: A Warning to England*, ed. Denis Knight (London: Lawrence and Wishert, 1984), p. 82.

6. John Houghton, *Houghton's Collection*, vol. II, p. 469. Quoted also in Salaman, *The History and Social Influence of the Potato*, p. 150.

7. Salaman thinks that, nevertheless, expeditions sponsored by Raleigh might have collected potato specimens that could have ended up on Raleigh's Irish estates.

8. Arthur Young, *A Tour in Ireland*, II (London, 1780), p. 23.

9. Arthur Young, *The Question of Scarcity Plainly Stated and Remedies Considered* (London: McMillan, 1800), p. 79.

10. E. P. Thompson, "The Moral Economy of the Crowd," in *Customs in Common: Studies in Traditional and Popular Culture* (New York: New Press, 1991), pp. 185–258. This quotation is from p. 188.

11. See Thompson, "The Moral Economy of the Crowd," p. 191 n. 5.

12. Thompson, "The Moral Economy of the Crowd," p. 193.

13. Young, *The Question of Scarcity*, p. 77.

14. The phrase comes from an anonymous poem of 1800; quoted in Thompson, "The Moral Economy of the Crowd," p. 232.

15. If by the 1830s the "cash nexus" had replaced the "bread nexus" as the central mechanism linking and creating conflict between country and city, laborers and governors, proletariat and bourgeois, and the moral economy was therefore merely a nostalgic memory, the bread nexus was nonetheless still a powerful ideal image of how things should be, which stood starkly opposed to the assumptions underlying the utilitarians' reform legislation. Hence, although it may be somewhat anachronistic to use Cobbett's potato rants as outbursts of the mentality of the food rioters of 1795, the anachronism throws into relief the threat that the tuber posed to "the moral economy of the crowd."

16. Thomas Malthus, *An Essay on Population,* I (1806; reprint, New York: E. P. Dutton & Co., 1967), p. 228.

17. Francis Place, *Illustrations and Proofs of the Principle of Population: Including an Examination of the Proposed Remedies of Mr. Malthus, and Reply to the Objections of Mr. Godwin and Others* (1822; reprint, London: George Allen and Unwin Ltd., 1967), p. 265.

18. Malthus, *An Essay on Population,* p. 230 n. 1.

19. "Ricardo to Miss Edgeworth. Bromesberrow Place, Ledbury, December 13th, 1822." Printed in *The Economic Journal. The Journal of the Royal Economic Society* xvii (1907): 433.

20. Malthus, *An Essay on Population,* p. 232.

21. Malthus, *An Essay on Population,* p. 232.

Chapter Five

1. The midrash is now genially revised in many contemporary Haggadoth to include daughters and mothers, but since this paper is about historical memory, it would seem misleading to do so here.

2. Similarly, it hears in the wise son's words "the Lord our God" the crucial recognition of participation.

3. Of course the child who reads the part of the wicked son is not refusing the supper but participating in the Seder, and indeed the character of the wicked son is himself participating, for his imagined self-exclusion enables the father to insist upon his own personal identification with the ancient events, an identification that would otherwise not be adequately marked. In this sense, the wicked son is essential to the reenactment, not despite but because he so clearly marks the fact that the events of the enslavement and liberation are in the past. If the present had genuinely collapsed into the past, there would be no place to ask the question of participation and meaning.

4. Dom Gregory Dix, among others, argues that the Eucharist was instituted not at a Passover Seder but at the formal supper on the night before the first Seder: "Our Lord instituted the eucharist at a supper with His disciples which was probably *not* the Passover supper of that year, but the evening meal twenty-four hours before the actual Passover. On this S. John appears to contradict the other three gospels, and it seems that S. John is right. Nevertheless, from what occurred at it and from the way in which it was regarded by the primitive jewish christian church it is evident that the last supper was a jewish religious meal, of some kind. The type to which it best conforms is the formal supper of a *chabiarah.*" Dom Gregory Dix, *The Shape of the Liturgy* (Westminster: Dacre Press, n.d.), p. 50. According to Anthony Grafton, the first modern scholar to recognize that the Eucharist originated in a Passover Seder was the Dutch Protestant philologist and historian Joseph Justus Scaliger. Scaliger analyzes the Haggadah, showing that the oldest elements are "This is the bread of

affliction" and "Next year in Jerusalem," and observing that the presence of the latter means that the Haggadah postdates the destruction of the Temple and hence is not identical to any ceremony that Jesus himself would have participated in.

5. In Sephardic communities it is customary for the father of the household actually to place the dish on the head of one of his children.

6. This anecdote is sometimes associated with Roman persecutions and the legendary martyrdom of Rabbi Akiba.

7. One telling measure of its radicalism is its effect on the medieval Jewish observance of the Passover: for centuries European Jews did not dare to drink red wine at the Seder for fear of the Blood Libel, the fatal accusation that they killed Christian children in order to drink their blood and bake their flesh into matzoth.

8. "He is present as a house is in a lease"; see Roger Hutchinson, *Works*, ed. Jo. Bruce (London: Parker Society, 1842), p. 251.

9. Thomas Becon, "The Jewel of Joy," *The Catechism of Thomas Becon*, ed. John Ayre (Cambridge: Parker Society, 1844), 2:453.

10. Miri Rubin, *Corpus Christi: The Eucharist in Late Medieval Culture* (Cambridge: Cambridge University Press, 1991), p. 288.

11. See Montaigne: "Most of the occasions for the troubles of the world are grammatical. Our lawsuits spring only from debate over the interpretation of the laws, and most of our wars from the inability to express clearly the conventions and treaties of agreement of princes. How many quarrels, and how important, have been produced in the world by doubt of the meaning of that syllable *Hoc!*" "Apology for Raymond Sebond," in *The Complete Essays of Montaigne*, trans. Donald Frame (Stanford: Stanford University Press, 1948), p. 392.

12. Louis Marin, *La Critique du discours: sur la "Logique de Port-Royal" et les "Pensées" de Pascal* (Paris: Minuit, 1975), p. 54ff.

13. For Protestant antimaterialism and its consequences for English culture, see Jeffrey Knapp, *An Empire Nowhere: England, America, and Literature from "Utopia" to "The Tempest"* (Berkeley: University of California Press, 1992).

14. *The Play of the Sacrament*, in *Medieval Drama*, ed. David Bevington (Boston: Houghton Mifflin, 1975), ll. 199–200.

15. Thomas Becon, *The Displaying of the Popish Mass*, in *Prayers and Other Pieces* (Cambridge: Parker Society, 1844), p. 278.

16. On priests as players, see Becon, *A Comparison between the Lord's Supper and the Pope's Mass*, in *Prayers*, p. 362; on Jesus' words as figurative speech, see *Displaying*, p. 271. See likewise Edmund Grindal, "A Fruitful Dialogue between Custom and Verity," in *Remains* (Cambridge: Parker Society, 1843): "scripture is not so to be taken always as the letter soundeth, but as the intent and purpose of the Holy Ghost was, by whom the scripture was uttered. For if you follow the bare words, you will soon shake down and overthrow the greatest part of the christian faith" (41).

17. See the references to Bullinger, Calvin, Zwingli, and others in Jaroslav Pelikan, *Reformation of Church and Dogma (1300–1700)*, in *The Christian Tradition: A History of the Development of Doctrine*, 5 vols. (Chicago: University of Chicago Press, 1984), 4:190.

18. Becon, *Displaying*, p. 270.

19. *Heresy Trials in the Diocese of Norwich*, 1428–31, ed. Norman P. Tanner, Camden series, vol. 20 (London: Royal Historical Society, 1977), p. 44.

20. "Et tunc dicta Mergeria dixit isti iurate, 'tu male credis quia si quodlibet tale sacramentum esset Deus et verum corpus Christi, infinite sunt dii, quia mille sacerdotes et plures omni die conficiunt mille tales deos et postea tales deos comedunt et commestos emittunt per posteriora in sepibus turpiter fetentibus, ubi potestis tales deos sufficientes invenire si volueritis perscrutari; ideoque sciatis pro firmo quod illud quod vos dicitis sacramentum altaris nunquam erit Deus meus per praciam Dei, quia tale sacramentum fuit falso et deceptorie ordinatum per presbiteros in Ecclesia ad inducendum populum simplicem ad ydolatriam, quia illud sacramentum est tantum panis materialis." In *Heresy Trials*, pp. 44–45. Translated in part and quoted in Rubin, *Corpus Christi*, p. 328.

21. Becon, *Displaying*, p. 272.

22. Quoted in Pelikan, *Reformation of Church and Dogma*, 4:199. In terms that are repeated almost verbatim by the Reformers, Berengar had ventured to argue that "the bread is present not symbolically but actually in its ordinary material or substance. It comes from the field into the granary, from the granary to the mill, from the mill on to the Lord's Table. Its nature is preserved, and it can be broken with the hands and ground with the teeth." He had concluded from this that "if the body of Christ were actually present on the altar, there would be in existence, every day and at the same time, a million bodies of Christ." Quoted in A. J. Macdonald, *Berengar and the Reform of Sacramental Doctrine* (London: Longmans, 1930), pp. 305, 310.

23. Luther expressed regret that he could not bring himself to reject the doctrine of Real Presence. "If you could show me," he wrote to the Reformers, "that there is nothing in the sacrament except bread and wine, you would have done me a great service, for I have suffered much, and would have gladly been convinced, because I saw well that with that opinion I would have given to the papacy the greatest slap. . . . But I am caught; I cannot get out: the text is too forcibly there, and will not allow itself to be twisted out of the sense with words." *De Wette Luthers Briefe* II:577 (1524), quoted in John A. Faulkner, "Luther and the Real Presence," in *The American Journal of Theology* 21 (1917): 227.

24. Quoted in Pelikan, *Reformation of Church and Dogma*, 4:54.

25. Quoted in Pelikan, *Reformation of Church and Dogma*, 4:189.

26. Quoted in Pelikan, *Reformation of Church and Dogma*, 4:189.

27. "Nous confessons bien que l'unité sacrée que nous avons avec Jésus-Christ est incompréhensible à notre sens charnel. . . . Mais faut-il

pour autant songer que sa substance soit transfusée en nous pour être souillée de nos ordures?" Quoted in Bernard Cottret, "Pour une Sémiotique de la Réforme: Le *Consensus Tigurinus* (1549) et la *Brève résolution* . . . (1555) de Calvin," in *Annales ESC* (1984): 280.

28. "Nous rejetons donc comme mauvais expositeurs ceux qui insistent ric à ric au sens littéral de ces mots: Ceci est mon corps, Ceci est mon sang. Car nous tenons pour tout notoire que ces mots doivent être sainement interprétés et avec discrétion, à savoir que les noms de ce que le pain et le vin signifient leur sont attribués. Et cela ne doit être trouvé nouveau ou étrange que par une figure qu'on dit métonymie, le signe emprunte le nom de la vérité qu'il figure. . . ." *Consensus Tigurinus* (1549); the French translation, cited here, was published in 1551 and entitled "L'accord passé et conclu touchant la matière des sacrements, entre les ministres de l'église de Zurich et maître Jean Calvin, ministre de l'église de Genève." Quoted in Cottret, p. 268. In *Brève résolution* (1555), Calvin writes similarly: "Mais selon que l'Écriture parle partout des sacrements, que le nom de la chose signifiée s'attribue au signe, par une figure qu'on appelle métonymie, qui vaut autant comme transport de nom" (268).

29. Quoted in Pelikan, *Reformation of Church and Dogma*, 4:201.

30. Becon, *Displaying*, p. 259; the passage, partly omitted by the Parker Society editor, is here restored.

31. Quoted in Kilian McDonnell, *John Calvin, the Church, and the Eucharist* (Princeton: Princeton University Press, 1967), p. 231.

32. John Jewel, *The Reply to Harding's Answer*, in *The Works of John Jewel*, ed. John Ayre, 4 vols. (Cambridge: Parker Society, 1847), 2:786.

33. Catholics like Rastell argued that the change in substance had taken place and that we should be able to see the body "with our bodily eyes, except divers causes were to the contrary, of which this is one, lest some horror & lothsomenes might trouble us, if it were geaven in visible forme of flesh . . . unto us." (Cf., similarly, Harding: the form of wine remains, covering the blood, "ut nullus horror cruoris sit, that there might be no abhorring of bloude. . . . Thus the bread and wine are changed in substance and yet kepe stil their olde outwarde formes." Quoted in John E. Booty, *John Jewel as Apologist of the Church of England* (London: SPCK, 1963), pp. 154, 158.

34. See Rubin, *Corpus Christi*, pp. 337–38. According to Andrew Willet, Cardinal Bellarmine says that "the body of Christ goeth downe into the stomacke, but no further: but when the formes of bread and wine begin to be corrupted there, the body of Christ goeth away." *Synopsis papismi, That is, a Generall View of Papiestrie* (London, 1600), pp. 515.

35. Anne Askew, in *The Paradise of Women: Writings by Englishwomen of the Renaissance*, ed. Betty Travitsky (New York: Columbia University Press, 1989), p. 175.

36. *The First Examination of Anne Askewe*, in John Bale, *Select Works*, ed. Henry Christmas (Cambridge: Parker Society, 1849), p. 154.

37. Becon, *Comparison*, p. 378. Cf. Willet, *Synopsis:* "If a Mouse chance to creepe into your pixe, and fill her hungry belly with your god-amight, what is it that the Mouse feedeth vpon? trow you they be accidents onely? for your say that the consecrated host goeth no further then the stomacke: and yet it is to much that the housell of Christians should be hosed in a mouses belly. These are but ridiculous and light questions, yet such as haue troubled your grauest and sagest heads, and remaine vnanswered." "The thirteenth generall controversie of the Sacrament of the Lord Supper," p. 516.

38. W. Lockton, *The Treatment of the Remains at the Eucharist after Holy Communion and the Time of the Ablutions* (Cambridge: Cambridge University Press, 1920), p. 2.

39. Yrjö Hirn, from whom most of these details are taken, refers to Bishop Anno's biography, which relates how "a fly, to the horror of the holy man, snapped up a portion of the Host, which, however, at Anno's earnest prayers, the creature brought back again." Yrjö Hirn, *The Sacred Shrine: A Study of the Poetry and Art of the Catholic Church* (Boston: Beacon Press, 1957; 1st ed. in Swedish, 1909), p. 497 n. 27.

40. On shipboard, priests celebrated a "*missa sicca,*" a Mass without consecration and Communion, for it was feared that the sea might cause the wine to be spilled out of the chalice.

41. Quoted in Hirn, *The Sacred Shrine*, p. 104.

42. Once again the controversy is associated with Berengar, who had written that if Christ was literally present in the bread and wine, His body would be subject to the digestion not only of human beings but also of animals. In c. 1073, the monk Guitmund (later bishop of Aversa) replied that the body and blood of the Lord remain in the Sacrament, even when the species are eaten by some animal. Some medieval theologians, including Odo of Ourscamp, Maurice Sully, the author of the *Commentarius Porretanus,* and Peter Comestor, concur. Others proposed counterarguments, for example, that the substance of bread miraculously returned when the mouse started nibbling. See Artur Landgraf, *Die in der Frühscholastik klassische Frage 'quid sumit mus,'* in *Dogmengeschichte in der Frühscholastik* (Regensburg, 1955), 3:2; Gary Macy, "Of Mice and Manna: Quid Mus Sumit as a Pastoral Question," in *Recherches de théologie ancienne et médiévale* 58 (1991): 157–66; Rubin, *Corpus Christi,* esp. pp. 65–68.

43. For the foregoing theological opinions, and others of the same kind, see Jewel, *Reply,* 2:783–84; and Rubin, *Corpus Christi,* pp. 65–68. The Peter of Palus quoted by Jewel is the Dominican Peter de La Palu (c. 1277–1342).

44. Thomas Wright, *The disposition or garnishmente of the soule to receiue worthily the blessed sacrament* (Antwerp [in reality, an English secret press], 1596), pp. 1, 99.

45. *Hamlet* 4.3.17–20. All citations of Shakespeare are to *The Norton Shakespeare,* ed. Stephen Greenblatt et al. (New York: W. W. Norton,

1997). *Hamlet* exists in three distinct early texts, two of which (the second quarto and the folio) have substantial authority. Passages that appear only in the second quarto text of the play and are omitted in the folio are indicated by an extra number: for example, 4.7.95.10 refers to the tenth line of a second quarto–only passage that appears immediately after act 4, scene 7, line 95.

46. The nightgown is indicated only in a Q1 stage direction. Both Q2 and F have a stage direction in the opening scene indicating that the ghost's "beaver"—that is, his visor—is raised, and the point is reiterated in the dialogue itself. When he is informed that the apparition was in armor, "from top to toe," Hamlet concludes, "Then saw you not his face." "O yes, my lord," Horatio replies, "he wore his beaver up" (1.3.227–28). In the closet scene, Hamlet addresses the "gracious figure" and notes "how pale he glares" (3.4.95, 116).

47. Erwin Panofsky, *Tomb Sculpture,* ed. H. W. Janson (New York: Harry Abrams, n.d.), pp. 39–66.

48. Quoted in Christopher Devlin, *Hamlet's Divinity and Other Essays* (London: Rupert Hart-Davis, 1963), p. 40.

49. John Bridges, "A Sermon Preached at Paules Crosse" (1571), p. 126. We owe this reference to Jeffrey Knapp.

50. Thomas Adams, *Mystical Bedlam, or the World of Mad-Men* (London, 1615), p. 70. We owe this reference to Christina Malcolmson.

51. Note the effect of the ghost's apparition on Marcellus and Bernardo, according to Horatio; they were, he says, "distill'd / Almost to jelly with the act of fear" (1.2.204–5). The image may be linked to the images of Foxe's *Book of Martyrs* that show the limbs of martyrs rendering their fat and water in the flames. There is perhaps some hint of this horrible process in the ghost's words to his son:

> My hour is almost come
> When I to sulph'rous and tormenting flames
> Must render up myself. (1.5.2–4)

52. *Hamlet,* ed. G. R. Hibbard (Oxford: Oxford University Press, 1987), 1.2.180n.

53. There are other images of entrails in the play, beyond those we have already noted: "Ere this," Hamlet declares in self-contempt, "I should have fatted all the region kites / With this slave's offal" (2.2.367–68). See also Hamlet on the dead Polonius: "I'll lug the guts into the neighbour room" (3.4.192).

54. Hamlet's way of laying the charge here does not present Gertrude as a mere passive accomplice to the murder, as the "Mousetrap" suggests, but seems to accuse her of being the murderer herself.

55. Another version of this image of inward corruption appears in a Q2 passage. Brooding on the apparent irrationality of Fortinbras's campaign against Poland for a plot of worthless ground, Hamlet declares:

This is th'impostume of much wealth and peace,
That inward breaks, and shows no cause without
Why the man dies. (4.4.9.17–19)

56. "You can see something like this," Galen writes of the female genitals, "in the eyes of the mole, which have vitreous and crystalline humors and the tunics that surround these . . . and they have these just as much as animals do that make use of their eyes. The mole's eyes, however, do not open, nor do they project but are left there imperfect and remain like the eyes of other animals when these are still in the uterus." *On the Usefulness of the Parts of the Body*, 2 vols., ed. and trans. Margaret May (Ithaca: Cornell University Press, 1988), 2:14.297, 628–29.

57. Shlomo Eidelberg, trans. and ed., *The Jews and the Crusaders: The Hebrew Chronicles of the First and Second Crusades* (Madison: University of Wisconsin Press, 1977), p. 90. We owe this reference to Aaron Greenblatt.

58. It is worth noting that these words are spoken when Hamlet believes that Claudius is engaged in the "purging of his soul" through prayer. We have been told by William Bouwsma that Hooker uses the phrase "fullness of bread" to mean "prosperity."

59. Without the divinity that shapes our ends, there would be no escape from the charnel house, no possibility of redemption, for the works of the flesh are necessarily corrupt. There is in *Hamlet* a passing allusion to this Protestant conception of grace that interestingly conjoins the Eucharist and the playhouse. When Polonius declares that he will use the players "according to their desert," Hamlet exclaims, "God's bodykins, man, much better. Use every man after his desert, and who should scape whipping?" (2.2.519–20). The lines pull away from the immediate dramatic exchange (the minor disagreement between Polonius and Hamlet about how the players should be "used") and from the specific social question of the status of the actors (with Hamlet arguing that they should be treated especially well because they are the bearers of reputation after death). Hamlet's words swerve rather in the direction of larger questions that have a moral and ultimately a theological resonance. We are all sinners and breeders of sinners, and by our own deserts we should all be punished; only through unmerited grace can we hope to be treated well. That grace, in theological terms, was linked to Christ's sacrifice to redeem the sins of mankind. It is the commemoration, the anamnesis, of this sacrifice, that lies at the heart of the Mass, and it is this anamnesis that has evidently called forth Hamlet's exclamation: "God's bodykins." For the diminutive "bodykin" refers specifically to the consecrated Host of the Holy Communion. The diminutive is a mark not only of affection but of the reduced size of the object as it figures in the Mass.

60. Montaigne, "Apology for Raymond Sebond," in *Essays*, trans. Donald M. Frame (Stanford: Stanford University Press, 1948), p. 339. G. F.

Stedefeld argues that "Shakespeare sought by the drama of *Hamlet* to free
himself from the impressions left upon his mind by the reading of the
book of the French skeptic, Montaigne" (*Hamlet, ein Tendenzdrama
Sheakspeare's* [*sic*] *gegen di skeptische und kosmopolitische Weltanschauung
des Michael de Montaigne* [Berlin, 1871], cited in Horace Howard Furness,
ed. Variorum *Hamlet* [New York: Dover, 1963; reprint of 1877 original],
2:344). If this is so, it is not clear to us that Shakespeare succeeded in
freeing himself, since his play seems haunted by Montaigne's most skeptical essay. Florio's translation of the passage we are looking at may convey
some further sense of this haunting presence: "There is nothing wherein
the world differeth so much, as in customes and lawes. Some things are
here accompted abominable, which in another place are esteemed com-
mendable. . . . Marriages in proximity of blood are amongst us forbidden
as capitall, elsewhere they are allowed and esteemed;

> "—gentes esse feruntur,
> In quibus et nato geitrix, et nata parenti
> Jungitur, et pietas geminato crescit amore.
>   Ovid, Met. x.331
> There are some people, where the mother weddeth
> Her sonne, the daughter her own father beddeth,
> And so by doubling love, their kindnesse spreddeth.

"The murthering of children and of parents; the communication with
women; traffick of robbing and stealing; free licence to all manner of sen-
suality: to conclude, there is nothing so extreame and horrible, but is
found to be received and allowed by the custome of some nation. It is
credible that there be naturall lawes; as may be seene in other creatures,
but in us they are lost: this goodly humane reason engrafting it selfe
among all men, to sway and command, confounding and topsi-turving
the visage of all things, according to her inconstant vanitie and vaine in-
constancy. . . . Nothing can be imagined so horrible, as for one to eate
and devoure his own father. Those people, which anciently kept custome, hold it neverthelesse for a testimonie of pietie and good affection:
seeking by that meane to give their fathers the worthiest and most honorable sepulchre, harboring their fathers bodies and reliques in themselves
and in their marrow; in some sort reviving and regenerating them by the
transmutation made in their quicke flesh, by digestion and nourishment.
It is easie to be considered what abomination and cruelty it had beene,
in men accustomed and trained in this inhumane superstition, to cast
the carcases of their parents into the corruption of the earth, as food
for beasts and worms." Montaigne, "Apology of Raymond de Sebond,"
in Montaigne, *Essays*, trans. John Florio, 3 vols. (London: Dent, 1965),
2:298–99.

61. In "De la coustume" (I.23), Montaigne cites from Herodotus the
story of Darius asking some Greeks, "What price would persuade them to

eat their fathers' dead bodies. They answered that there was no price for
which they would do it." In the "Apology" then, Montaigne is being
effortlessly classicizing in his anthropological speculations.

62. A "bung-hole" (5.1.189) is usually glossed as the opening of a cask,
but it could also, by transference, refer to the anus, as is made clear by
Cotgreve's 1611 definition of a sea anemone: "a small and ouglie fish, or
excrescence of the Sea, resembling a man's bung hole" (*OED*).

Chapter Six

1. Karl Marx, *Capital: A Critique of Political Economy*, I (New York:
Modern Library, n.d.), p. 83.

2. Marx tells us that, in addition to the unacknowledged fetishism of
commodities, capitalism also required such "abstract" conscious religious
beliefs as "Protestantism, Deism, etc.," for "the religious reflex of the real
world can, in any case, only then finally vanish, when the practical relations of everyday life offer to man none but perfectly intelligible and reasonable relations with regard to his fellowmen and to nature." Marx,
Capital, p. 92.

3. C.-A. Sainte-Beuve, *Causeries du Lundi* I (Paris: Garnier Frères,
1849), p. 38. This is a quotation that had Burkean overtones for English
writers. George Eliot, for example, uses it in "Debasing the Moral Currency," *Impressions of Theophrastus Such*.

4. For a thorough and evenhanded survey of more recent concepts of
ideology and forms of ideology critique, see John B. Thompson, *Studies in
the Theory of Ideology* (Cambridge: Polity Press, 1984).

5. Marx can also be read (against the grain of *Capital*'s "Fetishism of
Commodities" section) to stress his understanding that commodity fetishes retain their power even when thoroughly understood. Slavoj Žižek
argues that Marx did not intend to make fetishism a matter of subjective
belief, but instead referred it to an objective state of things, in which
"they know very well how things really are, but still they are [behaving] as
if they did not know. The illusion is therefore double: it consists in over-
looking the illusion which is structuring our real, effective relationship to
reality. And this overlooked, unconscious illusion is what may be called
the ideological fantasy." *The Sublime Object of Ideology* (New York: Verso,
1989), p. 33. To concentrate on what one knows, and to stress one's dis-
believing penetration of the fetish's real nature, according to Žižek, only
increases the ideological fantasy that demystification can free one from
ideological determination. Our analysis is certainly indebted to Žižek's,
but we do not find his conclusion—that the concept of ideology should
be retained—completely convincing. It seems not to take into account
the extent to which one can know that one's behavior is based on an "as
if" premise and can consciously stipulate to its exigencies. These exigencies may be phantasmatic, driven by unconscious desire, but they are not

necessarily illusionistic, in the usual sense of that word. For this reason, we've substituted the idea of credit for his notion of the "objectivity of belief."

6. "Our" pleasure might be, however, quite different from that of Shakespeare's contemporaries, for one mark of the shift that gave rise to the "literary" is our indifference to a historical Hamlet. It is difficult to say how much Shakespeare or his audience were invested in the assumption that Hamlet had been a real person, but it does seem that the playwright had a much harder time than we do imagining that tragic heroes had no prior bodily existence. Our "literary" appreciation, however, dispenses with a historical Hamlet to clear the field for a purer invention. Hamlet's story, too, can then be Nobody's story. For a discussion of the differences between the Shakespearean idea of "invention" and that which becomes prevalent with the rise of the novel, see Catherine Gallagher, *Nobody's Story* (Berkeley: University of California Press, 1994), pp. 158–61.

7. Charles Dickens, *Great Expectations* (New York: Oxford, 1989), p. 1. All quotations are taken from this edition.

8. For a thorough canvassing of the theme of cannibalism in Dickens's work, see Harry Stone, *The Night Side of Dickens: Cannibalism, Passion, Necessity* (Columbus: Ohio University Press, 1994), pp. 1–45 . His discussion of *Great Expectations* is on pp. 125–39.

9. Peter Brooks uses this term for the second encounter between Pip and Magwitch in his chapter on *Great Expectations* in *Reading for the Plot: Design and Intention in Narrative* (Cambridge: Harvard University Press, 1984), pp. 117–18.

10. In *The Way of the World: The Bildungsroman in European Culture* (London: Verso, 1987), Franco Moretti contrasts Dickens's heroes, including Pip, with those of the continental novelists—Goethe's Wilhelm Meister, Stendhal's Julien Sorel, and Balzac's Lucien de Rubempré—rightly pointing out that the trajectory of an English hero's career usually returns him to a state of childhood innocence rather than worldly disillusionment. Moretti, however, does not note that of all Dickens's heroes, only Pip altogether ignores his genealogy and seeks to leave it behind. Like other critics, he tends to exaggerate Pip's passivity.

11. An overview of the concept's history, as well as a set of analytical categories for organizing its major theorists, can be found in David Frisby and Derek Sayer, *Society* (London: Tavistock, 1986).

12. However, we must note that the novel thereby also impedes our attempts to take "the social" for granted as a stable framework for an ideological critique. Instead of providing a frame of reference for our analysis, the social in this novel repeatedly seems to emerge from the object under consideration, as the corner of a frame of some impossible Escher painting seems to project from inside the picture itself. Of course, historians of the novel are often forced to acknowledge that our attempts to ground its appearance in "society" become circular because the genre seems to inaugu-

rate the very discourse of the social; the novel as a genre and "society" as a concept are not only twin discursive formations, but also mutually delineating discourses, like Escher's drawing hands. But we encounter another arc of the hermeneutic circle when we notice that our analytical tool is not itself detachable from the object under analysis.

13. This fact has been analyzed repeatedly. F. R. and Q. D. Leavis call the London of *Great Expectations* "Newgate London" in *Dickens the Novelist* (New York: Pantheon Books, 1970), p. 331; and Foucauldian analyses of the novel have also focused on its fascination with the margins of criminality. See, for example, Jeremy Tambling's "Prison-bound: Dickens and Foucault," *Essays in Criticism* 36 (1986): 11–31. We claim that the novel figures more primitive ways of determining the boundaries of the social: expulsion and execution. Those inside are all locked up, one way or another, as in numerous Dickens novels; in this one, though, the emphasis is on being forbidden to "come back" into this prison.

14. David M. Craig argues that the London descriptions in *Great Expectations* emphasize the metaphoric work of Pip's imagination. See "The Interplay of City and Self in *Oliver Twist, David Copperfield*, and *Great Expectations*," *Dickens Studies Annual* 16 (1987): 17–38.

15. Among the critics who discuss Magwitch and Miss Havisham as vengeful parents born out of Pip's survivor guilt are Brooks, *Reading for the Plot;* Michael Peled Ginsburg, "Dickens and the Uncanny: Repression and Displacement in *Great Expectations*," *Dickens Studies Annual* 13 (1984): 115–24; and Douglas Brooks-Davies, *Fielding, Dickens, Gosse, Iris Murdoch and Oedipal Hamlet* (London: Macmillan, 1989), pp. 60–107.

16. The recognition (which followed from reading Foucault) that bringing previously self-evident notions into discourse was the main ideological move of the modern period led critics of modern literature to turn their attention away from "ideology critique" and toward "discourse analysis." Since any discourse can be seen as promoting at least its own operations (that is, as augmenting the discursive current), it seemed unnecessary to specify in what way a discourse supported the conditions of exploitation. "Discourse analysis" thus seemed either politically disinterested, a mere variety of intellectual history, or radically scornful of every variety of writing on the grounds that it was all necessarily part of the disciplinary web.

17. For analyses of the underlying bio-energetics of the labor theory of value, see Catherine Gallagher, "The Body versus the Social Body in the Works of Thomas Malthus and Henry Mayhew," *Representations* 14 (1986): 83–106; and "The Bio-Economics of Dickens's *Our Mutual Friend*," in *Subject to History: Ideology, Class, Gender*, ed. David Simpson (Ithaca: Cornell University Press, 1991), pp. 47–64.

18. John Ruskin, *The Seven Lamps of Architecture* (1849; reprint, London: Century, 1988), pp. 149–50.

19. William A. Guy, *Principles of Forensic Medicine* (New York: Harper & Brothers, 1845), p. 371.

20. James Curry, "Introduction," *Observations on Apparent Death* (London: E. Cox, 1815; 1st ed., 1792).

21. J. Fothergill, *Observations on the Recovery of a Man Dead in Appearance by Distending the Lungs with Air* (London, 1745). For a thorough overview of the history of apparent death, see Martin S. Pernick, "Back from the Grave: Recurring Controversies Over Defining and Diagnosing Death in History," in *Death: Beyond Whole-Brain Criteria*, ed. Richard M. Zaner (Boston: Kluwer Academic Publishers, 1988), pp. 17–74. We are very grateful to Thomas Laqueur for helping us locate all of these sources.

22. Pernick, "Back from the Grave," pp. 54–55.

23. Pernick, "Back from the Grave," p. 32.

24. For an overview of mesmerism in nineteenth-century Britain, see Alison Winter, *Mesmerized: Powers of Mind in Victorian Britain* (Chicago: University of Chicago Press, 1998).

25. John Elliotson, *Human Physiology* (London: Longman, 1835), p. 662.

26. Chauncy Hare Townshend, *Facts in Mesmerism, with Reasons for a Dispassionate Inquiry into It* (1841; reprint, New York: Da Capo, 1982), p. 15.

27. In *Possible Worlds of the Fantastic: The Rise of the Paranormal in Fiction* (Toronto: University of Toronto Press, 1996), Nancy H. Traill argues that Dickens, in his late fiction, implies that the "'supernatural' is merely a label for strange phenomena latent *within* the natural" (17). See also pp. 46–73. For a discussion of Dickens's use of the occult in his social criticism, see Christopher Herbert, "The Occult in *Bleak House*," *Novel: A Forum on Fiction* 17 (1984): 101–15.

28. Elliotson, *Human Physiology*, p. 692. We are indebted to Fred Kaplan's pioneering *Dickens and Mesmerism: The Hidden Springs of Fiction* (Princeton: Princeton University Press, 1975) for an overview of Dickens's connections among the mesmerists. However, we take issue with his contention that Elliotson believed in "the existence of an external invisible fluid of pervasive magnetic force suffusing the universe" (19). Elliotson disliked hypothesizing invisible entities and only writes of the fluid, in *Human Physiology*, to say that there is no evidence of such a thing and that if there were, it would augment materialism (30–33).

29. Elliotson, *Human Physiology*, p. 615.

30. Elliotson, *Human Physiology*, p. 615; all quotations in the paragraph are from the same page.

31. Elliotson, *Human Physiology*, pp. 616–17.

32. Quoted in John Forster, *The Life of Charles Dickens* (London: Chapman and Hall, n.d.), p. 558.

33. Quoted in Forster, *The Life of Charles Dickens*, p. 557.

34. Samuel Taylor Coleridge, *Coleridge's Shakespeare Criticism*, ed. Thomas Middleton Rayson (London: Constable & Co. Ltd., 1960), vol. 1, p. 116.

35. Quoted in Forster, *The Life of Charles Dickens,* p. 557.

36. Quoted in Forster, *The Life of Charles Dickens,* pp. 555–56.

37. Quoted in Forster, *The Life of Charles Dickens,* p. 551.

38. Forster, *The Life of Charles Dickens,* p. 551.

39. George Eliot, a more thoroughgoing psychological associationist and a more consistent materialist, worried that the culture's suspended beings could be robbed of their power by farcical productions. See her "Debasing the Moral Currency" in *Impressions of Theophrastus Such.*

40. Douglas Brooks-Davies points out several associations between Miss Havisham and both Gertrude and Ophelia (op. cit., pp. 73–88).

41. Among the critics who have discussed Pip's entanglement in various female plots are Hilary Schor, *Dickens and the Daughter of the House* (Cambridge: Cambridge University Press, 1999); Gail Turley Houston, "'Pip' and 'Property': The (Re)production of the Self in *Great Expectations,*" *Studies in the Novel* 24 (1992): 13–25; and Susan Walsh, "Bodies of Capital: *Great Expectations* and the Climacteric Economy," *Victorian Studies* 37 (1993): 73–98.

Index

absence, 31, 64, 74, 83, 171, 173, 185–88

accidents, 52, 66, 81–109 passim, 113, 118, 145, 147, 181. *See also* body; Real Presence; substance

Adams, Thomas, 154, 155

Advancement of Learning, The (Bacon), 37

aesthetic, the, 6, 10–13, 16–17, 23, 101–3, 104, 106, 191. *See also* art

Akiba, Rabbi, 140, 223 n. 6

Albertus Magnus, 147

Alexander, Sally, 58, 59

Alexander the Great, 162

allusion, 80–81, 92, 95

Alpers, Paul, 211 n. 1

Alpers, Svetlana, 211 n. 1

Altdorfer, Albrecht, 32

Althusser, Louis, 2, 62, 65

Althusserianism, 60, 61, 65

anecdote, 49–74
    in Auerbach, 36–40, 46
    in Barthes, 50–51
    in Fineman, 49–51
    in Foucault, 66–71
    in Geertz, 21–31
    and narrative, 47–51, 67
    and new historicism, 19, 35–36, 47, 51, 54
    in Williams, 63–64

Anglicanism, 197

animal magnetism. *See* mesmerism

animation, 66, 68, 74, 165–68, 171, 184–207 passim. *See also* fetishism; undead; vital force; vivification

Annales school, 53, 59

Anno, Bishop, 226 n. 39

anthropology, 5, 7, 20–31, 60

anti-Semitism, 78–108 passim

"Apology for Raymond Sebond" (Montaigne), 162

aporia, 14, 96, 109. *See also* holes; rupture

apparent death. *See* death, apparent

appetite, 125, 130, 160. *See also* desire
    sexual, 155–60 passim

Aquinas, Thomas, 4, 216 n. 4

Arnold, Matthew, 64

art, 6–18 passim, 67, 78, 191, 193. *See also* aesthetic; canon; imagination; representation

artificiality, 21–22, 25

Askew, Anne, 147–150

Atatürk, Kemal, 43

Auerbach, Erich, 31–47
    "Figura," 34
    Mimesis, 31–47

Augustine, Saint, 71, 145–46

235